EXITING THE FACTORY

Strikes and Class Formation beyond the Industrial Sector

Volume 1: Global Labour Studies and Class Theory

Alexander Gallas

First published in Great Britain in 2024 by

Bristol University Press
University of Bristol
1–9 Old Park Hill
Bristol
BS2 8BB
UK
t: +44 (0)117 374 6645
e: bup-info@bristol.ac.uk

Details of international sales and distribution partners are available at bristoluniversitypress.co.uk

© Bristol University Press 2024

British Library Cataloguing in Publication Data
A catalogue record for this book is available from the British Library

ISBN 978-1-5292-1211-2 hardcover
ISBN 978-1-5292-1213-6 ePub
ISBN 978-1-5292-1212-9 ePdf

The right of Alexander Gallas to be identified as author of this work has been asserted by him in accordance with the Copyright, Designs and Patents Act 1988.

Cover design: Andy Ward
Front cover image: iStock/FG Trade
Bristol University Press uses environmentally responsible print partners.
Printed and bound in Great Britain by CPI Group (UK) Ltd, Croydon, CR0 4YY

FSC
www.fsc.org
MIX
Paper | Supporting
responsible forestry
FSC® C013604

Contents

List of Tables

List of Abbreviations

AKSU	Arbeitskreis Strategic Unionism (Working Group Strategic Unionism, University of Jena, Germany)
GEW	Gewerkschaft Erziehung und Wissenschaft (Education and Science Workers' Union, Germany)
GLU	Global Labour University
NRS	National Readership Survey (Britain)
NUM	National Union of Mineworkers (Britain)
PRA	power resources approach
SALB	*South African Labour Bulletin*
SWOP	Society, Work & Politics Institute (formerly Sociology of Work Programme, University of the Witwatersrand, Johannesburg)
ver.di	Vereinte Dienstleistungsgewerkschaft (United Services Trade Union, Germany)

Acknowledgements

The road to completing this manuscript was long-winded, rocky and, in parts, steep. Considering my personal circumstances – precarious working conditions, the trials and tribulations of family life and the effects of the COVID-19 pandemic – it sometimes felt like an over-ambitious endeavour. If that was not enough, I opted for tackling an intellectual challenge that at certain points seemed insurmountable, which consisted in reconciling materialist class and state theory with global labour studies. It is for my readers to say whether I succeeded or not. In any case, I am glad that I got to where I am now, and I feel the need to stress how much I benefited from the help and support I received along the way.

My venture into strike research started in 2011 with a project on political strikes against austerity that was funded by the Rosa Luxemburg Foundation. I partnered with Jörg Nowak on this project, and our research led us to write a number of jointly authored publications. I would like to thank Jörg for the comradely spirit of our collaboration and for our discussions on the subject matter of strikes, which laid the foundations for this later book project. To a degree, the concepts we developed back then still inform my analysis today.

A great number of people have read draft chapters of my book or draft articles that later ended up as book chapters at different points in the writing process, and their recommendations were invaluable. I am grateful to Mark Anner, Maurizio Atzeni, Peter Birke, Anne Engelhardt, Elaine Hui, Katherine Maich, Jörg Nowak, Agustín Santella and Joscha Wullweber for their advice. I hope I have done justice to it, and, needless to say, I am solely responsible for any shortcomings and mistakes.

I would like to thank Ian Bruff, Sian Moore and Edward Webster for pointing out to me literature and sources that were important for the development of my conceptual framework and my empirical analysis, and Niklas Holzhauer for transcribing interviews and assisting me with the bibliography. Special thanks also go out to Stefan Krupp, who gave expert advice on bibliographical questions and, more generally, on matters of life and death. I am grateful to Georgina Bolwell, Isobel Green, Ellen Pearce and Paul Stevens at Bristol University Press for being such patient editors, and to the anonymous reviewers of my book proposal and my first manuscript for detailed and helpful recommendations. My sincere thanks also go out to Andreas Bieler, who supported me in the process of my *Habilitation*, the arcane rite of passage that is still a prerequisite for obtaining tenure in Germany. The manuscript for this book also served as my *Habilitation* thesis, and Andreas agreed become my external reviewer and examiner, an arduous task that is not recognized much in German academia and beyond. At various points in the last few years, Sonja Buckel offered guidance on how to navigate the partly feudal, partly neoliberal university system that I am part of. I would like to thank her for her advice – and for offering me a contract towards the end of my stint at the University of Kassel ensuring that I was still in work when I revised this manuscript. Like any other academic worker in Germany, I faced, and continue to face, a university system that is characterized by a combination of neoliberal competitive pressures, casual employment and steep, feudal hierarchies. My comrades at Uni Kassel Unbefristet, the grassroots campaign that we started in 2017 to fight against fixed-term contracts and precarious work on campus, offered invaluable support and unconditional solidarity whenever I experienced the toxic effects of this system. Thank you so much!

On many occasions, my students were my first audience, and I benefited greatly from sharing and discussing my ideas with them. Teaching on the MA programmes in 'Global Political Economy and Development' and 'Labour Policies and Globalisation' was one of the most enjoyable aspects of my work in Kassel. Thanks to all of you for the intellectual stimulation!

In the fall semester of 2017, I was a visiting scholar at the Center for Global Workers' Rights, which forms part of the School of Labor and Employment Relations at the Pennsylvania State University. Even if I had started doing research on strikes and the Great Crisis in 2011, it only occurred to me there and then what my book would be about. I would like to sincerely thank Mark Anner for inviting me to Pennsylvania and enabling me to work in an environment that allowed my ideas to flourish.

During the writing process, I learned that a colleague and fellow Poulantzasian, Ed Rooksby, had passed away. Ed wrote an excellent review of my previous monograph, *The Thatcherite Offensive*. Sadly, I never got to thank him for his critical appraisal of my work. I fondly remember a panel that I had organized and he participated in at the 2011 Historical Materialism Conference, and I hope that his contribution to materialist state theory will be remembered.

Last but not least, I cannot stress enough how grateful I am to my family. I would like to express my gratitude to my siblings, Elisabeth and Max, who were as reliable and consistent in their support as ever. My wife Verena and my sons Milo and Ben helped me through all the ups and downs of the research and writing process, and I know that it was not easy sometimes. Thank you so much!

Unfortunately, my father Andreas did not live to see the publication of this book. I owe to him my passion for politics and for reading, writing and debating, and he took great interest in my academic ventures. Undoubtedly, he would have liked to discuss the subject matter of my book with me, and I am equally sure that we would have disagreed at certain points. I dedicate this book to him.

Preface

In 1996, a monograph written by two Australian sociologists, Jan Pakulski and Malcolm Waters, was published. The message conveyed by title – *The Death of Class* – could not have been clearer. In the book, Pakulski and Waters suggest that the concept of class has lost any usefulness for understanding contemporary societies: '[C]lasses are dissolving and ... the most advanced societies are no longer class societies. ... [C]lass societies are specific historical entities. They were born with industrial capitalism, changed their form under the impact of organised or corporatized capitalism, and are disappearing in the face of post-industrialization and postmodernization' (Pakulski and Waters, 1996: 4).

I reference Pakulski and Waters not because their claim was unique or innovative, but because it is a very forceful expression of the widespread scepticism towards class among social scientists.[1] Throughout my intellectual

---

[1]   Even thirty years ago, the claim that class was dead was by no means new or original. At different historical junctures in the 20th century, scholars from a range of intellectual traditions and disciplinary backgrounds have questioned the viability and utility of the concept. The liberal economist Friedrich August Hayek was a leading anti-socialist intellectual in the postwar decades and one of the promoters of the free market (see Gallas, 2014). He put forward a principled, polemical critique of the concept at the level of social theory – not so much of the existence of 'income classes', whose existence he acknowledged (Hayek, 1988: 123), but of the notion of a 'dominant "class"'. According to him, one should reject the assumption of a 'conspiracy' in which this class manipulates society for its purposes because the latter is the complex product of 'abstract and spontaneous ordering patterns' (Hayek, 1988: 82). Needless to say, this critique rests on what is at most a caricature of Marxian thinking. Indeed, Marx could not have been clearer that he regarded class domination not a product of manipulation or conspiracy but of mechanisms inscribed in the capitalist mode of production (1976: 92, 201; see Part II in this volume). The reduction of social and economic inequality in the Global North after the Second World War caused a number of sociologists to question the empirical reality of class. As Pakulski and Waters acknowledge (1996: 17), Robert Nisbet already argued in the 1950s that 'the term social class ... is nearly valueless for the clarification of the data of wealth, power, and social status in contemporary United States and much of Western society' (1959: 11). Making a similar point around the same time, West German sociologist Helmuth Schelsky detected the '*emergence of a levelled, petty bourgeois, medium status society*'. According to him, this society was 'neither proletarian nor bourgeois' and

biography – as a student, a young scholar with a recently awarded PhD and a middle-aged lecturer – I have been encountering claims that the concept of 'class' is not or no longer relevant. These claims can be grouped into three categories, which are not mutually exclusive. The sceptics question the possibility of conceptualizing class at the level of social theory; of encountering, at the level of empirical social analysis, the existence of entities that can meaningfully be described as classes; and of advancing, in the present day and age, a politics of, by and for the working class. To my frustration, these claims are not exclusively made by people from the right and centre, but also from the left, among them scholars who profess to work in the Marxian tradition. Accordingly, one of my main motivations for writing this book is to demonstrate the enduring theoretical, analytical and political relevance of the concept of 'class'.

In what follows, I will argue that class is of crucial importance for understanding contemporary (and any other) capitalist societies. I follow the lead of Richard Hoggart (1989: vii), one of the founding fathers of British cultural studies, who remarked in a preface to *The Road to Wigan Peer*, George Orwell's classical study of the everyday lives of Lancashire and Yorkshire workers: 'Class distinctions do not die, they merely learn new ways of expressing themselves. ... Each decade we shiftily declare we have buried class; each decade the coffin stays empty.' My book is about showing that the coffin is empty still. There are novel ways in which class is expressed in present-day capitalism, and we can identify these expressions with the help of social theory and empirical analysis. In other words, my general research interest is to put forward an argument for the continued existence of class in the 21st century. Following the lead of materialist understandings of capitalism, I argue that class is intrinsically linked to the organization of work across society, which means that my book is also about labour relations.

In the neoliberal age, a number of important contributions to class analysis have focused on studying 'up': They have analysed capitalist classes and

---

'characterised by the loss of class tension and social hierarchy' (1952: 287; emphasis in the original). Likewise, French sociologist Raymond Aron wondered whether people really saw themselves as belonging to a class, or whether this was a sociological fiction (1960: 10). At the turn of the millennium, this found an echo in the work of Ulrich Beck and Elisabeth Beck-Gernsheimer, who recognized the existence of structured inequalities but argued that individualization had rendered class identity irrelevant (2002: 31; for a critique of conceptions of class based on inequality and identity, see Chapter 4). Last but not least, a strand in left thinking abandoned the idea of the working class as a privileged collective actor in the struggle for human emancipation, which reflected the rise of the 'new' social movements and the ossification of authoritarian, Soviet-style socialism. Among the authors in question were André Gorz (1982), Ernesto Laclau and Chantal Mouffe (1985) and Moishe Postone (1993). For a systematic critique of Postone's reading of Karl Marx, see Gallas (2006; 2011).

ruling blocs (van der Pijl, 1998; Sklair, 2001; Carroll, 2010). The decision to look in this direction may reflect the fact that it is impossible to understand social domination without considering how groups benefiting from it work to preserve it. But research pragmatics may have to do with it as well – for two reasons: First, it is comparably easy to make plausible the need for class analysis by pointing to the huge concentration of wealth among the owners of capital in contemporary societies. According to the British non-governmental organization Oxfam (2020), the 2,000 most wealthy people in the world own as much as 60 per cent of the global population – or 4.6 billion people. Observations like these make it difficult to defend the widespread scepticism towards class as a concept. Second, representatives of capital form comparably stable networks, which can be traced through network analysis (see Carroll, 2020) – even if their connections and links are often hidden from view and hard to access.

Arguably, researching working classes is more complicated. It may be tempting to study them in analogy to capitalist classes, that is, by looking at how workers have been building networks through the formation of trade unions und workers' parties. The problem is that there are ambiguities and contradictions surrounding the class effects of those organizations. A good illustration is the red-and-green government in Germany, which was in office from 1998 to 2005 and was based on a coalition between one of the eldest workers' parties in the world, the Social Democratic Party of Germany, and the Green Party. Initially, this coalition enjoyed broad support among trade unionists. Chancellor Gerhard Schröder liked to stress that he was from a family considered 'anti-social [die Asozialen]', and that his mother had been a cleaner (cited in Zastrow, 2004). Nevertheless, he and his government were responsible for the most comprehensive process of welfare state retrenchment in the history of the Federal Republic of Germany. Was this a government acting on behalf of the German working class? Was the Social Democratic Party still a workers' party? And were the representatives of German unions who sat on the commission that planned the restructuring process, and who consented to it, representing working-class interests? This key episode in recent German history underscores how difficult it is to capture the side of labour in class relations in capitalism. It may be necessary to consider that they are institutionalized in and through the capitalist state. Arguably, the latter's workings mean that working classes, as collective actors, exist in states of flux and fragmentation, and that many of the institutions facilitating their organization can also have adverse effects.

Next to these general points, there is a point to be made about the recent development of class relations in the global political economy. Despite countervailing trends at specific times and in specific places, there was, all in all, a long period of advances of working-class forces that started after the Second World War and ended in the 1970s; and a long period of decline after that point. The crises of the postwar settlements between capital and labour that emerged back then can be seen as a halt to 'the forward march of labour' – as historian Eric Hobsbawm (1978) concisely put it. Labour's weakness was further aggravated by the forward march of capital under the flag of the 'free market' and by the collapse of Soviet-style, authoritarian socialism, whose mere existence as an alternative social order had forced concessions from capital that workers had benefited from.[2] The aggressive liberalization of financial markets contributed to industrial decline in the former centres of capitalism and industrial growth in some areas located in the former periphery. In many countries of key significance for the global political economy, there has been a sustained decline in trade union membership and in support for labour parties – as well as a closure of political avenues that had been used for advancing the interests of workers (van der Linden, 2016). This makes for a fuzzy picture, in which huge sectors of different economies remain without forceful union representation, and where the representation of working-class interests at the political level is complicated by the fact that workers' parties are weak, have collapsed or have refashioned themselves as broad left organizations without a clear class constituency. The recurring and accelerating economic crises – first in the early 1980 and 1990s, then from 2007 onwards, and finally after the COVID-19 pandemic hit countries around the globe – mean that unions are further weakened. After all, getting embroiled in labour disputes is a high risk in times of a downturn, in particular when existing jobs are under threat. This makes identifying working-class forces harder than in periods of economic and institutional stability with comparably strong unions and labour parties, as was the case in Western Europe after the Second World War, and may lead us astray. 'In fact, there is the risk of continuing to bask in nostalgia for the forms and experiences of the past (or for those that are mere figments of our imagination), rather than recognizing the processes of class subjectivation that are taking place under our noses', remarks philosopher Cinzia Arruzza (2018). She has summarized succinctly the challenge faced, in the present moment, by scholars and activists aligned with the cause of labour.

So where is the working class in the 21st century? In my search, I have engaged with theories and analyses from the social sciences; media coverage;

---

[2] 'The main effect of 1989 is that capitalism and the rich have, for the time being, stopped being scared. All that made Western democracy worth living for its people – social security, the welfare state, a high and rising income for its wage-earners, and its natural consequences, diminution in social inequality and inequality of life chances – was the result of fear. Fear of the poor, and the largest and best-organised bloc of citizens in industrialised states – the workers; fear of an alternative that existed and could have spread, notably in the form Soviet Communism. Fear of the system's own instability' (Hobsbawm, 1991: 122).

quantitative and qualitative data; and, last, but not least, my own experiences, in the past 20 years, as a labour activist. But in recent years, I have also been drawing inspiration from the realm of fiction – and a number of recent novels that try to capture the present-day reality of class in their narratives.

A book that stood out for me was Thorsten Nagelschmidt's novel *Arbeit* [Work] (2020). In it, Nagelschmidt depicts a spring night in Kreuzberg in the early 2020s. Kreuzberg is an inner-city district of Berlin known for its vibrant nightlife. It used to be, and to a degree still is, a residential area for migrant workers and their families, but has become heavily gentrified in recent years. In a number of intersecting episodes, Nagelschmidt describes how the Kreuzberg nightlife and life in the city in general are sustained thanks to people working through this night – two paramedics and a pickpocket, two drug dealers and two police officers; two shopkeepers and a hostel manager; a delivery rider and a bouncer; a street sweeper and a taxi driver. The lives of the protagonists are connected because they all operate under same constraint – the constraint of capital accumulation, which forces them to keep going: '[T]he invisible hand burps with a feeling of satiety and contentment, wipes its mouth and says: *the sky is the limit* [English in the original], please carry on' (Nagelschmidt, 2020: 282).[3] And they are all connected insofar as they cross paths during this one night, with many of characters in some way or another taking care of other people.

The scenery is encapsulated in an inner monologue of a stressed paramedic called Tanja, a young woman originally from the Southern German city of Erlangen. After the delivery rider, a migrant hailing from Colombia and also a young female, has a road accident, Tanja and her colleague are called to the scene. They take the badly wounded woman to hospital, and Tanja recognizes herself in the person in her care:

> It could have been me, thinks Tanja, while they hoist the narcotized patient to a hospital stretcher. People have pain, people are hungry, and people are lonely, we drive to their homes – for a pittance and always in a hurry. We arrived in this city some time ago from somewhere with some expectations, and we now try to get by somehow, and sometimes someone kisses the dust, at some time everyone kisses the dust. (Nagelschmidt, 2020: 94–5)

Later in the night, while carrying an ailing older woman to hospital in her ambulance, Tanja offers a reflection on the general situation: 'The people who govern this city are at all nicely at home now, she thinks, it is just us, us

---

3   All quotations contained in this book from non-English language publications have been translated by the author.

and the sick, the beaten up, the helpless and the fakers, it is now up to us and we have to get this done somehow, together' (Nagelschmidt, 2020: 104–5).

If we follow Nagelschmidt, it does not matter so much where workers are from or what exactly they are doing – they are connected, and aware of their connection, which is expressed through Tanja's use of the words 'we' and 'together'. What they have in common is that they have to work to survive and their work is a struggle; that they earn very little; that they are not among those who make decisions over how things are run (those who 'govern'); that they cooperate with and support one another, and also help those who are even less fortunate; and that they keep society going. They operate in the cover of the night and at the margins of public attention, which is focused on the endless spectacle of the Berlin nightlife, and their work in its connectedness, as well as their acts of solidarity, are rendered invisible. Thanks to existence of those links and of solidarity, they can be said to be a class-in-formation – but a class that is constantly undergoing changes and is in flux because of the fleeting nature of their encounters.

Notably, none of Nagelschmidt's characters have a job in manufacturing and conform to the classical image of proletarian as a young to middle-aged White man with limited formal education, and none mention being aligned with a union or a workers' party. They are a diverse group of people – they differ in their educational backgrounds and their skills, are of different ages and genders, and hail from different parts of Berlin, Germany and the wider world. Nevertheless, as is expressed in Tanja's thoughts, there is a feeling of belonging together, and of not being among those who are in charge.

Despite Nagelschmidt's gritty, detailed descriptions of everyday life in Berlin, the imaginary he produces – like most literary narratives – lends itself to somewhat idealizing interpretations. It follows a storyline, and it is crucial for this storyline that the lives of the characters intersect. The police and the hostel manager may be trying to help other people. But is this enough to believe that they are on the same footing as everyone else? And importantly, my claim that Nagelschmidt describes a class-in-formation is based on my interpretation of the book. He does not even mention the word 'class'. Yet the strength of literature of this kind is that it expands our fields of vision and gives us clues on what to look for when we try to make sense of the world – and where to find it.

My book is about working classes, and I have been guided somewhat by Nagelschmidt when I looked for them – in non-industrial sectors, among diverse groups of workers, and in acts that connect people and are based on solidarity, namely strikes. Indeed, a key assumption guiding my research is that strikes are points where class relations crystallize in greater clarity than in other social situations. It is here that the connection between the organization of work in capitalist societies and social conflict comes into view, as well as the fact that people organize around their work. It is also here that people show expansive forms of solidarity – which is solidarity not just with those affected by exactly the same challenges and grievances in exactly the same place, but also with those facing similar challenges in different social and geographical spaces. And by focusing on such connections and acts of solidarity, I attempt to draw attention to working classes. If we follow Pierre Bourdieu (1987: 9), the act of making classes visible at the level of scholarship contributes to their formation as collective actors. In this sense, this book is an attempt to connect to a range of scholarly and literary books that, taken together, may make a small contribution to facilitating working-class formation in an age of deep crisis.

Alexander Gallas
Berlin, October 2022

Introduction

> [T]he global working class [is not] comprised exclusively of those who work for wages in factories or mines. Equally central are those who work in the fields and in private homes; in offices, hotels, and restaurants; in hospitals, nurseries, and schools; in the public sector and in civil society – the precariat, the unemployed, and those who receive no pay in return for their work. Far from being restricted to straight white men, in whose image it is still too often imagined, the bulk of the global working class is made up of migrants, racialized people, women both cis and trans – and people with different abilities, all of whose needs and desires are negated or twisted by capitalism.
>
> Arruzza et al, 2019: 24

'Walking down the stairs': the significance of strikes for labour movements

From a North Atlantic vantage point, it may be tempting to think that strikes are a relic from the industrial revolution, and that they share the fate of food riots or machine wrecking and play a marginal role as a mode of protest in contemporary societies. A superficial look at existing data suggests that there has been a steep decline in strike activity in Europe and the US in recent decades. According to the European Trade Union Institute, the weighted European average of days not worked due to industrial action was 62.7 per 1,000 employees in 2000 and 26.4 in 2020.[1] Likewise, numbers for the US from the Bureau of Labor Statistics say that 'days of idleness' due to strikes were 34 times higher in 1970 than in 2021 (see also Brecher, 2009: 75).[2] It is tempting to conclude that workers rarely choose the strike weapon as means of negotiating of wages and working conditions or of protesting more

---

[1] Data source: https://www.etui.org/strikes-map [Accessed 6 October 2022].
[2] Data source: https://www.bls.gov/web/wkstp/annual-listing.htm [Accessed 6 October 2022].

generally. In fact, some commentators suggest that labour relations have been pacified (Pakulski and Waters, 1996: 86; Meyerson, 2012), rendering the collective act of refusing to work meaningless.

Unsurprisingly, scholars sympathetic to labour disagree with this assessment. There are roughly five responses to the claim that strikes are superfluous, which are not mutually exclusive. The first centres on the argument that workers' reluctance to 'down tools' does not result from a general contentment with working conditions or from their ability to negotiate good conditions individually, but from a weakness of organized labour that is the result of attacks by capital in the form of processes of neoliberalization, which have been happening around the globe from the mid-1970s onwards (Harvey, 2005; Gallas, 2016b). In fact, neoliberalization has brought wage stagnation, cuts to benefits and persistent pressures on working conditions (Brecher, 2009: 75; Hein and Detzer, 2016; Palley, 2016) – and this has not just resulted in a hike in income inequality, but also in a 'demand gap' that causes sluggish growth and prevents capital from investing in the productive sector (Herr et al, 2014; Herr and Ruoff, 2016). It follows that organized labour needs to be strengthened not just for the sake of addressing the huge number of social problems that follow on the heels of high economic inequality (see Wilkinson and Pickett, 2014), but also for dealing with the economic failings of neoliberalism.[3] In a nutshell, the first response is that it does not follow from a sustained decline in strike incidence that going on strike is irrelevant from an economic point of view – quite the contrary.

The second response is concerned with the forms of collective action that workers are resorting to at the moment. Some labour scholars highlight that the strike is by far not the only form of collective action used by workers to air their grievances (Silver, 2003: 189; Gall, 2014; Vandaele, 2016). There is 'action short of a strike', which consists not in refusing to work altogether, but in carrying out only certain aspects or working slowly ('working-to-rule'). Furthermore, there are actions that do not directly affect the work process, for example, demonstrations, solidarity campaigns and consumer boycotts. This suggests that the decline of strike incidence cannot be equated with a pacification of labour relations; in fact, there are still a range of collective practices of protest with the help of which workers air their grievances.[4]

---

[3]   In light of this, some scholars have given serious thought to identifying strategies for the revitalization of organized labour (Voss and Sherman, 2000; Milkman and Voss, 2004; Lévesque et al, 2005; Gall, 2009; Urban, 2012; Gallas et al, 2016), and opting for a more antagonistic approach that includes using the strike weapon more often is seen by some authors as an important step in the revival of labour's fortunes (Connolly and Darlington, 2012; Hodder et al, 2016).

[4]   Existing data, however, raise doubts as to whether alternative forms of labour unrest really compensate for the fall in strike incidence (see Gall and Kirk, 2018).

The third reaction is similar. It highlights that strike data are by no means always valid and reliable, and that there are questions surrounding the methods of measurement. In some countries, official strike data have never existed; in the case of others, they stop at some point or are incomplete. A related problem is that small strikes are underreported or deliberately left out of statistics, which distorts findings, in particular if labour relations become fragmented. Last but not least, the methods of data collection diverge considerably (Dribbusch and Vandaele, 2016; Gall, 2022; Lodewick, 2022).

The fourth response highlights geographical shifts. It is encapsulated in a remark by Beverly Silver (2014: 50), who argues that 'where capital goes, labour-capital conflict shortly follows'. This statement suggests that the relocation of industrial production from the old capitalist centres to 'emerging' economies results in a shift of conflicts around work to new places. In other words, just because strike incidence is on the wane in the Global North does not mean that it is declining in other parts of the world.

But even so, the persistent decrease in strike incidence in the Global North calls into question the need for dedicating an entire book to strikes. If even labour scholars highlight the existence of other forms of collective action by workers and the fact that industrial militancy has moved elsewhere, why bother? This is where the fifth point becomes relevant, which is also the one I develop in this book. In this view, 'strikes matter' for organized labour (Van der Velden, 2007: 12; see Vandaele, 2011: 38–9; Nowak, 2018): They have a specific strategic significance because they can strengthen workers vis-à-vis capital, and it cannot be inferred from a sustained decline in strike incidence that they have become insignificant or are about to die out.

There are several arguments supporting the claim that strikes continue to be important. To begin with, it cannot be inferred from the existence of a sustained trend that this trend is irreversible. To examine this issue, it is worth going back to the immediate postwar period. In 1960, Arthur M. Ross and Paul T. Hartman asserted in a monograph called *Changing Patterns of Industrial Conflict* that there was 'a pronounced decline in strike activity throughout the world'. They argued that '[m]anagement and labor have outlived this instrument', and that '[t]he right to strike survives and is accorded its customary veneration but is seldom utilized in practice' (Ross and Hartman, 1960: 3). Ross and Hartman even went as far as observing a 'withering away of the strike, the virtual disappearance of industrial conflict in numerous countries where collective bargaining is still practiced' (1960: 6). In their view, changes such as the reduction in 'extreme poverty' and the proliferation of 'middle class mores' (1960: 44–5); the promise of advancing into white-collar work (1960: 45); 'profound changes in managerial attitudes' (1960: 47); new management techniques (1960: 49); 'organization among employers' (1960: 49); a greater degree of state involvement as 'supervisor of industrial disputes' (1960: 50); and the possibility to influence political outcomes without resorting to strikes had all contributed, in different ways, to this outcome (1960: 58). In a nutshell, the message was that the restructuring of labour relations after the Second World War was the death knell of worker militancy. Importantly, however, the industrial peace announced by Ross and Hartman only held for so long. From the late 1960s onwards, there was a surge in strike activities across the Global North (see Cohen, 2006: 9–29; Schmalz and Weinmann, 2016: 547–9). This shows that there is simply no guarantee that things carry on as they are. In fact, if capitalist development is tracked, it becomes clear from the data that there are cycles of strike action over longer periods, that is, significant increases followed by decreases and vice versa (Kelly, 1998; Cottle, 2017).

In addition, strike incidence does not tell us much about the quality of individual strikes. In this book, I discuss stoppages in detail that have occurred in recent years and have had a significant impact, in particular, on the political realm: the junior doctors' strikes in England and the general and feminist general strikes in Spain were actions not just demanding improvements to working conditions, but also forms of protest against the imposition of public sector cuts and austerity by governments; likewise, the strike action of train drivers in Germany did not just concern work hours and wages, but also the right of minority unions to enter collective bargaining negotiations and the right to strike more generally. This suggests that individual strikes may still have significant economic and political effects even if they occur in the context of an overall decline in strike action.

Correspondingly, labour scholars and activists have been highlighting the importance of strikes not so much because they occur rarely or oftentimes, but because they have a specific strategic purpose and symbolic content for labour movements. This is related both to the self-conceptions of labour activists and their organizations and to their effects in terms of developing force vis-à-vis an antagonist. A German-language volume I edited together with Jörg Nowak and Florian Wilde (2012) titled *Political Strikes in the European Crisis* contains interviews with union representatives and labour activists from a number of Western European countries. The interviewed were all involved in organizing protest strikes against austerity in the 2000s and early 2010s. Our conversations with them are relevant in the context of this book because they reflect on where strategic the importance of strikes lies – in particular the mass strikes that occurred in the context of the economic and financial crisis in Europe and conveyed a political message.

Michael Pieber, an official of the Austrian Union of Private-Sector Employees, Print, Journalism and Paper (GPA-djp), comments, for example, on a nation-wide, one-day strike against pension cuts that took place in his country in 2003. Pieber's reflections are important because he comes from a historically strike-averse country, which means that the effects of a single mass strike can be isolated more clearly than in countries with a high strike frequency. Pieber remarks:

> It was often said in advance [of the strike]: 'Actually, we thought that they can't do it anymore. They have been in their union headquarters since the war and they have not managed to walk down the stairs; they have even installed a lift.' For us as a union it was very important to recognize, on a fundamental level, that we can be a fighting organization – and of course people now believed that we are indeed capable of a forceful representation of the interests of employed people. (Pieber, 2012: 132)

What becomes clear from Pieber's statement is that the strike was significant because *workers collectively exercised power* ('a forceful representation of the interests of employed people').

Arguably, there are sources of power accessible to workers that are brought about by the organization of waged work in capitalism – and they can be tapped to redress, to a degree, the structural dominance of capital that is enshrined in the capitalist relations of production (see Wright, 2000; Silver, 2003; Dörre, 2011; Webster, 2015). What Pieber's statement also highlights, however, is that it was not enough to possess these sources of power. Workers have to collaborate in order to make use of them. And a standard practice of doing so is the strike. My working definition of this practice is as follows: *The strike is a collective practice of workers who stop working to make powerful and forceful demands vis-à-vis an antagonist* (see Hyman, 1989: 17; van der Linden, 2008: 182–3).

Importantly, the invocation of the need for collaboration points to an ethical-political commitment that workers need to make if they act in concert: They have to subordinate any individual needs and interests to a common cause. This commitment is generally referred to as 'solidarity'. It becomes clear here that part of the significance of strikes for labour movements lies in the fact that they activate the potential of workers to exercise power collectively.

According to Pieber, the act of going on strike did not just demonstrate that his union was capable of developing collective strength. It also challenged negative perceptions outsiders had of the union ('people now believed that we are indeed capable ...') as well as the self-perception of union members ('[f]or us ... it was very important to recognise that ... we can be a fighting organisation'). The strike had mobilizing and unifying effects, which were linked to cognitive shifts and learning processes: Through the experience of confrontation, it became clear – both to union officials and members as well as to other members of the public – that there is a fundamental conflict between capital and labour, and that workers can exercise power together. In this sense, the strike also acted as an instrument of spreading knowledge about the organization of work across society and the patterns of collective confrontation attached to it. In a nutshell, the strike was an act of self-affirmation and self-assertion of organized labour, to borrow from psychological terminology, or, more prosaically, of *working-class formation*.

In an interview in the same book, Sean Vernell – a representative of the University and College Union, which represents workers in the further and higher education sector in Britain – also touched upon this theme. Commenting on a nation-wide one-day strike across the entire public sector, which was about protesting against pension cuts and took place on 30 November 2011, he said: 'The working class is like a genie in a bottle. And on this day, the genie got out of the bottle. We haven't seen this for thirty, forty years. Millions of workers in the streets' (Vernell, 2012: 180–1). Following Vernell, the strike set free the spectre of a working class confronting a government that was seen as acting on behalf of capital. In other words, it was a collective practice that created links between workers, fostered a sense of acting in unison when making demands vis-à-vis an antagonist and thus contributed to working-class formation.

My argument could be taken to imply that each and every strike has such effects. But that would be too simplistic. Of course, strike calls usually fail to mobilize every single worker. In fact, very often certain groups of workers chose not to participate in strikes. They disagree with the latter's goals, are worried about a loss in income or expect other negative consequences for themselves, for example losing their job. Strikes often create two polarized camps among workers – those who walk out and those who continue working. A well-known example is the 1984–5 miners' strike in Britain, which was not just a fiercely fought confrontation between the National Union of Mineworkers (NUM) and the Thatcher government, but also created deep divisions between striking and working miners (Gallas, 2016b: 174–9).

Similarly, the solidarity underpinning strikes does not always take on an 'inclusive' form. Some strikes are 'exclusionary' (Marx Ferree and Roth, 1998: 628), that is, their demands are irrelevant to, or even work against, the needs and interests of other groups of workers. This can happen if they are strikes of small, specialized occupational groups. These stoppages do not contribute to class formation because their demands cannot be expanded to workers outside their constituency or connected to the latter's demand. In cases where they fortify privileges not available to others, they can even contribute to *class partition*, not class formation. Furthermore, strikes often result in defeats, and these can contribute to the demoralization of labour movements. And last but not least, it would be wrong to assume that all organizations of labour sooner or later use the strike weapon. In fact, some of them are averse to doing so because of the high risks attached to using it. Stoppages can damage businesses beyond repair, they can harm people through disrupting everyday life, and they can result in repression and job losses. The Pieber interview illustrates the reluctance of some unions to engage in militant action: The 2003 stoppage was the first large-scale political strike in Austria around a single issue after the end of the Second World War (Pieber, 2012: 132).

But labour movements, no matter what their goals and dominant orientations are, only qualify as such if they somehow try to exercise workers' power and invoke the need for solidarity in the process. Otherwise, it would not make sense to use the term 'movements', which is associated with a form of people acting in concert to achieve a goal. It follows that none of my critical observations disqualify the statement that strikes tend to have self-affirming and self-assertive effects – even if these may be temporary, limited to an in-group or overshadowed by other effects in certain contexts. Against this backdrop, I contend that the importance of the strike weapon for labour movements lies in the fact that they bring out what defines labour movements as movements. They bring out 'the genie in the bottle', to use Vernell's words, which may not always be the working class, but which is always a labour movement.

All in all, I contend that strikes have three key characteristics:

1. Strikes suspend competition between the workers participating in them, and by going on strike, workers subscribe to common demands and goals (solidarity).
2. Strikes are a form of collective disruption with the potential to enforce and reverse decisions and undermine decision-making capacities of other actors such as capitalists or politicians. They question existing decision-making authorities, for example management or the government, and attempt to transform workers into such an authority (workers' power).
3. Strikes facilitate learning processes on the side of workers about their collective power and collective goals (workers' self-affirmation and self-assertion).

In sum, I contend that strikes matter – both because they encapsulate, more than other forms of collective action, the goals and purpose of labour movements, and because there are still strike waves with a high economic and political significance.

From Halewood to Whitehall: on the changing faces of strikes

It is one thing to make principled arguments about the nature of strikes in capitalism in response to quantitative changes in strike incidence. But it is also important to ask whether there are qualitative changes behind the numbers. These come into view if one considers how the research field has evolved. A useful starting point for this purpose is to look, once more, at a seminal contribution to strike research – a monograph published in 1972 and written by Richard Hyman with the apt title *Strikes*. Today, *Strikes* is a classic text in labour studies, of which there are four editions. The book is mostly about Britain, which means that its general gist can be re-evaluated by considering more recent labour conflicts from the same country. This may give us some indications on how strikes have changed over time.

The cover of the first edition shows a black-and-white photograph of what appear to be miners wearing hard hats.[5] This was a fitting choice back in 1972 because in January and February of the same year, there had been a large-scale strike over pay in the British mining sector, the first official stoppage in the sector since the General Strike of 1926. The dispute led to power cuts across the country and culminated in the 'Battle of Saltley Gate', the mass picketing of a coke storage depot in Birmingham, which was supported by workers from other industries and secured victory for the miners (Cohen, 2006: 19–20; Gallas, 2016b: 167–8).

The opening passage of the actual text recounts a different, 'unremarkable dispute', which Hyman had chosen to discuss because it was the first workplace conflict to be covered extensively in the news after the book was commissioned (1989: 11). In June 1971, a shop steward was fired at Ford's Halewood plant in the Northwest of England. As a reaction, the workers downed their tools and spontaneously walked out. According to Hyman (1989: 13–17), the fact that the dismissal and the walk-out took place at all are a reflection of tensions caused by a drawn-out dispute over pay at Ford, which had started in January 1971 and took nine weeks to settle. It appears that management wanted to crack down on the activities of shop stewards in the aftermath of the dispute; the strike ensured that the fired shop steward was reinstated.

Both the cover and the narrative at the beginning of the book evoke the image of the classic economic strike where presumably White, male, industrial workers 'down tools' with the aim of fighting over their pay and working conditions. What is remarkable is how clichéd this image of labour struggle seems today. The Halewood plant still exists – it is partly owned by Ford and partly by Jaguar today – but the car industry in Britain employs far fewer people, and industrial decline in the country has accelerated in recent decades.[6] Strikes in manufacturing are not as common anymore, and strike

---

[5] See https://tinyurl.com/44wtee6t for a reproduction of the cover [Accessed 19 December 2023].

[6] In Britain, the number of people employed in motor vehicle manufacturing has fallen from 500,000 in 1971 to 166,000 in 2018 (Rhodes, 2019: 6). The share of the people working in the industrial sector amounted to almost a third of the entire workforce in the early 1990s and is less than a fifth today (see Volume 2, Figure 5.1).

incidence in Britain is significantly lower than in the 1970s or 1980s (see Volume 2, Figure 5.3 and Table 5.3 and Volume 2, Chapter 7).

This is neither to say that workers no longer go on strike, nor that industrial strikes of the Halewood type have ceased to exist. But an initial observation on what appears to have changed is the constituency of strikes, that is, the location of striking workers in the social division of labour. It may be impossible to capture the striker of today in Britain, Europe or the wider world in a single image. But if we ask what an iconic image resembling the cover of Hyman's book would look like in the present day and age, a worthy contender is the frontpage of *i newspaper* from 2 September 2016. It shows a doctor who appears to be female and of non-European descent holding up a placard with a slogan in defence of the British National Health Service.[7] In fact, in a conjuncture marked by a deep crisis, numerous strikes with mass support in Britain and beyond have taken place in the public sector, and they have involved women workers with professional backgrounds who traditionally would have been considered rather averse to militant forms of trade unionism. This observation is in line with the facts that the public sector is the stronghold of British trade unionism today (see Volume 2, Table 5.2), and that there is a feminization of the union rank-and-file in the country.[8]

In fact, the frontpage with the picture of the protesting medic was published in the context of a strike wave that took place in 2016 in all of England and involved junior doctors. It made headlines and was widely supported both within the medical profession and in the general public, and part of it was a demonstration in Whitehall in April 2016, which was attended by the then leader of the Labour Party, Jeremy Corbyn. The Whitehall event points to what is potentially a second, important shift: Whereas the Halewood episode was an economic strike in a narrow sense, this is much less the case if workers fight against deteriorating working conditions, are employed by the state and are faced with public sector cuts. Public sector strikes are economic and political strikes almost by default because they do not just concern the conditions of the consumption of labour power at the level of

---

[7] See https://tinyurl.com/4mu29775 for a reproduction of the frontpage [Accessed 18 December 2023].

[8] In 1995, union density was significantly higher for male than for female workers (32.2 per cent overall; 35 per cent for males; and 29.7 per cent for females). By 2021, the numbers had fallen significantly, and the gender discrepancy had been reversed: 23.1 per cent overall; 20 per cent for males; and 26.3 per cent for females (data source: BEIS, Trade Union Membership Statistics, May 2022, https://assets.publishing.service.gov.uk/government/uploads/system/uploads/attachment_data/file/1078005/Trade_Union_Membership_Statistics_Tables_May_2022.ods [Accessed 1 October 2022]).

production but also political decisions concerning public expenditure and the public infrastructure.

A third shift concerns strike tactics and the legality of strikes. In contrast to the Halewood strike, the junior doctors' dispute had an official status. There were strike ballots in line with British trade union law, and to my knowledge, no wildcat strikes took place in the context of this dispute. Correspondingly, the parties involved and the object of conflict were clearly defined: it was a conflict between junior doctors and National Health Service employers in England over work hours. The available data from Britain on unionization and industrial action confirm that there has been move from unofficial to official action.[9]

Even a superficial comparison of the two strikes yields interesting results. If they are representative of anything, there seems to be a move away from wildcat strikes and towards legalism; away from industry and towards the public sector; away from the classic constituency of male, industrial workers to a more mixed crowd; and, last but not least, away from highlighting economic issues to becoming a form of political protest. In short, there may be a shift in strike tactics, a changed composition of the working class and a shift in the politics of striking.

Correspondingly, I will chart, in my book, the passage from Halewood to Whitehall. I will examine the reasons why people go on strike and assess the impact of their actions on the social context within which they operate. In doing the latter, the political dimension of strike wave will move to the foreground. In recent years, strikes mobilizing large groups of workers appear to have contributed significantly to heated political debates not just on labour, but also on economic and fiscal policy.

The research problem: strikes and working-class formation

The discussion of the changing faces of strikes underscores that the constituency, the goals and the effects of strikes change according to time and

---

[9]   For obvious reasons, numbers on unofficial actions are hard to come by. For 1964–6, the Donovan Commission – a commission tasked by the government with making proposals for the restructuring of labour relations – reported that only 74 out of 2,275 strikes were official (Donovan Commission, 1971: 96); numbers provided by Gregor Gall and Sheila Cohen based on newspaper coverage suggest that the share of unofficial strikes has fallen considerably between 1990 and 2010 – from 30 to 17 per cent – even if they still take place (2013: 95–6). Despite the fact that Gall and Cohen's study is dated, it is plausible to assume that there are far fewer wildcat strikes than in the 1970s. The reason is that the Thatcher and Major governments introduced, in the 1980s and 1990s, legislation directed at curbing wildcat strikes (see Gallas, 2016b: *passim*).

place. As such, this is of course a rather trivial claim – most social phenomena show a significant degree of variation when they are examined over time and in different contexts. The challenge lies in identifying whether general trends exist concerning the changes – and if so, why they have emerged, and what their effects are on the contexts in which they occur. If we want to comprehend what drives change in the area of strikes, it is necessary to examine their broader social contexts.

From this perspective, materialist approaches to labour studies are useful. They look at labour relations as class relations and, in so doing, highlight the latter's link with the organization of work in capitalism. And they thus connect with my general research interest described in the preface.

Karl Marx (1976: 416) famously argued that the historical emergence of the working class as a *collective actor* was a reaction to the emergence of industrial production along capitalist lines and the tendency of capitalist competition to extend the working day ever more ('the production of absolute surplus value'). One of the first films ever shot, *La Sortie de l'Usine Lumière à Lyon* from 1895, is emblematic for the close connection between industrial work and class formation. One of its English-language titles is 'Exiting the Factory'; in a single shot, it shows the open gate of a factory located on the periphery of Lyon, and the workers leaving for their lunch break.[10] In an age where parts of the world experience sustained processes of deindustrialization (Rodrik, 2016; Kollmeyer, 2018), this raises the question of what happens to working classes when the factory gates are shut for good. Taking up Silver's point about how labour unrest follows on the heels of capital being shifted to novel sites of production, one also needs to ask what happens to labour struggles in the former industrial strongholds that now experience deindustrialization.

There are broadly two positions in the literature on this issue. One side argues that the type of collective agency that Marx and his followers used to ascribe to industrial workers is vanishing. This claim can be found, for example, in Manuel Castells' classic study *The Rise of the Network Society* (2010; see Gorz, 1982; Mason, 2015). His book is a useful starting point because it heralded the rise of a new society and was widely discussed after being published in the mid-1990s. Castells argues that we have entered a 'post-industrial period' characterized by the emergence of 'informational capitalism' (2010: 225, 18). He adds that class relations have changed fundamentally in the process: 'Capital tends to escape in its hyperspace of pure circulation, while labor dissolves its collective entity into an infinite variation of individual existences' (2010: 506–7). The counterclaim is that the decline of manufacturing does not amount to an end to waged work, and

---

[10] Source: www.youtube.com/watch?v=HI63PUXnVMw [Accessed 24 March 2022]

that working classes are being reconstituted outside industrial production. Among others, Leo Panitch is taking this position (2001: 367; see also Moody, 2017; Arruzza et al, 2019: 24): 'in the advanced capitalist world the decline in the size of the traditional industrial labour force is accompanied by the proletarianization of many service and professional occupations and the spread of more unstable, casual and contingent employment'. This creates space for new forms of collective agency – or 'new strategies for labour', as Panitch puts it (2001: 367).

This debate may sound scholastic at first, but it has far-reaching political implications: If the working class is in terminal decline thanks to deindustrialization, recent attempts to revitalize class politics are futile; if new working classes are emerging, the opposite is the case.[11] To advance in both the class theoretical and the political debates, it makes sense to resort to systematic empirical research. This may tell us whether it is possible to identify processes of class formation outside manufacturing, which would suggest that Panitch is right, or whether this is not the case, which would imply that Castells is correct. And one possible area where this can be examined systematically is indeed strike research. If we follow Marx, labour disputes are catalysts of class formation. For the sake of the argument, it is worth operating with a research heuristic, that is, focusing exclusively on strikes that occur outside the industrial sector. Consequently, my research question in this book is as follows: *What are the class effects of non-industrial strikes – or to what extent do they contribute to working-class formation?*

A useful starting point for a conceptualization of strikes along these lines is to return to the question of their potentially inclusive or exclusionary nature. Some strikes are based on inclusive solidarity, which means that they have the potential to expand beyond their original constituency and address workers in general, that is, people who depend on the sale of their labour power to make a living. An obvious example is the wave of public sector strikes against pension cuts in Britain from 2011 to 2014, which were not just about pensions for public sector workers, but about public sector cuts in general (Gallas and Nowak, 2012; Gallas, 2018a: 249). Since working people use public services and access to public services is part of their social wage, the demands made in the context of the strikes in question resonated far beyond their original constituency. Other strikes are exclusionary because they have a clearly defined constituency and are built on demands that are only relevant to this specific group or are even about denying other groups of workers equal access to resources. An extreme example is the 1922 Rand

---

[11] For some of the latest scholarly interventions aimed at reviving working-class politics, see Devine and Sensier (2017), Ainsley (2018), Blanc (2019), Candeias et al (2019) and Demirović (2020).

Rebellion in South Africa. White mineworkers struck against relaxing the colour bar, a ban that prevented Black workers from being hired for certain jobs. The mine owners wanted to weaken the existing regulations with the intention of cutting wage costs (Simons and Simons, 1969: 271–99; Johnstone, 2023: 125–36).

Importantly, it needs to be considered that strike demands can change over time or depending on their context – and the same can be said about their effects on third parties. Many commentators portrayed the strikes in the German railway sector, which I discuss in Volume 2, Chapter 6, as exclusionary because they were driven by inter-union competition. But as I demonstrate, the case is far more complicated.

The existence of different types of solidarity suggests that a simplistic account of strikes portraying them, in every single case, as instances of the exercise of workers' power is not adequate. Instead, a theoretical framework is needed that captures conceptually their ambiguous effects. I propose that this framework is offered by materialist class and state theory. The version that I put forward in this book is centred on Nicos Poulantzas' conception of class as laid out in *Classes in Contemporary Capitalism* (1974), and is dynamized by an account of class formation and class partition informed by Rosa Luxemburg's seminal study *The Mass Strike* (2008). It is the latter account in particular that caters for the ambiguities surrounding class effects: If strikes are inclusive, they contribute to class formation because they promote a unifying form of solidarity that addresses workers as workers; if they are exclusive, they can be seen as playing part in class partition because they deepen divisions among workers. As I show in my empirical analyses of strikes contained in this book, this can be assessed by examining the demands, constituencies and mobilization dynamics of strikes.

Obviously, these are not clear-cut criteria because demands and practices have contradictory effects. This is surely the case with the strikes I look at, whose class effects are not transparent. I contend that a specific strength of materialist class and state theory lies in catering for such ambiguities. A useful conceptualization of trade unions from this vantage point can be found in the works of German state theorist and labour scholar Josef Esser (1982: 225–46; 2014). It allows for producing nuanced accounts of strikes, which refrain from simply equating the activities of unions with class agency. One needs to ask to what extent these activities benefit labour as a pole in the relation of forces with capital (see Gallas, 2018b). This means that a case study-type, situation-specific analysis is required when the class effects of industrial action are assessed. Against this backdrop, it can then be asked whether there are reasons to assume that the effects of the strikes in question have contributed to working-class formation.

In so doing, I hope to contribute to a debate that has guided labour studies in recent years – the question of how to revitalize organized labour in an age of crisis. My research is based on a wager: If we understand the class effects of strikes, we are better positioned to advocate for strategies that are, on the one hand, in line with the ethical-political orientation of labour studies and, on the other hand, produce outcomes that conform to the interests of workers. In a nutshell, my book is about promoting a *class-analytical agenda for labour studies* and a *class-oriented strategy for organized labour*.

Zooming in and out: an incorporated comparison of strike waves in Western Europe and beyond

Hyman's book was exclusively focused on Britain, but the issue at stake has a far wider resonance. As the global nature of the multifaceted crisis of contemporary capitalism shows – whether it concerns finance, ecological issues, health or geopolitics – most of the grievances experienced by workers are by no means exclusive to any single national state. Consequently, strikes are not specific to any zone of the global political economy, and a study of strikes with an exclusively national focus threatens to ignore the transnational forces at work in the current conjuncture of an ongoing and protracted global crisis. As the proponents of global labour studies have suggested (see Silver, 2003; Webster et al, 2008; Brookes and McCallum, 2017), it is not enough, considering the global nature of capitalism and its crises, to focus exclusively on a single national state. And yet, the endeavour of analysing labour relations from a global vantage point comes with the challenge of paying enough attention to detail. Arguably, it is only possible to understand the social significance of qualitative shifts in strike patterns if one conducts a detailed analysis of strikes and their effects. This suggests that there is a need, in the field of strike research, for research designs that are based on a compromise between breadth and depth.[12]

This monograph is the result of such a compromise. I draw on Philip McMichael's method of 'incorporated comparison' to work towards a reconciliation of the needs for generality and specificity (see Volume 2, Chapter 1). To reach sufficient breadth, Volume 2, Chapter 4 comprises an empirical analysis of non-industrial strikes in the conjuncture of crisis around world. If one wills, I am zooming out to the global level in that chapter.

In contrast, Volume 2, Chapters 6–8 contain a comparative analysis of three country cases, Britain, Germany and Spain. It is integrated via a research

---

[12]   In the preface to the first edition of his book, Hyman already acknowledges that his exclusive focus on Britain is 'regrettably insular' (1989: 7). In later works, he branched out and became a prolific writer on labour relations and trade unionism in Western Europe (see Hyman, 2001).

design that is called a 'most-different comparison'. I contend that it is justified to see the country cases as different because they represent diverging regimes of labour relations (individualist-repressive, corporatist and mixed).

To reach sufficient depth, the country case studies cover one strike wave in each of the countries – in this sense, I am zooming in. These strike waves were located in the service and public sectors. They all occurred at roughly the same time, that is, within the conjuncture of a global crisis of neoliberal capitalism that commenced in 2007 and is still ongoing. Furthermore, they were marked by mass participation, with thousands of workers across the respective country getting involved; and they were widely discussed at the political level and fed into political confrontations. Consequently, examining them may allow me to identify key traits of the conjuncture of crisis in the area of labour relations.

The disputes in question are the railway strikes in Germany 2015; the junior doctors' strike in England in 2016; and the general strikes in Spain, which were directed against austerity in the early 2010s and, making a reappearance as feminist general strikes in the late 2010s, against the gendered division of labour as well as violence against women. Notably, none of these strike waves, despite being located in different sectors, conform to the classic image of the strike that Hyman created with reference to Halewood.

My sample may be limited considering the variety of present-day labour relations and movements around the globe. But it allows for a comparison of countries with significant differences within a fairly integrated economic-political setting that has been affected considerably by deindustrialization. In this sense, the book is not just about the passage from Halewood to Whitehall. It also about the journey from Rheinhausen in the West of Germany, the site of a 164-day steelworkers' strike in 1987, to Berlin Central Station, one of the German railway hubs heavily affected by the stoppages in that sector in recent years. And it is about moving from Asturias, where coalminers walked out in order to protest the Franco regime in 1962 and 1963, to the plazas in the city centre of Madrid, where numerous large-scale protests and strikes have been taking place from 2010 onwards against austerity, neoliberalism and patriarchy. I wager that it is possible to identify general trends if these detailed accounts are compared systematically and taken together with my observations at the global level.

Structure of the book

I planned and wrote this book as a standard research monograph, but my manuscript turned out to be far too long for this format. As a result, it is now a two-volume book. For ease of use, each volume contains an individual table of contents, distinct lists of abbreviations, figures and tables, and a standalone bibliography. Likewise, the parts and chapters in either volume are numbered separately. Whereas the preface and the introduction to this volume as well as the conclusion to the second volume concern the entire text, this does not apply to the afterword to this volume and the preface to the second volume. The sole purpose of the latter two sections is to summarize the story so far, and to explain what will happen next. In other words, they are about identifying where in the overall line of argument the passage from one volume to the next is located.

Importantly, the volume divide is not arbitrary: It reflects the distinction between theory and empirical research. Whereas the chapters contained in the first volume primarily concern conceptual issues, those in the second volume mainly offer detailed examinations of strikes in their socioeconomic and political contexts.

Volume 1 is divided into two parts. The first one contains Chapters 1 to 3. Its function is to describe the broader research field my work is located in, global labour studies, and where it connects with, and departs from, the existing literature. As I show in Chapter 1, there is a normative commitment implicit in key contributions to global labour studies, which consists in being in favour of the collective organization of workers. This commitment can be made explicit and justified by drawing upon arguments of social philosophy, namely a position called 'qualified ethical naturalism'. It consists in supporting working-class formation. What this exactly means for scholarly practices is the topic of Chapter 2. I contrast and compare different ways in which global labour scholars have conceptualized their relationship to workers, and explain how I see this relationship. In line with the claim of 'being on the side of workers', much of the literature aims to identity the power resources of workers. Arguably, the power resources approach (PRA) has become a dominant paradigm in the field of global labour studies, but it suffers from a serious limitation because it does not systematically discuss the concept of 'class' – and thus equates union power and class power. I discuss the limitations of the PRA and the ambiguities they result in when labour relations are analysed in Chapter 3.

Against this backdrop, I lay out, in Part II of this volume, a class theoretical foundation for global labour studies. In Chapter 4, I discuss critical realist ontological assumptions to highlight the specificity of a materialist conceptualization of class, which sees it as resulting from the organization of work across society. On this basis, I develop, in Chapter 5, a Poulantzasian understanding of class as a set of social relations inscribed in the capitalist mode of production, which is focused on class struggle and class domination. I supplement this, in Chapter 6, with a Luxemburgian, conjunctural take on class formation that emphasizes the importance of strikes. In Chapter 7, I discuss what the existence of the capitalist state means for class relations in capitalism and for working-class formation.

Equipped with the conceptual tools developed in Volume 1, I focus, in Volume 2, on strikes and their socioeconomic and political context. Again, the volume is divided into two parts. In the first part, I look at the subject matter from a global vantage point. In Chapter 1, I explain how McMichael's method of 'incorporated comparison' can be brought to be bear in the field of global labour studies and strike research. I contextualize my analysis in Chapter 2. With a concept inspired by Antonio Gramsci, I describe the global conjuncture of crisis as a 'catastrophic disequilibrium', which results from processes of neoliberalization in the last five decades. In the succeeding chapter, I discuss, with the help of descriptive statistics, how the latter have affected labour relations in the service and public sectors around the world. Chapter 4 follows, which brings my reflections on research from a global perspective to a conclusion. I present a mapping of non-industrial strikes around the world in the conjuncture of crisis, which is based on systematically analysing newspaper coverage.

In the second part of Volume 2, I shift my perspective and zoom in on Western Europe. It contains my comparison of the three strike waves in Germany, Britain and Spain. In Chapter 5, I discuss how labour relations and trade unionism have developed in the three countries, and how they have been affected by deindustrialization and neoliberalization. Chapter 6 contains my account of the railway strikes in Germany; Chapter 7 my discussion of the stoppages by junior doctors in Britain; and Chapter 8 my reflections on the general and feminist general strikes in Spain. In my conclusion, I present a systematic comparison of the three cases, connect them to my observations at the global level, assess Castells' claim and Panitch's counterclaim and provide an answer to my research question.

It should be clear that there is a rationale for dividing the book into two volumes, and yet they remain connected. Volume 1 offers insights into the nature of class in capitalism, but they may remain abstract, and their relevance for understanding real-concrete conjunctures of capitalism may stay obscure if they are not discussed with reference to actual events and processes. And Volume 2 contains detailed accounts of strikes in the present day, but their general socioeconomic and political significance beyond the individual case may not present itself if they are considered without consulting the theory. Consequently, the two volumes should be seen as constituting an organic whole and should be read together. The theory guides the empirical research process by stipulating what to look for, and the empirical research ensures that the social world is captured in its multifaceted, ambiguous and contradictory nature.

PART I

Global Labour Studies: Conducting Research on the Side of Workers

1

Being on the Side of Workers: On the Normative Foundations of Global Labour Studies*

The normative gap in global labour studies

Karl Marx and Friedrich Engels famously ended the *Manifesto of the Communist Party* with a call to arms – '*Proletarier aller Länder, vereinigt euch!*' [Proletarians of all countries, unite!] (1959: 493; emphasis in the original). Ever since, the issue of transnational solidarity and labour internationalism has formed part of the debates on the strategies and aims of labour movements. And through the ages, these debates have been of concern to scholars, who have not just discussed the prospects for solidarity that cuts across national boundaries, but also – and relatedly – the specificities of labour relations in different parts of the world, the issue of labour migration and the geographical scales of labour struggles (see van der Linden, 2008; Gallas, 2016a). In response to the emergence of global production networks from the 1970s onwards, 'global labour studies' has emerged as an academic project and a demarcated research field. Sociologists and other social scientists have committed to moving beyond the 'methodological nationalism' of industrial relations research and examining labour relations and movements from a global perspective (see Nowak, 2021a). This endeavour has become institutionalized in various ways – for example through the establishment of the Research Committee on Labour Struggles (RC44) of the International Sociological Association in 1990, the Global Labour University (GLU) in 2002 and the *Global Labour Journal* in 2010.[1]

---

* A previous version of this chapter forms part of the book *Marxism, Social Movements and Collective Action*, which was edited by Adrián Piva and Augustín Santella and published by Palgrave in 2022.

1 Obviously, some scholars have studied labour from a transnational angle long before this point (see van der Linden, 2005: 227–8). But from today's vantage point, it seems fair to say that these endeavours reached a new degree of institutionalization only around 40 years ago, and that this process roughly coincided with the rise of global labour production

In recent years, several authors have made programmatic statements in which they seek to explain the aims and challenges of global labour studies. Marissa Brookes and Jamie McCallum, for example, suggest that there is a community of scholars from a variety of social science disciplines committed to a 'new labour transnationalism' that attempts 'to steer economic globalisation towards more equitable ends' (2017: 202). Similarly, Maria Lorena Cook and others (among them the author of this book) call for focusing global labour studies on 'who is being pushed to, or has continuously remained on, the side-lines' (2020: 75). It is clear from the context that they refer to people performing productive and reproductive labour who are at bottom of work-related hierarchies and to the distribution of wealth created through global divisions of labour. And in the most recent contribution of the three, Jörg Nowak emphasizes 'labour agency', that is, the capacity of the workers around the globe to actively shape their social surroundings, which he locates not just in the workplace, but also in 'popular and political traditions of mobilisation' that are often community-based, and in struggles around the reproduction of labour-power (2021a: 9).

Notably, none of these programmatic statements highlight the challenges of managing multinational corporations, recruiting highly skilled staff capable of operating in transnational settings or ensuring a steady supply of labour power to keep global production networks intact. They are not primarily concerned with obstacles faced by managers, business owners or investors but by workers – people who carry out surplus labour for the benefit of others, be it in the realm of production or reproduction. And in so doing, the authors in question seek to validate the economic, political and cultural significance of workers' collective activities and struggles in different parts of the world. In this regard, they resemble the US sociologist Howard S. Becker, who famously declared that he and his colleagues 'usually take the side of the underdog' (Becker, 1967: 244).[2]

But this raises a question. Alvin Gouldner, another eminent figure in US postwar sociology, responded to Becker by asking: 'Why should we

---

networks. Importantly, the moniker 'global labour studies' was not used from the start. There was a *Newsletter of International Labour Studies* from 1978 to 1990, which was edited by Peter Waterman (see Munck, 2009: 625), and a number of books and article that also spoke of international rather than global labour studies (Taylor, 2009: 437–40). Taken together, the contributions to international labour studies can be seen as constituting the first phase of what was later called global labour studies.

[2] At the time, Becker's observation concerned sociology in general, and he sought to point out the partisan nature of any research endeavour in the social sciences. According to him, 'we cannot avoid taking sides' (Becker, 1967: 239); he added that it is unavoidable to prioritize certain perspectives on social settings over others because making sense of society means looking at it from a certain position (Becker, 1967: 245). For him, it followed that it is impossible 'to do research that is uncontaminated by personal and political sympathies' (Becker, 1967: 239).

undertake our studies from the standpoint of the subordinate, underdog?' (Gouldner, 1968: 105). Gouldner's question of course also applies to global labour studies, and it is relevant because a pro-worker stance is by no means immune to critique or in line with the general intuitions of scholars or society more broadly. Indeed, it has been criticized fiercely – not just liberals, but also by left-leaning post-Marxists.[3]

Notably, global labour scholars are mostly silent when it comes to explaining why they are on the side of workers, and what being on this side exactly means.[4] It follows that they make themselves susceptible to being charged with bias if they uphold their pro-worker stance. This is a critical problem because it leaves them open to accusations that this an arbitrary commitment, and that the validity of their analyses stands and falls with other people being willing to honour it.[5] Indeed, scholarship for, and on behalf of,

---

[3]   Economic liberals traditionally take issue with the idea that capitalism is marked by an asymmetric relationship between labour and capital. They emphasize individual freedom and the beneficial effects of 'free' markets for everyone and thus question the right of workers to unionize (see Hayek, 1960: 267; 1973–7: 71; Friedman, 1962: 124). In contrast, post-Marxists do not deny this asymmetry, but emphasize the importance of collective struggles around issues other than work and question why the needs of workers should be prioritized politically over those of other social groups (see Laclau and Mouffe, 1985: 167–8; Postone, 1993: 371).

[4]   Of course, this is also a self-critique, and there are some exceptions. Edward Webster discusses partisanship and its practical implications in a book chapter called 'Choosing sides: the promise and pitfalls of a critically engaged sociology in apartheid South Africa', which was published in a German-language book in 2017. Webster is not so much concerned with my focus here, the normative justification of a pro-worker stance, but with a practical ethical dilemma faced by partisan researchers: As scholars, they are committed to openly sharing knowledge and research findings, but through sharing, they may do harm to allied people or organizations in their research field (see also Chapter 2). But he acknowledges the relevance of normative questions when he says that 'one takes sides on the basis of certain value commitments' (quote from the original manuscript). Tobias Schulze-Cleven also briefly discusses such commitments in a programmatic chapter on the future of work. His contribution is a more a comment on US labour studies than on global labour studies, but it can easily be transferred to the global level. According to him, '[t]wo beliefs about how to implement substantive democracy anchor the field: work should be rewarding for all workers, and all workers should be able to exercise voice in the design of labor processes' (Schulze-Cleven, 2021: 41). He also invokes the concept of 'social justice' and the need to assess whether 'broader legal structures and labor market institutions provide human beings with the capacity to self-actualize based on their innate creativity' (2021: 42). Similar to Webster, Schulze-Cleven's focus is not so much on providing justifications for these convictions, but on using them to highlight how labour studies differs from other fields in the social sciences, in particular how it diverges from neo-classical economics.

[5]   In my understanding, a critical problem is an issue producing contradictions in one's line of argument that cannot be addressed without changing one's ontological, epistemological or methodological assumptions.

labour could be rejected altogether on the grounds of representing a case of 'arbitrary partisanship' (Habermas, 1994: 276; see Urban, 2013: 396) if its proponents do not explain why they subscribe to the cause of labour, and what this cause consists in.

Arguably, the pro-worker stance of global labour studies is an implicit normative position – implicit because it is not clearly stated or explained, and normative in the sense of an assumption about what the social world should be like. This assumption is that the organization of the social world ought to be in line with the interests of workers, and that one should support collective mobilizations of workers advancing their interests because they may bring us closer towards this goal. The lack of a justification for this position means that there is a normative gap in global labour studies, which is open to charges of bias.

In this chapter, I argue that it is possible to close the normative gap. I look at two monographs and a collection of loosely connected articles that all have contributed significantly to shaping global labour studies as a field and project: Beverly Silver's *Forces of Labor* (2003), Edward Webster, Andries Bezuidenhout and Rob Lambert's *Grounding Globalization* (2008) plus the more recent contributions laying out the PRA, which build on the earlier interventions and aim to develop a 'research heuristic' for the study of labour from a global vantage point (Schmalz et al, 2018: 113; see also Webster, 2015). I identify similar normative themes in these texts and argue that the assumptions informing their claims can be justified with the help of a position in social philosophy called 'qualified ethical naturalism'. In other words, I show that there are good reasons for taking a pro-worker stance. Importantly, this is not merely an academic exercise. I wager that clarity about why we commit to the cause of labour, and what it means, will enhance our capacities to conduct empirical analyses and to engage in strategic-political thinking.

Problematizing value freedom

Before entering the debate on the normative themes in existing contributions to global labour studies, it is necessary to discuss whether taking an explicitly anti-normative position would be a potential response to charges of bias. One could argue that one should accept such charges and ditch the pro-worker stance instead of attempting to justify it. This would require global labour scholars to study global production networks and labour disputes around the world from the standpoint of the detached, purportedly neutral bystander. They would need to aspire to being 'value-free' in their research activities.

Such an approach would be compatible with a line of reasoning that is very common in the social sciences. According to this line, social scientists should refrain from engaging in normative arguments. It goes back to the

18th century and philosopher David Hume (1888: 469–70), who famously questioned that what ought to be the case could be derived from what is the case. In a similar move, sociologist Max Weber argued that it is impossible, in the empirical social sciences, 'to provide binding norms and ideals from which directives for immediate practical activity can be derived' (Weber, 1904: 52). Hume and Weber suggest that normative assumptions remain outside the reach of the social sciences, which means that it is impossible, on the grounds of social scientific reasoning, to justify or refute them.

If this line of argument is correct, global labour studies benefits if normative assumptions are dropped or avoided: observers refrain from adding unfounded beliefs and hunches to their descriptions, which mean that the latter are less biased and thus more precise. One could argue that a way to achieve this would be to avoid using normatively loaded language and to adopt apolitical and technical terms instead.

It needs to be asked, however, whether it is possible at all to describe work, a hotly debated issue in contemporary societies, in ways that do not lend themselves to being interpreted as 'being on a side'. A small decision like calling a teacher in a state school, for example, a 'public servant', an 'employee' or a 'worker' has significant analytical and political implications even if none of these terms seem overtly political at first sight. Indeed, each of the terms is associated with a different understanding of labour relations in the public sector and with distinct political agendas. And if we refer to entities, issues or activities that are characterized by conflict, it may not be possible at all to find 'distanced' language. Are factory owners who reorganize the labour process exercising their 'right to manage', or is this an instance of 'factory despotism'? Do we live in a 'market economy' or in 'capitalism'? None of these expressions are value-free in the sense of being detached from normative and political arguments over the nature of the society we inhabit.

Against the proponents of value freedom, I contend that it is not a critical problem per se if concepts are normative. Social theorist Andrew Sayer notes that there exists, in the social sciences, a 'zone of concepts which are simultaneously positive and normative' (Sayer, 2005: 215; see Lindner, 2013: 345) – they describe the world and also say something about what it ought to be like, which means that they have normative implications. As Sayer points out, openly normative terms often capture social reality better than terms that appear to be technical and non-normative (2005: 216). If one chooses to speak of flexibilization instead of precarization, for example, one says less and not more about the situation and experiences of the workers who are subject to the process of having to adjust to living with fixed-term contracts, limited access to benefits and unclear future employment prospects. This implies that if concepts are value-laden, this does not mean that they produce distorted or even wrong observations.

In light of this, I contest the assumption that there is, or should be, a clear separation between descriptions of what is, and descriptions of what ought to be, the case. Our descriptions of social reality always already lend themselves to normative evaluations, which is why it makes more sense to spell out these evaluations and critically discuss them rather than keeping up the appearance that we are arguing from a 'value-free' standpoint. Consequently, it makes no sense to respond to charges of arbitrary partisanship by opting for a purportedly 'value-free' approach.

It follows that it is not a critical problem that global labour scholars take a pro-worker stance, but that they are hesitant to justify their commitment. In my view, it is time to recognize this problem and work towards closing the normative gap in global labour studies. This can be done by providing sound reasons for why one should commit oneself to being on the side of workers. I wager that the pro-worker stance of scholars in the field is not located outside reasoning, and that engaging in a systematic discussion on how it can be justified is the best way to shield it from charges of bias.

Class domination and the suffering of workers

If a commitment to 'value freedom' is an unconvincing response to charges of bias, it makes more sense to examine existing contributions to global labour studies and identify implicit normative arguments informing them. In this chapter, I start with Silver's book. It is one of the first major interventions in the age of transnational production that analyses labour relations from a global perspective.

In the introduction, Silver discusses Karl Polanyi and Karl Marx and their respective theories of the commodification of labour power in capitalism. Silver argues that for Polanyi, the extension of the principle of the free market into the realm of work amounts to a dissolution of existing 'social compacts on the right to livelihood' (Silver, 2003: 17). In *The Great Transformation*, Polanyi provides an example of such a compact – the 'Speenhamland system', an informal legal arrangement in the English countryside introduced in the late 18th century (2001: 81–9). In today's language, the system was designed to ensure a living wage. Local authorities topped up the income of workers in line with the price of bread. The aim was to ensure that workers had the means to sustain themselves.

If we follow Silver's reading of Polanyi, the removal of such regulations triggered 'a sense of "injustice"' (Silver, 2003: 18), which in turn led to the formation of 'a strong countermovement from workers and other social groups' (Silver, 2003: 17). It is clear from the context that Silver broadly agrees with Polanyi and, by implication, with the view of workers that the expansion of the 'unregulated' labour market was unjust (Silver, 2003: 17).

Considering the overarching question at stake in this chapter, it is notable that Silver here discusses 'justice' – a key normative principle.[6]

But why should workers see the emergence of a liberalized labour market as 'unjust'? The obvious answer, if we follow Polanyi via Silver, is that they are forced to accept a system of work that does not ensure their survival – no matter whether they fulfil their side of the bargain struck with their employers or not. In *The Great Transformation*, Polanyi explicitly speaks of the 'right to live' in the context of the Speenhamland system (2001: 82). It follows that injustice, in this understanding, is the existence of a social arrangement that infringes on a basic human right.

If we return to our initial question of what a pro-worker stance is, a critical problem with the Polanyian line on justice emerges. It does not provide a justification for general partisanship in favour of labour – at least if we understand by 'workers' not a random collection of individuals who happen to work in order to make a living, but a (potential) collective social force. This is an issue because most of the programmatic statements and major research undertakings (including Silver's) see workers as such a force. There is a broad consensus among global labour scholars that one should welcome, in principle, the formation of labour movements and organizations of workers (see Silver, 2003: 18; Webster et al, 2008: ix–x; Brookes and McCallum, 2017: 201; Schmalz et al, 2018: 113; Cook et al, 2020: 79–80; Nowak, 2021a: 1339).

With reference to Polanyi, it possible to identify normative reasons for why there should be regulations, in capitalist social formations, that ensure living wages. But it is entirely conceivable to be in favour of such regulations, for example, minimum wage legislation, without supporting an agenda of workers organizing to advance their interests collectively. Put differently, the demand for a minimum wage is compatible with a liberal-individualist stance that recognizes individual rights of workers but denies them collective rights, for example, the right to unionize and the right to strike. The Blair government in Britain, for example, introduced a minimum wage in 1999, but decided to refrain from repealing legislation passed by the Conservative governments in the era of Thatcherism that severely restricted the room for manoeuvre of trade unions. Furthermore, it did not expand, in any meaningful sense, collective rights at work (Gallas, 2016b: 281). If taken in isolation, the Polanyian line does not help us to close the normative gap

---

[6] Silver's terminology is a nod to Polanyi, who speaks of 'unregulated competition' (Polanyi, 2001: 70) and the principle of a 'self-regulating market' (71–80) that emerges with the commodification of 'labor, land and money' (72). One can question whether it makes sense to use the attribute 'unregulated' in this context. If we follow Marx (1976: 178), durable economic arrangements in the capitalist mode of production only exist if there is a degree of formal or informal legal regulation enabling people to enter binding contracts.

in labour studies because it does not provide us with principled reasons to support organized labour.[7]

But importantly, Silver does not stop here. She moves on to Marx and briefly discusses his notion of 'justice'. Again, her reflections indicate that she broadly agrees with the view she ascribes to him:

> Marx's analysis ... emphasized power and injustice. Capitalism is seen as simultaneously producing growing mass misery and growing proletarian power. ... Toward the end of Volume I of *Capital* ... Marx described how the advance of capitalism leads not only to misery, degradation and exploitation of the working class but also to a strengthening of its capacity and disposition to resist exploitation. (Silver, 2003: 18)

In this passage, Silver supplies an explanation for why workers are faced with injustice that does not contradict Polanyi, but goes much further. It is not just that capitalism, if badly regulated, poses a threat to the life of workers. It is also that they experience misery even if their lives are not at stake. Silver appears be rehashing an argument found in *Capital* volume 1. Here, Marx describes the effect of capitalist development on workers:

> We saw ... that within the capitalist system all methods for raising the social productivity of labour are put into effect at the cost of the individual worker; that all means for the development of production undergo a dialectical inversion so that they become means of *domination* and *exploitation* of the producers; they distort the worker into a fragment of a man, they degrade him to the level of an *appendage of a machine*, they destroy the actual content of his labour by turning it into a torment; they *alienate* [entfremden] from him the intellectual potentialities of the labour process in the same proportion as science is incorporated in it as an independent power; they deform the conditions under which he works, subject him during the labour process to a *despotism* the more hateful for its meanness; they transform his life–time into working–time, and drag his wife and child beneath the wheels of the juggernaut of capital. But all methods for the production of surplus–value are at the same time methods of accumulation, and

---

[7]   This is not an argument against the normative content of the Polanyian position. Indeed, there are good reasons to assume that a 'right to live' exists. Social mechanisms ensuring the survival of people were 'widely accepted' before the onset of liberalization, as Silver points out (2003: 18), and a similar point can be made with reference to present-day welfare states. It appears that the existence of social support mechanisms that ensure people's survival conform with the normative intuitions of very many people, and there is a broad range of social and political forces in favour of them.

every extension of accumulation becomes, conversely, a means for the development of those methods. It follows therefore that in proportion as capital accumulates, the situation of the worker, *be his payment high or low*, must grow worse. Finally, the jaw which always holds the relative surplus population or industrial reserve army in equilibrium with the extent and energy of accumulation rivets the worker to capital more firmly than the wedges of Hephaestus held Prometheus to the rock. It makes an accumulation of *misery* a necessary condition, corresponding to the accumulation of wealth. Accumulation of wealth at one pole is, therefore, at the same time accumulation of *misery*, the torment of labour, slavery, ignorance, brutalization and moral degradation at the opposite pole, i.e. on the side of the class that produces its own product as capital. (Marx, 1976: 799; own emphasis)

The first observation to make is that according to Marx, capitalist development, increasing productivity and the resulting growth in wealth across society is accompanied by the subjugation of workers. They are faced with immiseration, but 'misery' here does not refer to absolute material poverty, but more to a general state of suffering. As Marx emphasizes, it is very well possible that wages increase over time. The misery of workers has two facets: First of all, they are exposed to exploitation. Their wages only represent the material means that they need to reproduce themselves. The remainder of the value product they have produced goes, in the form of profits, to the capitalist class. If workers can only ever reproduce themselves while capitalists amass profits, this means that there is a tendency for a growing material divide to emerge in capitalist society. It follows that the first facet of misery in a capitalist context is relative poverty or economic inequality – the fact that the ratio between the wealth of capital and the wealth of workers usually increases. Second, the transition to industrial capitalism is accompanied by a shift in power relations. Workers are subjected to a regime of work that they have no say over, and the more is done to increase productivity and change the labour process by using science and technology, the harder it becomes for the individual worker to challenge capitalist control over the labour process. Accordingly, Marx argues that the capitalist organization of work undermines the humanity of workers: They are transformed into 'an appendage of a machine', which also means that they cannot use – and thus are prevented from developing – their full abilities and skills when they work.

Taking up a key term used by Marx in the quoted passage, one can argue that workers in capitalism are at the receiving end of class domination. They are placed in the capitalist mode of production in such a manner that they are systematically disadvantaged in three ways: Their wages amount only to part of the value they have produced (exploitation); they have no say over the organization of the labour process (despotism); and they have to follow plans that are developed by people not directly involved in production, for example scientists, engineers and managers, which means that they are obstructed from fully using and developing their skills and intellectual capacities (alienation). Needless to say, there is also a class that benefits from this arrangement – the capitalist class. As Silver points out, Marx differs markedly from Polanyi by systematically addressing the question of power: As long as the capitalist mode of production exists, class domination means that the capitalist class has a systemic advantage over the working class when it comes to exercising power, and this is reflected in the unequal access to material and ideational resources.

Coming back to Silver, a justice issue does not just occur if capitalism is weakly regulated. Marx's argument is that we are dealing with a mode of production causing collective suffering on the side of workers no matter whether or not there are safeguards ensuring that they are paid 'decent' wages. One may add that the different varieties of capitalism harm workers to different degrees, and that it is on the whole preferable to be a car worker in Sweden than a garment worker in Ethiopia. But the point is that capitalism is causing harm no matter how well it is regulated. Even in Sweden, the capitalist class makes profits; has the right to decide, in the last instance, on how to organize production; and insists on having privileged access to the knowledge necessary to run firms. Following Silver, the injustice of capitalism is systemic in the sense that class domination does not cease to exist because regulations are put in place that improve the lot of workers.[8]

In a nutshell, there is a normative theme in Silver's work according to which the injustice of capitalism lies in the fact that workers are exposed to unnecessary suffering that they are not responsible for. They are subject to class domination as a form of oppression that results from the organization of work in capitalist societies and not from individual behaviour.[9] In this

---

[8]   There is a critical problem with this interpretation, whose discussion is beyond the scope of a book chapter. Notably, Marx takes great pain to demonstrate, in *Capital* volume 1, that the capitalist mode of production is not based on unequal (and by implication, unjust) exchange (Marx, 1976: 270–80), which raises the question of whether capitalism can be 'unjust'. In other words, it remains an open question whether the concept of 'justice' can be applied to the line of argument developed in *Capital*. On the conceptual challenges surrounding this issue, see Wood (1972) and Lindner (2013: 350–3).

[9]   One may object here that workers voluntarily enter employment contracts. But Silver's and Marx's point is that workers in capitalism are in a significantly weaker bargaining position than capitalists unless they possess very rare skills or are able to form very strong coalitions – or unless there are 'labour shortages'. After all, capitalists tend to employ more than one person. It follows that the individual worker is usually far more dependent on being employed by an individual capitalist than vice versa. Whereas capitalists can compensate the fact that a position remains vacant by ordering other employees to fill

sense, they can also be said to be in a state of unfreedom. And importantly, Marx suggests that things do not need to be this way: Workers produce an immense and increasing amount of wealth that does not belong to them. It follows that their subjugation is not a result of general poverty resulting from low productivity and limited resources but from the way work is organized in capitalism.

Accordingly, there is a strategic theme that is linked to this normative argument. Silver talks of 'growing proletarian power'. This suggests that workers are not just a social group affected by injustice, but they are also equipped with specific capacities when it comes to changing society. Following Erik Olin Wright, Silver argues that they possess two kinds of power. The first is 'structural power' (Silver, 2003: 13), the specific power that arises out of their place in the capitalist process of production, which allows them to disrupt the accumulation of capital, for example, by going on strike or using a tight labour market to make demands vis-à-vis capitalists. The second is 'associational power', which refers to the power arising out of their ability to form coalitions (Silver, 2003: 13).

This theme is also present towards the end of Silver's book, where she assigns to workers the role of a collective social force that is, in principle, capable of triggering fundamental social change. She says: '[T]he ultimate challenge faced by workers of the world in the early twenty-first century is the struggle, not just against one's own exploitation and exclusion, but for an international regime that truly subordinates profits to the livelihood of all' (Silver, 2003: 179). In this sentence, Silver revives the Marxist trope of a 'historical mission' of the working class, which consists in a global effort of liberating humanity from capitalism through rising up against it (see Marxhausen, 2004).[10]

---

the gap or by hiring someone else, the worker does not have an income, which is a potential threat to their survival. Consequently, workers tend to be forced to accept their working conditions and pay no matter whether they find them inacceptable and are not even able to sustain themselves through their wages. The injustice lies in being systemically disadvantaged in negotiations with one's counterpart, so that one is forced to accept binding contracts with unfavourable conditions.

[10] Silver does not discuss the political implications of this observation, which is unsurprising given that she is not primarily concerned with questions of strategy in her book. It is worth mentioning that there are at least three practical challenges that need to be addressed if one argues for a worker-led global liberation effort: (1) how to deal with the possibility (of which there are many historical examples) that working classes enter compromises with capital at the national level that benefit core workforces on the 'inside' but not outsiders; (2) how to build alliances across national boundaries under those circumstances; and (3) how to deal with the fact that there are many people in capitalist societies inhabiting 'contradictory locations within class relations' (Wright, 1978b: 74), who cannot be placed easily on either side of the labour or the side of capital.

In sum, siding with workers means, for Silver, siding with a social group encountering systemic injustice in the form of class domination and capable, with the help of the power resources at its disposal, not just of ending the injustice they are facing but of liberating humanity. Importantly, Silver associates injustice with human suffering – 'misery, degradation and exploitation' – and makes it clear that this suffering is not simply the fate of workers. Her line of argument is based on the wager that it is possible, in principle, to advance to a society where workers no longer face injustice and, by implication, no longer suffer the ills arising out of the capitalist organization of work.

Neoliberalism and the imperative of the market

Webster et al's pro-worker stance is not fundamentally different from Silver's. They regularly refer to her and have similar theoretical reference points: Polanyi (Webster et al, 2008: 1–21) and, to a lesser degree, Marx (Webster et al, 2008: 38). And just like Silver, they also discuss a normative theme in Polanyi's work. Echoing Silver's take on Polanyi with its emphasis on people's right to live, they argue that he was driven by a 'moral concern over the psychological, social and ecological destructiveness of unregulated markets' (Webster et al, 2008: 4). They identify what I propose to call a 'collective humanism' in his work. This is the recognition that people are social beings – they are members of communities and part of a society – and that the social world ought to be organized around their collective needs: 'Polanyi's moral intervention is grounded in the notion of the innate value of persons, hence the centrality of constructing a just and free society. … In this vision, persons, communities and society are the priority' (Webster et al, 2008: 4–5).

Notably, Webster et al's analysis of present-day global capitalism is informed by this idea. In their view, Polanyi is still relevant 'because such a relentless drive towards a market orientation lies at the very heart of the contemporary globalization project' (Webster et al, 2008: 4). If Polanyi observed a 'First Great Transformation', that is, the expansion of the market principle in the transition to industrial capitalism, we are now witnesses to a 'Second Great Transformation' (Webster et al, 2008: 52): after a phase of regulated capitalism, at least in the Global North, a 'global environment' has emerged that is characterized by 'market-driven politics and restructuring of work and society' (Webster et al, 2008: 55). And it is clear from the book that Webster et al criticize neoliberalism on much the same grounds as Polanyi when he criticized 19th-century economic liberalism: As a project that is subsuming the 'innate value' of people to the imperative of the market. In a first approximation, one could argue that the normative dimension of Webster et al's take on contemporary society lies in their opposition to neoliberal globalization. Following their interpretation of Polanyi, one could argue that it produces injustice and unfreedom – normative concepts that they use when they talk about the 'innate value of persons'. This injustice and unfreedom, again, consists in unnecessary human suffering that is not the responsibility of those who suffer – and in the great threat to people's livelihood posed by ecological destruction.[11]

Importantly, Webster et al are discussing Polanyi not just to point out a threat to people's survival posed by liberalized labour markets. They emphasize how the 'Second Great Transformation' affects all areas of society. Reiterating a point made with reference to Silver's reception of Polanyi, it is worth pointing out that criticizing liberalization and marketization as such does not necessarily mean that one is taking a pro-worker stance. It is compatible, for example, with promoting an authoritarian–corporatist form of capitalism that fortifies class domination. Correspondingly, the primary conflict in a Polanyian framework is the conflict between the market principle and society, which is also visible in the fact that parts one and two of *Grounding Globalization* are titled 'Markets against society' and 'Society against markets'. It follows that Webster et al's invocation of Polanyian notions of 'justice' and 'freedom' provides a normative justification for being on the side of society, but not necessarily for being on the side of workers.

But if we follow Webster et al, it may be possible to establish a link between a pro-society and pro-labour stance by introducing Marx through the backdoor. They complement the Polanyian narrative with a class analysis. In their view, at the heart of the countermovement against the First Great Transformation in the Global North was the 'historical compromise between

---

[11] Economic liberals may reply to this line of argument that a huge number of people in different countries around the world, among them many 'emerging economies', have benefited materially from the push for economic liberalization at the global level from 1970s onwards, and that the environmental record of authoritarian socialism was abysmal (see Wolf, 2004; 2014; Petersen and Hartmann, 2020). But in defence of Webster et al, one could respond to the first point that there has been a sustained rise of economic inequality, at least in the Global North, during the neoliberal age (see Alvaredo et al, 2018: 8–13) – and that societies with highly developed economies are facing more social problems if they are more unequal, as epidemiologists Kate Pickett and Richard Wilkinson have argued with reference to quantitative data (Pickett and Wilkinson, 2009; 2014). Concerning the second point, it does not matter so much if past social formations with a high degree of regulation did badly in terms of environmental protection because the issue at stake here is not whether or not authoritarian-socialist regimes would be capable of addressing the climate crisis, but what the track record of present-day neoliberal capitalism is in this respect. In a recent statement signed by 11,000 scientists under the heading of 'climate emergency', the authors argue that '[d]espite 40 years of global climate negotiations, with few exceptions, we have generally conducted business as usual and have largely failed to address this predicament' (Ripple et al, 2020: 9).

capital and labour', which resulted in 'the creation of welfare states' (Webster et al, 2008: 52). This suggests that workers are affected in specific ways by the liberalization of markets, which is also why they are at forefront of the resistance against it.

Indeed, there are two themes in *Grounding Globalization* that connect the general normative-critical assessment of neoliberalism with the situation of workers. First of all, Webster et al observe, drawing upon Michael Burawoy's work, that the neoliberal age and the 'global industry restructuring' that comes with it (Webster et al, 2008: 51) produce a regime of work that they call 'hegemonic despotism', where mechanisms of negotiation such the 'institutions of collective bargaining' change insofar as they are used to impose measures of liberalization on workers. This is done through 'concession bargaining' (Webster et al, 2008: 53). At this point, Webster et al reiterate the Marxian motive of a systematic subjugation of workers, but link it to a specific regime of work within capitalism, not with capitalism per se. This regime emerges with neoliberalization and the extension of the market principle – a development that they also call, using Polanyian terminology, a 'Second Great Transformation' (Webster et al, 2008: 52) of capitalism. So, one reason for Webster et al's pro-worker stance is that workers are suffering because they are subjugated by a regime of work that they have no control over.

There is also a second theme in Webster et al's account, which is also linked to the 'Second Great Transformation'. This theme is the insecurity that workers are facing if markets are extended:

> When large numbers of workers in different factories, in different countries, experience the same feelings of insecurity, it is no longer a personal trouble only, it is a public issue. To understand insecurity, it is not enough to identify the sense of helplessness, fear, depression, anger and sadly, often self-destructive behaviour such as suicide, substance abuse and domestic violence. It is necessary … to identify the broad social forces, institutions and organization that manufacture this insecurity. (Webster et al, 2008: 2)

Here, siding with workers means, again, siding with people who are exposed to a regime that prevents them from taking control over their own lives. In a nutshell, the issue is suffering once more – this time the suffering caused by the proliferation of vulnerability and instability that follows on the heels of neoliberalization. One can conclude that the injustice and unfreedom resulting from the emergence of a global neoliberal order is experienced across classes, but that workers are hit particularly badly by the effects of neoliberalization. They find themselves in a situation of injustice and unfreedom because they suffer from despotism and insecurity – and their suffering is neither the product of their own making, nor a necessary state of affairs.

Taking up the Polanyian idea of a counter-reaction from society to marketization, Webster et al analyse the conditions of, and opportunities for, a 'global counter-movement' (Webster et al, 2008: x) to neoliberal globalization to emerge, which is capable of challenging the extension of the market principle across the globe. In keeping with their Polanyian-Marxian leanings, they argue that this countermovement should be carried by an alliance of intellectuals, labour movements and other social movements as well as political parties (Webster et al, 2008: xi–xii, 53–5, 214, 222). Importantly, they see 'global unionism as a core constituent of a global counter-movement' (Webster et al, 2008: 17) and discuss new forms of labour internationalism (Webster et al, 2008: 186–211). Furthermore, they advocate utopian thinking: Following Erik Olin Wright, they call for 'a real utopia, grounded in the actual experiments and institutional forms that are emerging, which link the local to the global' (Webster et al, 2008: 21).

It follows that Silver and Webster et al use similar normative themes. They suggest that social arrangements are unjust if they are unnecessary, and if their existence is not the responsibility of those who are suffering. And they agree that workers are not just suffering from such injustices, but are also a potential collective social force capable of eradicating them.

Trade unionism and social critique

Taking up Silver and Wright's considerations on workers' power, the PRA offers a set of categories for studying systematically how workers around the world respond, in their collective efforts to advance their interests, to the 'contexts' and 'challenges' they encounter. A stated aim is to facilitate 'union renewal' through highlighting 'the ability of organised labour to act strategically' (Schmalz et al, 2018: 113). Put differently, the proponents of the PRA – among them Webster himself – see their role as empowering workers with the help of a set of categories that allows organized labour to make decisions on the grounds of systematic strategic considerations (Schmalz et al, 2018: 113; see also Dörre and Schmalz, 2013: 14; Schmalz et al, 2019: 85). These categories refer to sources of workers' power. The PRA refers to structural and associational power as identified by Wright and Silver and adds two other power resources – first of all, institutional power, that is, the capacity to use one's 'influence in institutional set-ups', for example, consultation fora with governments; and, second, societal power, that is, the ability to operate through 'coalitions' (Schmalz et al, 2018: 122) with other collective actors and to 'offer credible interpretation patterns or "frames" and solutions to problems' (Schmalz et al, 2018: 124).[12]

Just like Silver and Webster et al, the various contributions to the PRA do not explicitly discuss, to my knowledge, the normative underpinnings of their endeavour. But there is a German-language monograph on *Strategic Unionism* by Ulrich Brinkmann and others (2008), which is taking a line towards labour relations that is informed by the PRA (see Volume 1, Chapter 2). This book is particularly relevant in the context of this chapter because the authors explore, in one section, why social scientists should study unions. In these considerations, they allude to what their pro-worker stance is, and why they take it.[13]

Brinkmann et al's entry point is the foundation of 'science-based social critique' (Brinkmann et al, 2008: 146). Citing Luc Boltanski and Eve Chiapello, they imply that such a form of critique sides with people whose access to '(economic, educational and social) resources' is limited. Its object is 'social insecurity'. Brinkmann et al indicate that this insecurity reflects the 'transformations of capitalism', presumably neoliberalization, and that it affects the 'world of work' (2008: 147). It follows that the people with limited resources are workers, and that they suffer thanks to being in this state of insecurity.

Accordingly, Brinkmann et al highlight the need for critical scholars to forge alliances with organized labour. They argue that there is 'mutual dependency' (Brinkmann et al, 2008: 147) between scholars promoting social critique and trade unions. The reason for this is that trade unions are 'not just one, but the key, presently irreplaceable actor for [increasing] the relevance of a renewed social critique', and that trade unions 'need an intellectual frame of reference that is based on empirical research' to 'decipher the on-going transformations of society and the world and to translate them into productive exigencies for action' (Brinkmann et al, 2008: 147). Put differently, unions are a collective force for eradicating the suffering of workers, which is why they give the social critique uttered by scholars practical relevance. And conversely, critical scholars are also needed in the process of improving the lot of workers because they provide the

---

[12] The focus of this section is the normative dimension of the PRA. For detailed, critical accounts of the analytical purchase of the PRA, see Chapter 4 and Nowak (2018); for a detailed account of how the PRA has evolved over the years, see Marticorena and D'Urso (2021: 181–91).

[13] The book contains several references to *Forces of Labor* and to Webster's work, which shows that there is a direct link to the other authors discussed in this chapter. There are no references to *Grounding Globalization*, which is probably down to the fact that both Brinkmann et al's and Webster et al's book were published at roughly the same time.

intellectual tools needed for making sense of the social world and making strategic decisions.

This line of reasoning is entirely consistent with Webster et al's critique of neoliberalism and broadly compatible with Silver, who is also concerned with the connection between the unequal access to resources and human suffering. Importantly, there is an implicit normative assumption at work here. The critique of insecure working and living conditions of disadvantaged groups signals that the world is not how it should be.

Importantly, Klaus Dörre and Stefan Schmalz, in another programmatic statement, confirm that Boltanski and Chiapello's notion of social critique was an important point of departure for the development of the PRA (Dörre and Schmalz, 2013: 16). This demonstrates that it is justified to use Brinkmann et al's account as a template for identifying a normative theme in the PRA, which consists in a critique of the suffering of workers as a systematically disadvantaged group in contemporary capitalism, and in the need to work with unions to drive back the causes of their suffering.

It follows that there are similar normative themes in the works discussed in this chapter. Following our authors, a social arrangement is unjust if it is unnecessary and if its existence is not the responsibility of those who are suffering. Their pro-worker stances also overlap broadly: Being on the side of workers means being on the side of a group that is faced with systemic injustice and unfreedom; workers are locked into arrangements that cause them to suffer.

A key difference between Silver and Webster et al lies in where they see the cause of this suffering: Whereas Silver sees the 'world capitalist system' (Silver, 2003: 34) as the reason for why workers are being treated unjustly, Webster et al highlight the 'global neoliberal project' (Webster et al, 2008: 159). The proponents of the PRA are less clear where they stand on this matter. The account of social critique provided by Brinkmann et al suggests a proximity to Webster et al's rejection of neoliberalism; a more recent programmatic statement highlights the need to 'bring capitalism back into the analysis of trade unions' (Schmalz et al, 2019: 85).

What can be said is that there are two different objects of social critique. In the case of Silver, the pro-worker stance is coupled with a critique of capitalism; in the case of Webster et al with a critique of neoliberalism. In my view, the Silverian-Marxian line is more convincing because it is more comprehensive – it does not spare interventionist-welfarist forms of capitalism from critique and allows us to focus on class domination. Marx's critique of the latter is borne out by historical facts insofar as there was strong worker discontent with the socioeconomic and political arrangements in Western Europe in the 1960s and 1970s. At the time, strong and militant labour movements emerged in Britain, France, Italy and West Germany (Nowak and Gallas, 2013).

Qualified ethical naturalism as a normative foundation

If we follow Aristotle, ethics crucially revolves around the question of how to lead a 'good life' (1999: 12, 94). From this perspective, it is possible to identify an ethical common ground in the observations of Silver, Webster et al and the proponents of the PRA. They are concerned with human suffering and would agree, in all likelihood, to the proposition that workers in present-day neoliberal capitalism suffer because of societal forces that subjugate them and prevent them from taking control over the social environment they inhabit. From an ethical perspective, workers are faced with unnecessary obstacles to leading good lives (see Miller, 1981: 326).

Notably, this line of reasoning is fully compatible with a position in present-day social philosophy – Sayer's 'qualified ethical naturalism', which he defines thus:

> It is ethically naturalist in that it considers that the very meaning of good or bad cannot be determined without reference to the nature of human social being. As a first cut, we can say that the meaning of good and bad ultimately relates to human needs and to human capacities for flourishing or suffering. (Sayer, 2005: 218)

Building on Sayer (2005: 222) and on philosopher Urs Lindner's reading of Marx (2013: 393–4; see also Bruff, 2011), there are three types of needs that result from human nature – and that have to be met for humans to lead good lives and flourish. First of all, there are bodily needs that directly concern people's physical survival and wellbeing, among them permanent access to food and water, clothing, shelter and healthcare. Second, there are social needs in the sense that any individual depends on other people. In other words, people need opportunities to socialize, and they rely on social relationships that provide them with recognition, support and care. Finally, there are developmental needs, that is, the ability of people to use and develop their capacities. People suffer if their capacity to learn and to use what they have learned is stunted – and this does not just concern children and adolescents, but also adults. Marx points this out when he criticizes the fact that industrial workers are turned into 'appendages' of machines. If these three types of needs are met, people are able to make free choices, that is, they are able to consciously reflect on, and actively shape, their social environment and enter social relationships on a voluntary basis. Put differently, humans flourish if they are in a state of freedom, which is based on 'agency, reflexivity and self-realisation' (Lindner, 2013: 350), and they suffer badly if they are imprisoned (Sayer, 2005: 222).[14]

---

[14] Following Lindner, the early Marx already has a similar understanding of human nature. Lindner identifies three groups of needs in Marx's writings, namely 'bodily facilities, reflexivity as well as sociality' (Lindner, 2013: 349).

Importantly, Sayer adds that it is necessary to qualify this position because needs are not simply given across time and space (2005: 219). They are conditioned by social influences, which means that they take on specific forms in different spatio-temporal contexts. Following Lindner, we can speak of a 'socio-historic, dynamised conception of human nature' (2013: 349). In other words, needs are transhistorical and transgeographic, but they take on diverging, historical-specific forms in different social formations.

The need for shelter, for example, means something different in the context of urban life in capitalist metropolises in the 21st century than in the context of pre-Columbian nomadic communities in North America. Likewise, the capacity of human beings to socialize and forge close bonds with others can be identified across time and space, but people's patterns of interaction in the locally centred, tightly knitted rural communities in medieval Europe diverge significantly from those prevalent in diaspora communities of migrants in the internet age, which spread across countries and continents.

Against this backdrop, a general foundation for normative evaluations of the social world emerges: Social arrangements and broader social orders ought to be organized in a manner that is conducive to human flourishing, which results from people engaging in activities that allow them to meet their needs. These needs are transhistorical yet overdetermined by spatio-temporal contexts. If people are constrained in their attempt to meet their needs thanks to social arrangements or orders, the latter contribute to human suffering and ought to be abolished. Importantly, this is not a claim that any type of human suffering can be abolished – people's relationships with others (or their breakdown) can be a source of pain, and the same can be said about sickness and death. The point here is to say that changeable structures, mechanisms, institutions and processes contributing to suffering should be transformed or removed.[15]

This normative foundation is fully compatible with Marx's famous '*categoric imperative*', according to which our aim should be to 'overthrow all relations in which the human being is a debased, enslaved, abandoned, despicable essence' (Marx, 2009a; emphasis in the original, translation amended). Marx here calls for driving back and abolishing social domination in all its forms. If his categoric imperative is taken together with Sayer's qualified

---

[15] Admittedly, the 'changeability' of social arrangements is difficult to assess. Even if all social arrangements are produced by human beings and are, in principle, changeable, calls for transformation need to address a number of questions if they are supposed to gain political traction. Examples are: What is a plausible alternative to the status quo, and does it magnify human flourishing? Do the benefits in terms of human flourishing of transforming an arrangement outweigh the costs? And what kind of changes should be prioritized over others?

ethical naturalism, one can argue that human suffering is caused by social domination, and human flourishing by its absence (see Lindner, 2013: 347). It becomes clear that critical evaluations of the social world do not just require normative arguments concerning human nature, but also a critical theory of social domination that explains to what extent its different facets harms people, and how it can be driven back or even abolished.

The normative-critical subtext of global labour studies

In the cases of Silver and Webster et al, the critical theory of social domination consists in Marxian and Polanyian takes on present-day capitalism. Both perspectives agree that workers are faced with similar circumstances because they share a location in the social division of labour – and that their unfreedom results from being in this location. One can argue, on these grounds, that they form part of a social class or of social classes, which can be called the working class(es). They are subject, according to the Silverian-Marxian line, to capitalist class domination – or, for Polanyians like Webster et al, to neoliberal despotism and insecurity. This also means that workers do not control the conditions under which they live; much rather, they are faced with circumstances beyond their control that constrain their choices.

As has been indicated, Marx's account of the capitalist mode of production, due to its comprehensive nature and level of detail, is particularly useful for illuminating how these circumstances emerge and what their effects are. According to Marx, the capitalists as owners of the means of production are driven by the profit-motive – not because they are greedy, but because competition forces them to accumulate. Otherwise, they would risk their own economic existence (Marx, 1981: 353): Not making gains means falling behind one's competitors. Marx speaks of the 'silent compulsion of economic relations' (Marx, 1976: 899) in this context.

If we look at the three types of needs listed by Sayer, we can see that their fulfilment is affected directly by the way work is organized under the capitalist mode of production and the profit-motive. Marx (1976: 275–6, 875) argues that workers' wages tend to be at a level that allows them to reproduce themselves – and if they are unemployed or underemployed, they struggle to reach even this basic level. This also means that their access to material resources is usually restricted, and they have little choice but to continue selling their labour power if they want to survive. Consequently, there is a constant threat of capitalist competition taking place at the expense of workers, for example through work intensification, longer work hours, the creation of hazardous working conditions, wage depression or redundancies. Capitalist competition poses a threat to the bodily needs of workers not being met fully and thus to their physical wellbeing.

Likewise, the ability of workers to meet their social and developmental needs is also limited through the exigencies of having to work under capitalist command. They do not determine their work hours, the geographic location of their workplace or the composition of the team they are part of – and the same applies to the rhythm and content of their work. This strictly limits the choices of workers concerning how they socialize, and how they develop their capacities. Their working conditions, again, reflect the need to turn a profit, not the need of people to connect with others or learn and use new skills.

Importantly, the physical, social and developmental needs of workers in capitalist social formations change and develop (see Lebovitz, 1992: 17–18). The competition-induced drive for capital to accumulate constantly 'revolutionizes production and social relations', as Silver puts it. Changes in the labour processes force workers to develop new skills and change jobs (Marx, 1976: 617–18). They learn, make modified and novel products as well as entering new social relations. This affects what they desire to consume, what kind of connections with other people matter to them, and what kind of things they know and can do. Thanks to their ability to build coalitions and engage in collective struggles, they tend to force capital to recognize some of these changed needs, for example, through winning wage increases (including changes of the social wage) or successfully campaigning for regulatory change (see Lebovitz, 1992: 21–3, 57).

At the same time, the competition-induced drive for capital to accumulate does not cease to exist. This directly impacts on the ability of workers to lead a good life. As long as the capitalist mode of production remains in place, they are only ever able to meet a set of basic needs allowing them to survive (and sometimes not even this), but never the full set of needs enabling them to flourish (Lebovitz, 1992: 28). So even if they gain concessions, they continue to face exploitation, despotism and alienation. Despite the constant evolution of what workers can do and need, they remain in a state of unfreedom.

This Marxian perspective on workers' needs is broadly in line with the contributions to labour scholarship discussed here. Silver speaks, with reference to *Capital* volume 1, of a 'dialectic between workers' resistance to exploitation at the point of production and the efforts of capital to overcome that resistance by constantly revolutionizing production and social relations' (Silver, 2003: 19). The reference to 'resistance' suggests that the workers find themselves in a subordinate systemic place vis-à-vis capital. Webster et al (2008: 67, 145) put it in a more concise manner and simply refer to the 'structural domination of capital'. And likewise, Schmalz et al, as proponents of the PRA, speak of 'the structurally asymmetric and antagonistic relationship between capital and labour' (Schmalz et al, 2018: 115). In a nutshell, the different texts contain reflections on how capitalism is marked by the systematic subjugation of labour by capital, which means that they refer to class domination.

In conclusion, the pro-worker stance of global labour studies rests on a qualified ethical naturalism and a critical evaluation of class domination in capitalist societies. Human flourishing depends on people's ability to meet their needs, but labour relations in capitalism seriously constrain this ability on the side of workers. I propose to speak of a normative-critical subtext of global labour studies. It is a subtext because the arguments presented are implicit in the texts discussed in this chapter; they can be found in side-remarks in passages that do not explicitly focus on the pro-worker stance. Furthermore, it is critical – it indicates that it is bad for people to be in the state thus described. And it is normative: to criticize this state is only possible if one also assumes that, in principle, things could and should be different, which can also be understood as a statement about what the world ought to be like. 'Being on the side of workers' means being for workers exercising their class power and advancing their interests against capital, and for workers resisting and challenging capitalist class domination in the process.

Analytical and political implications

If taken together with arguments from social philosophy and theory, the identified subtext can serve as a normative foundation for global labour studies. It can be used to close the gap discussed in the introduction to this chapter. At the same time, the encounter of global labour studies with normative reasoning helps clarify what the analytical tasks of global labour scholars are. If 'being on the side of workers' signifies being in favour of workers exercising their class power, it follows that global labour scholars should seriously engage with class theory and class analysis. They should identify, in their research, how labour relations reflect relations of class domination, and what kind of opportunities, constraints and dilemmas this gives rise to when workers act collectively.

Importantly, the encounter also give rise to an analytical challenge. If we take Marx's categoric imperative seriously, it is necessary to acknowledge that he speaks of overthrowing all forms of oppression, not just class domination (Buckel, 2015: 30). There is no principled reason, from this normative perspective, to foreground the critique of class domination.[16] This calls for

---

[16] Even if one acknowledges the 'ecological dominance' (Jessop, 2000: 328–9) of capital accumulation in present-day societies – and the fact that it entails the continuous reproduction of capitalist class relations – it does not follow that other relations of social domination are of lesser importance for understanding the character of those societies. In a nutshell, capital accumulation feeds off difference – both because it can only take place if unpaid reproductive work is carried out ensuring a constant supply of labour power, and because a degree of socially produced heterogeneity among workers is functional for ensuring the constant extraction of surplus labour (see Volume 2, Chapters 3 and 8).

grounding global labour studies in a systematic conceptualization of capitalist class relations as relations of social domination, but also considering their articulation with other such relations. If global labour studies, as programmatic statements suggest (Cook et al, 2020: 75, 77; Nowak, 2021a,b: 1343), are about work in all its different forms – productive, reproductive; waged, unwaged; secure, precarious; formal, informal; employed, self-employed, bonded, voluntary – and about all kinds of divisions of labours – be they along class, gender, racial or caste lines – then such articulations should be part and parcel of the empirical research carried out.[17]

Next to clarifying analytical tasks and challenges, the encounter also contributes to illuminating issues of high political and strategic relevance. If one takes the issue of class domination seriously, one should take seriously an important insight of materialist class and state theory – the activities of trade unions cannot simply be equated with the exercise of class power. After all, unions are apparatuses that both facilitate the mass integration of workers and the advancement of the interests of labour vis-à-vis capital. It follows that union activities are not pro-worker activities per se. This is demonstrated by the long track record of how some unions collude with management and neglect the needs and interests of their members and other workers in the process.[18] Various scholars, among them the author (Gallas, 2018b; Nowak, 2018; 2021a; Atzeni, 2020; 2021; see Volume 1, Chapter 3), have recently argued that global labour studies should not, in each and every situation, align themselves with the causes of unions.

In conclusion, reflecting on the normative foundations of global labour studies contributes to clarifying the tasks and challenges of scholars in the field. It becomes clear what commitments they make when they claim that they are on the side of workers, and what the analytical and political ramifications of these commitments are: They need to operate at

---

[17] Admittedly, this may result, from a pragmatic point of view, in researchers being overburdened with complexity (see Buckel, 2015: 30–1). It is beyond the scope of this chapter to discuss feasible research strategies that take on this challenge. For a more detailed discussion of the articulation of gender and class relations in present-day capitalism, and how it figure in strikes, see Volume 2, Chapter 8.

[18] On the day I finished writing this chapter, *Süddeutsche Zeitung*, a leading German quality newspaper, published an article (Hägler, 2021) about Bernd Osterloh, the trade unionist heading the works council of Volkswagen. According to the article, Osterloh had decided to resign his position to become an executive board member of Traton, a subsidiary of the carmaker. Apparently, his annual remuneration was in seven figures (in euros). This random example illustrates how trade union leaders can become deeply entangled with business networks, in particular in corporatist settings like the German system of labour relations, which is based on principles such as 'social partnership' and 'co-management'.

a distance from organizations claiming to represent the interests of workers and ask what the effects of the latter's activities are on relations of social domination. Obviously, this is not just a scholastic question, but of great strategic relevance. Global labour studies as a field and project benefits from embracing the need of, and a systematic reflection on, normative arguments. What is and what ought to be are closely connected.

2

From Organic Intellectuals to Academic Workers: How Knowledge Handlers Connect with Organized Labour

The pro-worker stance and knowledge production

In the preceding chapter, I argued that there is a normative foundation of global labour studies, which remains implicit in recent contributions to the field. I explained *why* there are sound reasons for global labour scholars to take a pro-worker stance, and that this means being in favour of workers exercising their collective power to undermine class domination. What I have not discussed so far, however, is what taking this stance means in practice. In other words, I have not examined *how* global labour scholars should operate if they take the normative foundation of their field seriously. This is what I will do in this and the next chapter.

There is an obvious starting point for the how-question. If 'being on the side of workers' means supporting them in their efforts to contest capitalist class domination, this means supporting organized labour broadly understood, that is, any attempts of workers to organize and mobilize. In a nutshell, siding with workers means supporting workers' struggles. If one considers that scholars are professional handlers of knowledge, this suggests that scholars with a pro-worker stance should make available knowledge to workers that is useful for their struggles – and that helps them make good strategic decisions. The theoretical critique of social domination needs to be articulated with forms of practical critique – collective practices that contest social domination. In the bellicose language of the young Marx, '[t]he weapon of criticism cannot, of course, replace criticism of the weapon' (2009a).

These observations raise two questions: How can global labour scholars make useful strategic knowledge available for workers? And what kind of research designs do they need for this purpose? I will respond to the first question in this chapter, considering, again, the important contributions to global labour studies by Silver, Webster et al and the scholars promoting the PRA – but also interventions by authors operating in their vicinity, that is, from South African and German labour sociologists. Furthermore, I will discuss the reflections of two eminent Marxist intellectuals, Antonio Gramsci and Nicos Poulantzas. The second question will be my main subject in the next chapter, which is exclusively about the PRA. I have chosen this focus because it represents a conceptual framework that has been designed for labour research, and whose proponents explicitly commit themselves to the cause of labour.

The class analyst's dilemma

In her book, Silver only addresses the relationship between global labour scholars and workers in passing. Consequently, I have chosen to examine what kind of implicit assumptions she makes when she presents her findings. The final chapter of her book ('Contemporary dynamics in world-historical perspective') is particularly useful in this regard. In it, she discusses how key claims in the social science literature on the state of labour compare with her insights. Most importantly, she argues against the claim by some scholars that there is a 'race to the bottom' in terms of an ever-weaker working class – and retorts that according to her data, labour unrest is to be expected in regions of the world 'that have been experiencing rapid industrialization and proletarianization' (Silver, 2003: 169). Similar observations that can be found in the chapter are that the economic gap between the Global North and South is not closing (Silver, 2003: 170); that the significance of forming organizations and of the political context of trade unionism is likely to increase (Silver, 2003: 173); that the wars of today differ from those that emerged in the late 19th century in that workers in the Global North are better insulated from them, which means that the explosive reactions of working classes to armed conflict seen in the first half of the 20th century are unlikely to be repeated (Silver, 2003: 174–5), and that it is not a given that labour internationalism will be revitalized (Silver, 2003: 177).

Notably, these findings are of significant strategic relevance for labour movements. One could argue that Silver identifies key conditions for the organization of workers in the present day and age from a global perspective – and does so from the standpoint of the social scientist who commits to being on the side of workers. From the way Silver presents her findings, we can conclude that her role is to produce and present knowledge of strategic relevance, and that the role of workers engaging in struggles is to make use of this knowledge. In other words, Silver's presentation of her findings implicitly presupposes a double relationship between scholars and workers: The former study objects that the latter form part of, and the latter are supported by the former in struggles against class domination. Inherent in this double relationship is a clear-cut division of labour, which is institutionalized thanks to the existence of academia: Scholars are responsible for studying labour relations and producing strategically relevant scientific knowledge; workers struggle against class domination and make strategic decisions in the process for which this knowledge can be helpful.

Importantly, Silver's monograph by no means stands out in this respect. The division of labour described is presupposed in many writings of labour scholars and other social scientists with normative and political commitments – and this of course includes the author of this book. Arguably, it is a standard mode of operation used by social scientists when they attempt to make their research politically relevant. If one takes the normative foundation of global labour studies seriously, however, it is worth reflecting critically on the class effects of this division of labour.

The passages quoted in Volume 1, Chapter 1 from Marx's *Capital* offer a reflection on the function of science in the capitalist mode of production. Marx argues that 'science is incorporated' in the work process 'as an independent power'. With the attribute 'independent', he suggests that the creation and application of scientific knowledge takes place in different domains. Such knowledge is applied all the time in capitalist work processes. But its production usually takes place away from the workplaces where it is used – in research departments of private firms, but also, and importantly, in public institutions such as universities and research institutes.

According to Nicos Poulantzas, the capitalist relations of production entail the existence of a state-controlled and mostly state-run sphere of science, which exists in separation from most other work processes in society (see Poulantzas, 1978: 55–6; Stützle, 2011: 177–8). There is a separation between experts (scientists, scholars and intellectuals) and laypeople (workers) enshrined in a 'Scientist-State', which produces 'a knowledge and discourse from which the popular masses are excluded' (Poulantzas, 1978: 56) – in short, a 'state-monopolized science-knowledge' (Poulantzas, 1978: 58). Most of the scientific knowledge production is carried out by people whose expertise is approved by state apparatuses in the form of degrees and academic titles. The latter give them the authority to speak, intervene in public debates and make decisions. Those who do not possess state-certified expertise tend to be relegated to jobs where they execute orders and follow plans made by people who are presumed to possess superior knowledge because of their academic credentials (Poulantzas, 1978: 60). Poulantzas describes the connection between experts, the capitalist state and science thus:

[T]he State structures intellectual labour through a whole series of circuits and networks ... it subordinates and marks down for itself the *intellectual-scientific corps* ... Intellectuals have been constituted as a specialized professional corps through their reduction to functionaries or mercenaries of the modern State. In the universities, institutes, academies and societies of learning, these bearers of knowledge-science have become state functionaries. (Poulantzas, 1978: 57; emphasis in the original)

Conversely, Poulantzas observes that the existence of the capitalist state is crucial for shutting out workers from creating or possessing knowledge that is universally accepted as expertise. They tend to submit to arrangements in the work process that are planned and devised by people such as managers, lawyers and engineers (Poulantzas, 1978: 55–6; see Stützle, 2011: 173). As I have argued in the preceding chapter, this results in workers becoming alienated from their own intellectual capacities, which Marx describes as one of the key aspects of their subjugation to capital. Following Poulantzas, a 'corps of licensed intellectuals' – or professional knowledge handlers – tends to play an important role in the reproduction of class domination because it creates the knowledge needed to organize work processes or, through its mere existence, justifies the hierarchies in the workplace (1978: 61). In a nutshell, the capitalist mode of scientific knowledge production facilitates the continued extraction of surplus labour.

Importantly, global labour scholars are not exempt from these mechanisms just because they claim to be on the side of workers. They usually do not produce knowledge that is used for organizing work processes. And they make productive use of the distance of scientists to corporate agendas by highlighting and criticizing class domination. But they are still state-appointed 'labour experts' – usually, they are affiliated with universities or research institutions that are either publicly funded or at least certified by the state. Just like all scientists with institutional affiliations, global labour scholars are perpetuating the separation described by Poulantzas. Accordingly, workers are supposed to somehow receive their expertise and apply it in their struggles (see Webster, 2004: 32; Buhlungu, 2006: 427).

It follows that global labour scholars (and any other social scientists taking a pro-worker stance) become entangled in a performative contradiction. They are facing what I propose to call the class analyst's dilemma. It is their aim to produce knowledge that helps workers contest capitalist rule, but they can only do so with the help of state-sanctioned scientific practices – and these have unintended consequences: They contribute to the reproduction of class domination insofar as any kind of science, under capitalist conditions, rests on the separation between experts and laypeople and thus perpetuates the alienation of workers from their skills and intellectual powers. As a result, global labour scholars are facing a contradiction, which concerns the form and the content of scientific knowledge production under capitalist conditions: They tend to a have a degree of freedom when it comes to deciding what the content of their research activities is, which means that they can criticize the status quo. But their expertise is certified by the state authorities in a manner that also creates non-experts who are denied this status. Consequently, their existence as academics separates them from laypeople – and this in turn serves as a legitimation for subjugating workers and disconnecting the latter from their intellectual capacities.

In class-analytical terms, academics 'occupy contradictory locations within class relations' (Wright, 1978a: 10), which are, in a Marxian understanding, relations of production. They are not much different from workers in the sense that they are dependent on selling their labour power, which also creates opportunities for solidarity between both groups. But they also have a great degree of control over their work, which sets them apart from workers, and enjoy expert status, which means that they cannot avoid being complicit, to a degree, in the subjugation of workers. Scientists committing to the cause of workers do not just have to cross the social distance between academia as a location in the social fabric and other workplaces; they also have to find ways of dealing with this unavoidable complicity. Consequently, the relationship between global labour scholars and workers is fraught with difficulties.

Importantly, my critique of expertise is not meant to advocate epistemic egalitarianism. It would be wrong to assume that everybody knows as much as everybody else. Hierarchies of knowledge are as opaque as they are real.

They are opaque because different social groups and individuals know different things – and the claim that 'experts' are always best suited to speak about a certain topic is questionable on various grounds. Professional knowledge handlers are socially situated just like anyone else, which means that they have biases and blind spots, and that they may not understand aspects of their objects and subjects of study because of their social distance to the latter. In fact, practitioners may know more about certain aspects of the social world than 'experts' even if their knowledge is not formally or socially recognized. Thanks to their practical experience, nurses may know more than doctors, mechanics more than engineers and labour activists more than labour scholars in many areas – and this knowledge is usually not recognized as expertise because its bearers lack formal credentials for being seen as experts. Besides, there is tacit, practical knowledge that is highly useful in day-to-day activities but is difficult to transfer from one person to the next because it is hard to verbalize. The much sneered-at ineptitude of some professional footballers to explain in post-match interviews what they have done on the pitch is testament to this. As a result, it would be plain wrong to say scientific knowledge is superior to other forms of knowledge in every regard and social context or the only kind of valid knowledge (see Sayer, 1992: 14–15; Nowak, 2019: 11; Scherrer, 2020: 291; Yudken and Jacobs, 2021: 154).

And yet, hierarchies of knowledge are also real and not just a product of ideology or academic imagination. Scientists possess access to data, conceptual tools enabling them to make sense of the world and technical knowledge on how to use such tools (Althusser, 1969: 182–9; Sayer, 2000: 19). Consequently, they possess and produce reservoirs of knowledge that other people cannot easily tap into, but that can be of high practical relevance if applied the right way. And global labour scholars usually wager that they produce knowledge that is strategically relevant to workers – and this of course also applies to the author of this book.

This wager is based on the experience that labour activists and trade unionists draw upon scientific knowledge in their day-to-day dealings. There are further- and higher-education programmes specifically geared towards their needs and interests, for example those offered by the GLU – and there are gateway publications like the *Global Labour Column* or the *South African Labour Bulletin* (SALB) that aim to disseminate the findings of social scientists, among them global labour scholars, to a wider audience of labour activists, trade unionists and workers.[1] Besides, the research units of unions produce and engage with scientific knowledge. Indeed, many labour practitioners produce strategic, and in parts even scientific, knowledge and sometimes publicize it through the same channels as pro-worker academics (see Barker and Cox, 2000/2001: 1, 23; Buhlungu, 2009: 153; Cox, 2015: 39–41; Pillay, 2016: 171).

It follows that the class analyst's dilemma cannot be resolved by simply declaring scientific knowledge superfluous for labour practitioners. In other words, anti-scientific relativism is not the answer. Much rather, the fact that labour practitioners sometimes say that scientific knowledge is of no use to them points to an additional challenge. This is the challenge of knowledge transfer. It is difficult to transport scientific knowledge from academia into the world of work – and to transform it, in the process, into practical knowledge that can be used by workers in their collective struggles. This is obvious to anyone involved with academic teaching and science communication; it is a common experience that people struggle with accessing knowledge – and even if that is not case it may be that it is, or appears to be, useless for them. But importantly, this challenge also exists if one works the other way round. The point of labour research is that workers possess pools of experiential, practical and practical-strategic knowledge that are not transparent to the scientific community – and that it is worth tapping into those pools and examining their contents systematically to close information gaps and challenge prejudices and untested assumptions. Consequently, the question

---

[1] For detailed accounts of the histories of the GLU and the SALB, see Hoffer (2006), Çelik (2013: 27–9), Fichter et al (2014) and Scherrer (2020).

of knowledge transfer concerns social science communication, but also methods of social research.

In conclusion, there is a double challenge for global labour scholars. On the one hand, they need to address the class analyst's dilemma if they are serious about the normative-political commitment of their field. On the other hand, they also need to bridge the gulf between themselves and workers to ensure that knowledge can be transferred from one side to the other.

The organic intellectual

In an important contribution to global labour studies, the monograph *Mass Strikes and Social Movements in India and Brazil*, Jörg Nowak identifies one way of tackling the double challenge: '[G]iven the fact that social movements themselves continuously produce intellectuals and scholars, the line dividing scholars and movement actors is not so easy to draw' (2019: 11). Following Nowak, the gulf between both sides is not unbridgeable because there are people who are located on both sides at the same time. His model for this type of scholar is Antonio Gramsci's 'organic intellectual' (Nowak, 2019: 11). Similarly, the South African sociologist Devan Pillay (2016: 171) speaks of a 'labor intellectuals' or 'intellectual activists', that is, 'labor scholars who remain within the labor movement'. But what exactly is this model?

Gramsci's reflections on the matter can be found in his *Prison Notebooks*. Their provisional, fragmentary and coded character mean that serious interpretative work is warranted if one wants to make sense of his considerations (see Hoare and Nowell Smith, 1971: x–xi). As a first approximation, Gramsci speaks of 'intellectuals' when he refers to people who handle knowledge – who shape, transform, elaborate and disseminate ideas (1971: 9, 323; see Wright, 1978a: 6). In principle, this applies to human beings in general, which is why Gramsci proposes, in a second step, tightening the definition. In this narrower sense, intellectuals are people who develop and promote 'an integral conception of the world' (1971: 9) – a coherent and stable worldview. Importantly, such a worldview has class effects in capitalist societies. If we take neoliberalism as an example, we see that its commitments to entrepreneurship, the 'small' state and individualism lends credence to the accumulation strategies pursued by financial capital. It perpetuates capitalist class domination by contributing to the formation of political projects that reproduce and consolidate it. Neoliberals – just like any other intellectuals aligned with a coherent worldview – universalize specific class interests by promoting their worldview and getting people across society to adopt it (or parts thereof). As my reference to 'class effects' indicates, this does not have to be an intentional process. Following Gramsci, class domination is both reproduced and contested not just with the material force of the baton or the gun, but also with the help of ideas – and intellectuals are the people who are taking leading roles in handling knowledge. It follows that through their characteristic activities, they facilitate processes of class formation (Gramsci, 1971: 5, 12).

According to Gramsci, it is necessary to distinguish two sub-types of the intellectual in the context of the capitalist societies. Invoking everyday understandings of the term, he refers to 'traditional intellectuals', who are not just 'ecclesiastics', but also 'administrators', 'scholars and scientists' (1971: 7) as well as 'journalists … philosophers, artists' (1971: 9). They see themselves as being 'autonomous and independent' (1971: 7), that is, as detached from their own location in the relations of production and committed only to ideas, for example, in the fields of religion and philosophy. Their mode of knowledge production is usually 'contemplative' (Barker and Cox, 2000/2001: 3); it is about producing knowledge for its own sake from the standpoint of the unbiased outsider. Accordingly, traditional intellectuals tend to see themselves as hovering above society – or above the masses of people who merely create and use knowledge in an instrumental manner, that is, for clearly defined, often work-related purposes. 'The traditional "scientific" stance is that of the *detached observer*', as Norman Blaikie and Jan Priest, two specialists on research practices, aptly describe this attitude (2019: 44; emphasis in the original).

Similar to Poulantzas, Gramsci mentions 'the formation of the *noblesse de robe*, with its own privileges, a stratum of administrators etc., scholars and scientists, theorists, non-ecclesiastical philosophers, etc.' (1971: 7; emphasis in the original). The 'nobles of the gown' were French aristocrats in the age of absolutism who worked in the state administration. However, Gramsci refers here not just to civil servants but also to the different categories of people who are affiliated with academic institutions, as the second half of the sentence shows. The main state apparatus endowing scholars and scientists with 'privileges' is the university. Consequently, I read this sentence not just as a critique of the civil service, but also of academia.

Following Gramsci, the existence of academic systems means that there is a small band of people – an intellectual 'aristocracy' – who enjoy not just the 'material advantage' of making a living based on knowledge production (Barker and Cox, 2000/2001: 5), but also the ideational advantage of being seen as experts. It follows that they have significantly more far-reaching capacities to be heard and shape discourses than people who are not, and they are often not even aware of, or choose to ignore, their location in the relations of production. Accordingly, many of their activities consist in engaging with a clearly delimited epistemic communities of co-experts – and compared to other people working in the public sector, they have a significant degree of autonomy.

Through working in and through these rather secluded epistemic communities, traditional intellectuals perpetuate monopolies of expertise.

There are 'canons' and 'states of the art' in their respective fields, and having sufficient knowledge about them, next to formal academic qualifications, is an entry requirement if one wants to join their illustrious circles. This is reflected in the importance of the 'literature review' as a scientific practice. Canonization and the assumption that there are 'states of the art' mean that traditional intellectuals usually handle bodies of knowledge that have sedimented into paradigms; 'scientific revolutions' that forcefully contest the received wisdom in a field are few and far between, rarely produce a complete rupture and take a long time to succeed (see Sayer, 1992: 72–3; Blaikie and Priest, 2017: 9, 31–2; 2019: 20, 79). The existence of such monopolies entails that traditional intellectuals operate in and through rather stable configurations of class domination. Gramsci's line of argument is fully compatible with Poulantzas' considerations on 'state-monopolized science-knowledge'.

Thanks to the institutionalized division of labour between academics as experts and non-academic as laypeople, there is a socially significant distance of the intellectual aristocrats of academia to the people whose professions are not focused on knowledge handling. If academics make observations on the social world, this distance is reflected in a tendency to produce ahistorical abstractions that are far removed from the lived reality of the people. This compromises the accuracy of their observations and reflections (see Gramsci, 1971: 400).

Importantly, Gramsci's critique of the form of academic knowledge production applies to scientists who are critical of capitalism just as much as those who defend it. They also display an in part wilful ignorance towards the class relations they are entangled in and often react with defensiveness towards demands that they reflect their own location in the social fabric and their material and ideational advantages (see Cox, 2015: 36). This is an important reason why it is so hard to tackle the class analyst's dilemma.

Importantly, Gramsci juxtaposes this critique of traditional intellectuals and academia with observations on the group of intellectuals that he views much more favourably, as befits a scholar and activist who mostly operated outside academic institutions and inside the Italian labour movement. He calls them ' "organic" intellectuals' (1971: 6), and they adopt a stance that can be characterized as 'conscious partiality' (Blaikie and Priest, 2019: 46). They are on the side of 'their' people, meaning that they take part in the latter's collective practices and universalize the latter's views and experiences by turning them into more coherent sets of ideas. In other words, they are engaged in practices of knowledge handling that are based on a deep awareness of their own location in relations of production, and of how work is organized across society. Through their activities, they directly engage with the people they side with – and help the latter learn about their joint class interests (Gramsci, 1971: 5, 10), but also tap into pools of popular knowledge inherent in the common sense that are critical towards the authority of traditional intellectuals and their worldviews. Gramsci refers to people's 'good sense', which consists in 'a contemptuous attitude to the abstruseness, ingenuities and obscurity of certain forms of scientific and philosophical exposition' (1971: 423) – an attitude that 'does not let itself be distracted by fancy quibbles and pseudo-profound, pseudo-scientific metaphysical mumbo-jumbo' (1971: 348). Their firm grasp of the organization of work forms the basis of their broader worldview: 'In the modern world, technical education, closely bound to industrial labour even at the most primitive and unqualified level, must form the basis of the new type of intellectual' (1971: 10). For Gramsci, the union leader or workers' party cadre with insider knowledge of the industrial scenery are the prototypes of the organic intellectual. They do not simply rely on their skills as speakers, which is an attribute of traditional intellectuals, but on their organizational capacities. This sets them apart from the latter: 'The mode of being of the new intellectual can no longer consist in eloquence, which is an exterior and momentary mover of feelings and passions, but in active participation in practical life, as constructor, organiser, "permanent persuader" and not just simple orator' (Gramsci, 1971: 10).

With reference to Gramsci's biography, it becomes clearer what he means by this. After the First World War, Gramsci was a militant in Turin, one of the hubs of Italian manufacturing, and the editor of *Ordine Nuovo* [New Order], a left-socialist newspaper. By invoking these activities in his reflections, he emphasizes the importance of organic intellectuals for working-class political projects. Their leadership is not exercised *ex cathedra*, but through active involvement in struggles, close social links with workers and detailed knowledge of the industrial world of work. Through their practices, they universalize a class-based, socialist worldview that takes up the good sense of the workers and gives it coherence (Gramsci, 1971: 9–10, 419–25; see Bieler, 2012: 366). Their dominant mode of knowledge production is not 'contemplative' but 'activist' (Barker and Cox, 2000/2001: 7); it is developed in the 'already-occupied terrain' that is controlled by the traditional intellectuals (2000/2001: 21), and thus is 'knowledge-in-struggle' and knowledge in opposition to the status quo (2000/2001: 23). In contrast to traditional intellectuals, organic intellectuals are linked with classes in formation (Gramsci, 1971: 5). They constitute the 'militant minority' of workers, to use Kim Moody's words (2017: 86), who have a fairly consistent worldview, are committed to fundamental social change, think strategically and are prepared to take the lead in confrontations with capital.

If we relate his observations back to the class theorist's dilemma, we can conclude that Gramsci proposes refusing to become a state-sanctioned expert. The organic intellectuals of the working class not only get directly involved in workers' struggles and engage with the workers' good sense, but they are also immersed in the lifeworld of workers. Operating this way, they circumnavigate the trap of becoming experts and accomplices in the perpetuation of class domination.

Implicitly, Gramsci's critique of traditional intellectuals is also a critique of a distinct mode of political intervention they engage in, which can be called 'enlightenment politics'. This mode is based on the premise that people will make better political choices if they are better informed about the social world – and that it is the job of experts to supply the information needed. In other words, social scientists produce ideas and insights, which then need to be communicated to the public in a convincing and accessible manner. This can happen through public speeches at political and cultural events in the broadest sense, as Gramsci points out. But it is also the dominant form of 'political education' offered by schools and universities, the news media and certain forms of the arts and literature. To a degree, this mode is inescapable in capitalist societies; it results from people being divided into experts and laypeople. If we follow Gramsci, enlightenment politics impedes advances of the working class. It reproduces and fortifies the separation between experts and laypeople and only transfers knowledge in a top-down fashion. In other words, it fails to address either of the two challenges faced by global labour scholars. To quote Marx, proponents of enlightenment politics forget that 'it is essential to educate the educator himself' (2005; see Hoffer, 2006: 31).

Against this backdrop, my response to the question I posed at the beginning of the section is this: According to Gramsci, intellectuals should be immersed in the world of workers and exposed to the latter's lived experiences. His model is the union organizer or the party leader rather than the critical academic. He hopes that the knowledge thus produced does not reinforce the distinction between experts and laypeople and is transferred back and forth between worker intellectuals and the workers themselves. Following Nowak, the lesson from Gramsci would be to promote forms of global labour scholarship where intellectuals remain immersed in labour movements; they should operate at a distance to academia.

At the same time, it would be naïve to claim that the relationship between organic intellectuals and workers is tension-free. As Nowak observes, movements are not spaces devoid of relations of social domination:

> [T]he question of representation will inevitably come up within social movements themselves: Movements regularly strive to represent a certain social group, community, neighbourhood and so on, and the question of legitimate leadership remains a permanent and at times conflictive issue inside of social movements. Thus, one can conclude that representation is rather an issue to be dealt with than one that can be entirely avoided. But it is for sure a landmark of progressive and left politics to permanently question types and forms of representation and

to not take them for granted, since representation is inevitably tied up with domination. (Nowak, 2018: 13; see also Barker and Cox, 2000/2001: 1; Cox, 2015)

Following Nowak, there is a double relation of representation inherent in labour movements. For one, they claim to represent a broader constituency of workers. Most of the time, not all workers in a workplace or sector walk out if there is a strike, but the striking workers usually still claim to represent the interests of a broader constituency. And of course, there are always spokespeople who take a leading role – the organic intellectuals Gramsci refers to. Consequently, it is likely that hierarchies emerge in labour movements, and that these hierarchies often perpetuate relations of social domination because people with material and ideational advantages occupy leadership positions. The professionalization of movement leadership in the form of full-time union officials tends to reinforce these tendencies because it creates a permanent division of labour between union leaders and the rank-and-file (see Voss and Sherman, 2000; Darlington and Upchurch, 2011; Camfield, 2013).

As Nowak suggests, the challenge of representation can only be addressed through mechanisms of accountability between leaders, movements and their broader constituency that allow for permanent critical discussions, that is, relative transparency concerning how and why leaders arrive at certain decisions and democratic mechanisms for their election and removal. Arguably, this also requires a degree of institutionalization, for example, regular meetings among leaders and officials and with the rank-and-file and unorganized workers (see Voss and Sherman, 2000: 305–6; Gumbrell-McCormick and Hyman, 2019: 101–5).

The organic academic

The Gramscian model offers a way of dealing with the double challenge for global labour scholars identified at the end of the last but one section, and it appears possible to address the accountability and representation issues that arise in its context. But in contrast to most present-day global labour scholars, the organic intellectual envisaged by Gramsci operates from a distance to academia.[2] Taking Gramsci seriously means posing the question whether academia is suitable as an operational base for global labour scholars, or whether they should head for other shores if they take

---

[2]   The main association for global labour scholarship, the Research Committee on Labour Struggles of the International Sociological Association (RC44), is a decidedly academic enterprise, and the same can be said of its publication, the *Global Labour Journal*.

their normative-political commitments seriously and work for trade unions, labour non-governmental organizations or journalistic outlets with links to labour. Put differently, it is far from obvious why pro-worker intellectuals should enter academia.

One could of course argue that the academic nature of global labour studies means that Gramsci is not one of the key authors in the field, which in turn would explain why important debates are not guided by his considerations on organic intellectuals.[3] Alternatively, one could speculate that labour intellectuals have pragmatic motives when they embrace academia. It may be a form of dealing with the 'silent compulsion of economic relations' and making a living (Marx, 1967: 899). In the neoliberal era, a decline of labour organizations around the globe coincides with a sustained expansion in higher education (see Schofer and Meyer, 2005; van der Linden, 2016). Under these circumstances, labour intellectuals have strong material incentives to retreat into academia (see Barker and Cox, 2000/2001: 7–8). All of this of course matters, but it may also not be enough. As I will argue in this section, there are substantive reasons concerning knowledge production that explain why global labour scholars tend to be academics. In brief – and coming back to Poulantzas – the nature of the capitalist state means that academia as a professional 'knowledge apparatus' is the key site of knowledge production in capitalist societies (Stützle, 2011), and this has to be considered in discussions on the relationship between intellectuals and labour movements.

Against this backdrop, I have chosen to critically examine two bodies of literature that discuss the practices of labour intellectuals. I have chosen these particular literatures because they connect with the reference points of my discussion in Chapter 1 – and because they reflect my interest in taking a global perspective. The literatures in question are the reflections offered by Webster and his colleague, fellow South African and sometimes co-author Sakhela Buhlungu, plus those of German PRA scholars. I start with South Africa in this section and move on to Germany in the next one.

In South Africa, a close connection between a group of White intellectuals and Black labour activists emerged after what has been called the 'Durban moment' (Webster, 1992: 89) – a conjuncture of labour activism and anti-Apartheid protests that started with a wave of wildcat strikes by Black workers in Durban in 1973, which were directed against low wages and poor working

---

[3] Notably, *Grounding Globalization*, *Forces of Labor* and the various contributions to the PRA do not engage with Gramsci's thought in detail. But saying that Gramsci is ignored by global labour scholars would be wrong. There is a range of authors for whom Gramsci is of great importance. I have already discussed Nowak's monograph, but names such as Andreas Bieler and Adam Morton (2004; 2018), Michael Burawoy (1979; 2008; 2012), Ercüment Çelik (2013) and Elaine Hui (2017) are also worth mentioning in this context.

conditions. The strikes served as a catalyst for some White intellectuals seeking to support Black workers in their struggles, both by becoming union officials and by supporting them from inside academia, which was done through education drives, research, publications and interventions in public political debates (Webster, 1992: 89–90; 2017; Buhlungu, 2006: 229–30; 2009: 146–9; Kalekin-Fishman, 2012: 162; Çelik, 2013: 25). Considering these experiences and the important contribution of organized labour to bringing down Apartheid, it is not surprising that South African labour scholars and trade unionists have been promoting 'social movement unionism' for decades – a mode of unionism based on organizing and mobilizing workers both in their workplaces and communities (Webster et al, 2008: 160, 180, 220; see also Fairbrother and Webster, 2008).

In this context, Webster relays his experiences as a labour sociologist. He discusses how he established a close working relationship with the National Union of Mineworkers in the 1980s, attempting to support them in efforts to improve working and living conditions. He and his colleagues from the Sociology of Work Programme (SWOP) at the University of the Witwatersrand in Johannesburg did so by starting a research project on health and safety in mines – and heavily drew upon the knowledge of workers concerning the issue in the process. In Gramscian terms, they tapped into the 'good sense' of the workers. By publishing the findings widely and confronting employers with them, they tried to give workers 'institutional voice' (Webster, 2017). Importantly, the project was a collaborative effort from start to finish:

> SWOP emphasised participatory research defined as a co-operative enquiry by both the researcher and the people who are the focus of the study. This included joint identification of the problem to be studied; sharing of ideas on the best way of conducting the study; and reporting back on the results. This involved making the research accessible. An example is the publication of *A Thousand Ways to Die*, a study on underground mine safety, into a popular pamphlet in Xhosa, Sotho and English for the members of the National Union of Mineworkers. (Webster, 1992: 90)

These experiences can be seen as part of the backdrop against which Webster and his co-authors reflect on the relationship between intellectuals and workers in *Grounding Globalization*. In line with my reflections on Gramsci, they propose organizing a regular exchange of ideas between global labour scholars and representatives of organized labour. In their view, global labour scholars should work at shouting distance to labour activists and vice versa: 'we see the relationship as a reciprocal one whereby the movements are as much shaped by the ideas of the intellectual as is the intellectual shaped by these movements' (Webster et al, 2008: 226). Two things follow on from the notion of reciprocity: participants need to recognize, from the start, that everyone involved has knowledge to contribute, and that no one – no matter what their standing in the worlds of academia or organized labour – possesses knowledge that is superior in every regard. Taking reciprocity seriously means subverting the division between experts and laypeople.

Accordingly, Webster et al suggest 'building institutional space within the university' in which reciprocal relations between academics and workers can blossom (Webster et al, 2008: 226). I understand this as a call for the creation of networks and forums where both sides meet and start a process of mutual learning. This is exemplified not just by SWOP, the South African GLU programmes and the SALB, but also by a number of zones of encounter mentioned by Webster and Buhlungu that emerged during the Apartheid regime, among them the Durban-based Institute for Industrial Education, the Labour Studies programme of the Federation of South African Trade Unions and several church-based initiatives (Webster, 1992: 89–90; Buhlungu, 2006: 444–5; Çelik, 2013: 25–9; Pillay, 2016: 171–6).

But despite a certain proximity to Gramsci reflected in the call for reciprocity and exchange, Webster et al stress that the model of the intellectual that they have in mind differs from Gramsci's:

> To be an engaged intellectual … is to actively ensure that the knowledge produced becomes part of these movements, through teaching, organizing or publishing in accessible journals and other outlets. But an engaged intellectual is not the same as an organic intellectual. Organic intellectuals operate inside organizations and, while they perform an intellectual function, they do not have the distance or the time to produce the concepts and theories that define the central characteristics of an intellectual. (Webster et al, 2008: 226; see also Kalekin-Fishman, 2012: 167)

Accordingly, Webster states in a separate piece that his experiences as a pro-labour academic differs from those of organic intellectuals:

> [T]he public is not some collective *tabula rasa* waiting passively with empty heads for the intellectual vanguard from the university to tell them what to think. They have ideas, traditions, political cultures, organisations and political leaders of their own. Indeed they have their own grassroots organic intellectuals whose task it is to interpret, and give direction to, the world around them. … I discovered this when, in 1973 in the wake of the Durban strikes, I developed a relationship with the workers' movement, which was emerging among industrial

workers in South Africa at that time. (Webster, 2004: 31; see also Webster, 1992: 88)

Webster signals that it is not the task of the engaged, pro-labour academic to lead workers in their struggles – this is the task of organic intellectuals, which exist no matter what is happening within the academic system. Importantly, he and his co-authors identify a substantive reason for supporting organic intellectuals in Gramsci's sense through operating inside academia: Whereas organic intellectuals need to subsume their reflections to the exigencies of the struggles they are immersed in as well as day-to-day practices of representation, organization and mobilization, academics operate at a distance to movements. Consequently, they tend to have more time and space to reflect critically on their observations and insights because they enjoy a degree of 'academic freedom' – a conditional autonomy concerning their activities that reflects the fact that political power as it is enshrined in the capitalist state tends to be separate from economic power (see Poulantzas, 1978: 44; Fichter et al, 2014: 568).

Furthermore, the state-sanctioned expertise emerging in academic contexts can be used for advancing the causes of labour, as Webster's remark about giving 'institutional voice' to workers indicates. It offers material and ideational resources to intellectuals that people operating on the outside do not have. These resources can be used provided that it is possible to enter a relationship of 'reciprocity' with workers, labour activists and – importantly – organic intellectuals in the Gramscian mould. Due to this close relationship, the model intellectual envisaged here can be possibly called an organic academic – or an 'organic public sociologist', as Michael Burawoy puts it with reference to his own disciplinary backdrop (2008: 354). This latter label is used approvingly by Webster, who is also a sociologist (Kalekin-Fishman, 2012: 167). In Blaikie and Priest's words, the organic academic is 'a *reflective* partner who is committed to the emancipation of the participants' (2019: 45; emphasis in the original).

This mode of intellectual practice is exemplified by the activities of Webster and his colleagues in Apartheid South Africa. It was extremely risky for the organic intellectual of the Black workers' movement to reach out beyond their direct constituencies. In contrast, there was degree of academic freedom in historically White, English-language academic institutions, which opened their doors, from the 1970s onwards, to some Black students and staff (Metcalfe and Cock, 2010: 67–70).

And yet, the engaged academics in Webster's mould also face significant constraints. By intervening in public debates, they keep on reproducing the separation between 'experts' and 'laypeople' and become entangled, time and again, in the class analyst's dilemma. And notably, the evaluation criteria applied to their academic work are neither neutral nor uncontested.

In fact, the selectivities of the 'scientist-state' tend to favour ideas and insights that legitimize and consolidate the status quo. This is visible in the long history of harrassing or marginalizing radical academics in academia, from McCarthyism in the US in the 1940s and 1950s to the present-day persecution of left-wing academics by the Erdoğan regime in Turkey or the Modi government in India; from the *Berufsverbote* [occupational bans] in 1970s West Germany to the prohibition of Gender Studies in present-day Hungary. Under the extreme example of Apartheid South Africa, being vocal about racial and class oppression could result in imprisonment and, in some cases, extermination.[4]

And under conditions of neoliberalization, there is a pressure to conform even if there are no direct threats of persecution. In many countries where education systems have been neoliberalized, academics are under heavy labour market pressures unless they enjoy tenure, which is thanks to a range of factors, among them the introduction of research metrics supposed to measure the quality of research output (but which favour certain styles of research over others and do not enjoy universal acceptance); the proliferation of fixed-term contracts; and public expenditure cuts that translate into department closures and job cuts. In other words, there is strong pressure on academics to prioritize career strategies and individual advancement over normative-political commitments. In many contexts, it may pay off for social scientists to neglect workers' issues in their research (see Cox, 2015: 49–50; Gallas, 2018c; 2018d).

All of this reflects the fact that academia is an ideological state apparatus. It has distinct selectivities operating in favour of capital, which turn intellectuals not just into 'bearers of knowledge-science' but also into 'state functionaries' (Poulantzas, 1978, 57; see also Gallas, 2018c; 2018d; Kutun and Tören, 2018; Nowak, 2018: 10). No matter what their politics are, they are likely to become entangled in mechanisms that facilitate the reproduction of capitalist class domination, which are difficult to escape from. It is unlikely that people will gain academic respectability who refuse to act as experts, and gaining this respectability usually means speaking and writing in a language that makes scientific knowledge difficult to access for workers.

The resulting distance between academics and workers is further aggravated because both sides tend to inhabit milieus in the lifeworld far removed from one another – and the number of academics from worker

---

[4] Webster himself was arrested and on trial for a year in 1976 for calling for the release of Nelson Mandela from prison (Kalekin-Fishman, 2012: 160). His colleagues Richard Turner and David Webster were murdered by the Apartheid police in 1978 and 1989, respectively (Webster, 2004: 32).

families is low in many academic systems. Under the Apartheid regime, the distance was institutionalized by racialized and classed patterns of settlement. White professionals lived in suburbs that were separated from Black residential areas. Accordingly, Webster observes that despite the efforts of establishing mechanisms of support, 'white intellectuals were never fully integrated into the movement with which they had decided to pledge solidarity' (2004: 32; see also Buhlungu, 2006: 435; 2009: 466). And following Buhlungu and Webster, the distance between academics and workers did not shrink in the post-Apartheid era. Indeed, the neoliberalization of higher education led to institutional changes that facilitated competition among academics and created close ties of certain sections of the social sciences with business (Webster, 2004: 35–8; Buhlungu, 2009: 154–9). It is worth mentioning the title of one of Buhlungu's articles in this context. The latter highlights 'The decline of labor studies', which roughly coincided with the neoliberal turn of the South African political economy during the Mbeki presidency (Buhlungu, 2006; see also Gallas et al, 2014: 145, 148).

In brief, Webster's 'engaged intellectuals' are located in universities because this allows them to present themselves as experts and give them access to ideational and material resources that the organic intellectuals in the Gramscian mould do not possess. The challenges posed by knowledge transfer and the class analyst's dilemma can ideally be addressed through the institution of regular exchanges with workers and organic intellectuals inside the movements. And importantly, organic academics can cooperate closely with organic intellectuals in the Gramscian sense in this process. But there is also a critical issue specific to academics linked with labour movements. They are accountable to two different constituencies – to academia and the movements they support – and this can create grave tensions.

Webster shows this with reference to a research project he was involved in. In the late 1980s, SWOP did research on migrant labour and AIDS. They found that the dependency of the mining industry on migrant labour gave rise to '[a] system of casual sex and prostitution' in mineworkers' settlements that facilitated the 'the rapid spread' of HIV. Representatives of the NUM reacted angrily when they read the first draft of SWOP's research report. They feared that the findings could be used to vilify Black mineworkers by fuelling discourses that portrayed 'the black man ... as diseased and promiscuous' (quotations from the original manuscript; see Kalekin-Fishman, 2012: 164). Against this backdrop, Webster et al highlight the 'contradictory location' (2008: 226) of academics who support organized labour. As the example shows, they are 'caught between the demands of the profession and its need for autonomous spaces for critical reflexion and theoretical development and attempts to make themselves accountable to organizations outside the university' (Webster, 1982: 2, cited in Webster, 2017) – or between a commitment to truth and a commitment to tactical and strategic gains for their constituency.[5]

Arguably, the AIDS study laid bare the dangers of HIV for workers' communities and the need to discuss gender relations in them. Indeed, taking the normative foundation of a principled opposition to social domination seriously requires us to refrain from sugar-coating it in one place for the sake of criticizing it in another. All of this speaks against suppressing valid observations and considerations. At the same time, Webster concedes that there are questions to be asked about the 'where' and 'when' of publicizing them (2017). To adapt an adage from the footballing world, strategy wins matches, but truth wins championships. Yet without winning matches, it is impossible to win championships. It follows that the commitment of academics to truth is not just an exigency in own right but also valuable from a long-term strategic point of view, and that it needs to be taken into account. It is a difficult challenge, however, to do so without compromising short-term strategic considerations.

Looking back, Webster points to this challenge in his own reflections. He is self-critical and says that he 'had not fully understood the cultural dynamics of sexuality in the context of apartheid and the history of colonialism' (2017). At the same time, he also stresses that the AIDS study 'made visible the patriarchal system and the exploitation of vulnerable women by the mineworkers' (2017). It must remain an open question whether it would have paid off to involve the NUM more in the research process. But it follows from Webster's reflections that it was right to conduct the study: for the sake of the sex workers, but also for mineworkers and their communities – and, in the end, for overcoming divisions between workers, which is fully in line with Marx's categorical imperative. And one could also hypothesize that suppressing the study could have damaged SWOP's standing as an academic institution and could have led to barring the people affiliated with it from academic debates. In other words, there is no simple, one-size-fits-all solution to the problem of the two constituencies. Viable strategies of using the material and ideational resources of academia to advance struggles outside of academia requires one to carefully consider this structural dilemma. One needs to take into account the existing institutional opportunities and constraints as well as conjunctural conditions. In certain circumstances, it

---

[5]   My invocation of 'truth' in this context is meant to mark the horizon of knowledge production inside academia – the fact that any commitment to academic debate implicitly presupposes the existence of an observer-independent reality that science seeks to discover. It should not be read as an emphatic truth claim signalling that scientific knowledge about the social world is beyond contestation, or that it is not affected by the social location of its producer. Drawing upon Sayer's work, I subscribe to the notions of 'epistemic relativism' and 'practical adequacy' (Sayer, 2000: 47–51; see also Sayer, 1992: 65–71).

may be the right answer to leave academia behind; and in others, working in and through it may make more sense – if done the right way.

The strategic-professional academic

The 'Arbeitskreis [working group] Strategic Unionism' (AKSU) is based at the University of Jena in Germany and had approximately 80 members in 2017. It is a network of academics and organic intellectuals that has been developing its distinct take on the PRA – the *Jenaer Machtressourcenansatz* – for more than a decade (Dörre, 2017: 106). These activities are relevant for my considerations because they have involved self-reflections by pro-worker intellectuals inside the group and in its vicinity on the relationship between labour sociology and trade unionism. I will focus on these reflections in this section.

The historical background to the Jena PRA is the fact that, much like in other Western European countries, organized labour was weakened profoundly in Germany thanks to neoliberalization. A process of political-economic restructuring started in the 1970s and 1980s, but was slow compared to Britain and the US. After the reunification in 1990, it accelerated. A key turning point was Gerhard Schröder's chancellorship. Schröder was in office from 1998 to 2005 and promoted a distinct take on 'third-way' social democracy, which was inspired, to a degree, by 'New Labour' (see Blair and Schröder, 1999). The Schröder government liberalized the labour market and cut benefits substantially. Initially, leading trade unionists reacted to these changes with acquiescence, which is unsurprising given the informal, but nevertheless strong links between the large German unions and Schröder's Social Democratic Party of Germany. The unionists aimed to avert the worst by showing their preparedness to enter concession bargaining. The calculation was that this strategy might protect the existing constituencies of their organizations, in particular the core workforces in manufacturing. And yet, liberalization allowed capitalists to compete via wages and working conditions and increased pressures on workforces to make concessions. Thanks to profound changes to labour law, a low-wage sector emerged, and a vicious cycle ensued: concessions created obstacles to organizing and mobilizing workers, which in turn weakened the unions and caused them to seek further concessions. In the end, the union leaderships turned against the government and spoke out against the restructuring of the labour market and the welfare state but did not manage to stop it (see Brinkmann et al, 2008; Urban, 2010; 2018: 382–7; Dörre, 2011: 22–4, 29–30; 2017: 106, 109; Dörre and Schmalz, 2013).[6]

---

[6] For a detailed account of the neoliberalization of the German political economy, see Volume 2, Chapter 6.

In this context, Hans-Jürgen Urban, a leading official of the metalworkers' union IG Metall and a key organic intellectual of organized labour in Germany, suggested drawing upon the existing literature on 'strategic unionism' and 'labour revitalisation' (2010: 447; 2012: 221). Like their South African counterparts, Urban and other German pro-labour intellectuals promoted 'social movement unionism'. But they added that the specific institutional conditions of German trade unions – labour relations in the country are based on corporatism and the notion of 'social partnership' – needed to be considered (Brinkmann et al, 2008: 45–69; Dörre et al, 2009: 47–8; Dörre and Schmalz, 2013: 14, 28; Dörre, 2017: 110, 121; see also Volume 2, Chapter 6). Accordingly, the AKSU, from the start, was a project that involved both academics and organic intellectuals from the trade unions (see Urban, 2010; 2013; 2018; Uellenberg-van Dawen, 2013). And some of the research and publications on power resources and union revitalization is funded by the Hans Böckler Foundation, which was founded by the German Trade Union Confederation (Brinkmann et al, 2008; Schmalz and Dörre, 2013).

Despite the geographical distance between the two countries, the deliberations by the German scholars are taking place, to a degree, in the vicinity of those by their South African colleagues. This is reflected in the fact that there are joint programmatic statements and a lively exchange of ideas between both groups (Schmalz et al, 2018; 2019; see also Aulenbacher et al, 2017: 9). Webster's autobiographical reflections on his relationship with organized labour during the Apartheid era has been translated into German and was published as a chapter in a book edited by Klaus Dörre, one of the key figures behind the PRA in Germany (Webster, 2017).[7]

Unsurprisingly, the relationship between pro-worker intellectuals and labour practitioners envisaged by the German scholars resembles the one developed by their South African counterparts. Both stress the importance of cooperation between pro-worker intellectuals and workers. Nevertheless, they have diverging views of what this means. The South African authors stress the need for a relationship of 'support' – academics strengthen organized labour with the help of the knowledge they produce and the discursive interventions they make (Buhlungu, 2009: 146; Webster, 2017; see also Cox, 2015: 39). This reflects the specific configurations of power and repression

---

[7] The close collaboration between German and South African scholars is noteworthy because there is still a language barrier between Germany and the Anglosphere. Despite the sustained internationalization efforts by a range of actors in academia in the German-language area, there is still a lot of scholarship made available by journals and academic publishers that only or mostly publish in German, and the working language of most universities in Germany and Austria is German. For example, the Webster chapter has not been published in English to my knowledge.

under the Apartheid regime: While White academics were not immune from persecution, they were in a more secure position than Black union leaders and reached audiences that the latter were denied.

In contrast, their German counterparts view the relationship as a 'partnership' (Urban, 2013: 396), which is characterized by 'mutual dependency' and a clearly defined division of labour (Brinkmann et al, 2008: 147). Accordingly, they argue that scholars committed to 'social critique' can only be effective in contributing to social change if they communicate with non-academics – and for this purpose they depend on unions, which can act as 'anchors' of social critique in society (Brinkmann et al, 2008: 147; see also Dörre, 2011: 22; Urban, 2013: 395). At the same time, they add that unions need 'an intellectual frame of reference based on empirical research' helping them to make sense of social change and identify 'requisites for action' [*Handlungsanforderungen*] (Brinkmann et al, 2008: 147; see also Dörre, 2011: 42; Urban, 2013: 396). In this model, unions serve as a gateway allowing academics to transport their insights to a broader audience of people who, in their everyday lives, suffer 'under the capitalist system' (Dörre, 2011: 22) – whose 'good sense', to use Gramsci's term, tells them that there is something wrong with the societies they inhabit. And conversely, academics provide unions with guidance when it comes to the identification of strategic decisions adequate to the conjunctures in which they operate. Rather than seeking an outright alliance, the German PRA scholars promote cooperation.

This approach reflects the existing division of labour between academics and organic intellectuals of organized labour in present-day capitalist societies – the fact that in many countries of the Global North, academia is institutionalized in a manner that keeps labour movements at a distance, and organized labour is dominated by union officialdom (see Darlington and Upchurch, 2011; Camfield, 2013; Cox, 2015; Volume 2, Chapter 7). And importantly, it leaves this division of labour intact and even fortifies it: What is required, according to Urban (2013: 396), is 'mutual respect concerning the specific social roles and cultures of recognition characterising the respective field'. By invoking the different 'cultures', Urban implicitly calls for upholding the criteria on the grounds of which the activities of academic and trade union intellectuals are evaluated. Accordingly, he stresses, for the academic side, the need to abide by 'scientific standards' and to refrain from compromising them out of strategic expediency in acts of 'over-politicisation' (Urban, 2013: 396). Brinkmann et al go even further. They argue that the success of the envisaged partnership between academics and trade unions depends on a preparedness to recognize uncritically the criteria for quality control in present-day academia: 'Such an endeavour will only be successful if research is carried out at a level that is seen as being satisfactory, at the levels of the empiric and of theory, in the world of rankings, excellence initiatives and peer-reviewed journals' (Brinkmann et al, 2008: 148).

Operating this way, the German scholars address the issue of the two constituencies in a manner that diverges fundamentally from how their South African colleagues approach it. They stress that academics have the freedom to choose their objects of research, which, by implication, can be strategic in nature. Consequently, they can cooperate with trade unions when they determine their research interests and research questions (Urban, 2013: 394; see also Dörre and Schmalz, 2013: 14) – but they are autonomous in their methods, which follow rigorous academic standards, and in publishing their findings. Of course, this also means that the suppression of research results for short-term strategic gains is not acceptable. Conversely, trade unionists are autonomous in deciding what they do with the strategic findings thus produced. This is at least what the phrase 'mutual respect concerning the cultures of evaluation' implies. In other words, academics have no say over the strategic choices of unions. All of this suggests that either side remains accountable to their own constituency, and tensions are supposedly fended off by saying that one side should not interfere with what the other side does. In a nutshell, the model intellectual for the Jena PRA is the strategic-professional academic – or, in Blaikie and Priest's words, 'the *empathetic observer*' who 'aims to achieve ... objectivity but insists that it is necessary for researchers to be able to place themselves in the social actors' position' (2019: 44; emphasis in the original).

There are, however, three critical issues with this model. First, it is highly unlikely that there will be no interference. Academics working on unions need to be able to comment on the latter's strategic choices when they carry out research. And conversely, it is not plausible that unions will play their roles as instances 'anchoring' research findings in the broader public if findings question their choices.

Second, the decision to leave the division between experts and laypeople fully intact does nothing to address the class analyst's dilemma. The labour academics can present themselves as experts on the matter of labour relations, and their knowledge is presented as being superior. This model is incompatible with the normative foundation of global labour studies because it refrains from addressing how the capitalist mode of scientific knowledge production perpetuates capitalist class domination.

And, third, it is contradictory to criticize neoliberalization while fully buying into its effects on higher education, which is the result of accepting existing criteria for quality control in the area of scientific knowledge production. The oft-encountered neoliberal obsession with competitiveness, rankings and other research metrics does not generate universally agreed modes of evaluating the quality of social research. Arguably, it fortifies dominant discourses and narrows the sayable through favouring '*problem-solving*' over '*critical*' research (Cox, 1981: 128–9; emphasis in the original). If pro-worker academics consciously decide not to criticize such forms of evaluating academic work, they strip themselves of the intellectual tools needed to criticize social domination. And they undermine efforts by activist-scholars who fight the neoliberalization of higher education and its disastrous effects on working conditions in academia. Indeed, Wright detected a tendency towards 'proletarianization' in academia in the US as early as the 1970s, and arguably, this tendency has been spreading beyond its borders and has been accelerating in the last 40 years (1978a: 13; see also Barker and Cox, 2000/2001: 5; Mountz et al, 2015; Gallas, 2018d; Brankovic, 2021). Defending the results of neoliberalization that harm academic workers does not just go against the normative foundation of global labour studies. It also compromises the legitimacy of global labour scholarship as a form of social critique.

I have discussed three models for how pro-labour intellectuals can connect with organized labour: Gramsci's organic intellectual, who operates inside the movement and outside academia; Webster et al's engaged intellectual or organic academic, who supports the movement from inside academia; and the Jena PRA's strategic-professional academic, who consults with unions with the aim of conducting strategically relevant research but operates at a distance to organized labour.

Unless one advocates spontaneism, the emergence of organic intellectuals in the Gramscian mould is unavoidable. After all, the precondition of any kind of organization and even self-organization of workers is that there are people who drive the process forwards, and these people are, by definition, organic intellectuals. And importantly, the South African and the German approaches can be combined with the Gramscian model, which shows that it works in different conjunctures. The more complicated question is which of the other two approaches is more suitable for advancing the cause of labour.

On balance, I wager that the South African model of the organic academic is more promising because it addresses the class analyst's dilemma. It does not seem plausible to completely leave an aspect of capitalist class domination untouched if one aims to shift class relations of forces. But admittedly, the South African model also gives rise to a danger. It comes with the risk of compromising one's position within academia if one prioritizes the strategic needs of organized labour.

Nevertheless, the example of Apartheid South Africa demonstrates that positions inside the university can be used to advance the cause of labour even under difficult circumstances. The activities of SWOP in the 1980s are exemplary in this context – and can be seen as a fruitful way of dealing with the class theorist's dilemma and the problem of knowledge transfer. But even so, the social location of academics creates a distance to the world of workers that Gramsci's organic intellectuals – who can also be described as 'movement intellectuals' – do not have. It would be wrong and politically fatal to simply ignore this distance. Thanks to the selectivities of academia as an ideological state apparatus, contesting capitalist class domination in and through the state is an uphill battle (see Poulantzas, 1978: 44–5). In other words, a strategy is needed, and this means simply 'doing one's work' and advancing through the ranks of academia will not do for labour academics if they take their normative-political commitments seriously.

The academic worker

Colin Barker and Laurence Cox, both scholars with a focus on social movements, have taken the freedom to turn a well-known feminist slogan on its head. According to them, '[t]he political is often very personal' (2000/ 2001: 20). If we locate the foregoing discussion in the field of the politics of being a labour intellectual, it follows that the issue at stake also merits personal reflection. Put differently, it would be inconsistent, in the context of this chapter, to refrain from addressing my own practices as a global labour scholar. There is a need for 'reflexivity' (Blaikie and Priest, 2019: 47). In the words of Barker and Cox, we need to ask 'how … "we" (activist/academics) live our contradictions' (2000/2001: 25), and what this has to do with our own locations in the social fabric.

My first observation is that it is difficult for academics in their everyday practices to subvert and circumnavigate the separation between experts and laypeople. Many of the routines in the academic world perpetuate it – and this includes all aspects of working as an academic: teaching, which is based on a clear-cut distinction between the expert/teacher and learner/student; research, which requires training in the handling of theories, methods and data; and committee work, which institutionalizes divisions between different 'status groups' inside the university. Undoubtedly, I am entangled in academic practices that perpetuate the separation, and it is impossible, in my experience, to completely avoid such entanglements if one works in a university setting.

And yet, my location in the division of labour is comparable to those of other workers in one important respect: I am wage dependent. And like the vast majority of scientists employed by German universities who are not full professors, I am on a fixed-term contract – and make this remark, at the time of writing, without having an immediate prospect of finding a permanent position.[8] Arguably, the proliferation of precarity in academia

---

[8]   For a more detailed account about the proliferation of precarity in academia and the prevalence of fixed-term contracts in the German university system, see Gallas (2018c; 2018d).

thanks to neoliberalization creates conditions under which the adsorption of university employees into the struggles of organized labour is a genuine possibility – even if they are different from people occupying the working-class locations in the relations of production because they usually enjoy a far greater degree of autonomy over their work and are state-sanctioned experts, which is why, according to Wright, they find themselves a contradictory class location.[9] The possibility of adsorption is demonstrated, for example, by the strikes in British higher education in recent years. These did not just voice 'narrow' concerns like the attacks on the existing pensions scheme, pay and working conditions, but also drew attention to broader, class-relevant political issues such as the role of organized labour in British society, the effects of neoliberalization on the public sector and the politics of austerity pursued by successive Conservative governments (Bergfeld, 2018; Hayes, 2018; Smyth, 2018; Evans, 2020).

Arguably, a fourth model of the pro-worker intellectual next to the organic intellectual, the organic academic and the strategic-professional academic may be the academic worker – someone employed by a university or research institute who is handling knowledge that is of strategic relevance to workers, who is immersed in labour struggles in higher education, and who aims to connect those with other labour struggles. In this model, there is no social distance to travel for connecting one's academic practices with struggles of workers. The challenge lies in reconciling the different practices one is involved in and aiming for a degree of coherence.

When I say this, I speak from my own experience. I am not just a global labour scholar, but also a labour activist on campus. I am a rank-and-file member of the German Education and Science Workers' Union (GEW) and have participated in organizing several one-day warning strikes. Furthermore, I am a member of a grassroots initiative fighting against fixed-term contracts of employees of the

---

[9]   For a more detailed discussion of the concept of adsorption, see Chapter 7. My claim that there are workers located in contradictory class locations may be confusing at first. I rely on a very broad understanding of the term 'worker', which refers to everyone who is wage dependent. My usage resonates with standard English, where terms such as 'white-collar worker', 'social worker' or 'education worker' are very common. In my understanding, there is no claim attached to this usage that everyone referred to with the term 'worker' necessarily belongs to the 'working class'. Of course, one could also use it in a narrow sense highlighting class. Then 'workers' would be people who are wage dependent, exposed to the despotism of capital and alienated from their skills and intellectual capacities. From this standpoint, scientists employed with a university would not be workers. It follows that the term 'academic worker' is an instance of the former, not the latter, usage. I have adopted it to highlight that there is still potential for the adsorption of academics into working-class networks – even if they are different from people clearly located on the side of labour in the capital–labour divide. For a systematic exposition of class locations in capitalism, see Chapter 6.

University of Kassel – Uni Kassel Unbefristet [Kassel Uni (for) Open-Ended (Contracts)] – which is supported by the two main trade unions active on the Kassel Campus, GEW and the United Services Trade Union (ver.di).

My own activism has helped me refine my understanding of labour relations and trade unionism in Germany and, in particular, of the dilemmas and challenges that labour activists operating in the public sector are faced with. An important motivation for writing this book has been my intention to understand better the class effects of the public sector struggles that I am involved in. At the same time, I experienced the challenge of reconciling my different practices first-hand. This concerns, first, time as a resource. Time spent researching and writing is time not available for talking with colleagues, organizing workers' meetings or reflecting on strategies directly tailored to my workplace. And conversely, time spent being an activist is not time used to enhance one's standing in academia and improve one's chances of finding a permanent position. Second, a treatise on strikes from a global angle does not easily translate into strategic guidelines in a very specific workplace in Germany, and vice versa. In other words, even if there no social distance between the academic and the worker in this model, there is an intellectual distance to be travelled. And finally, the academic worker model has a serious limitation in its scope. The experiences made as an academic worker are often far removed and specific compared to those of other workers – the mixture of high qualifications and significant job insecurity that German academia is known for is very different from most fields of work in the country. Even if there is no social distance to be travelled between the scholar and the worker, there is a significant social distance between the academic worker and other workers, all the more since academics are in a contradictory class location, which means that they enjoy significant advantages over other workers in terms of their wages and working conditions. Consequently, there is a danger of demands becoming particularistic, that is, non-expandable beyond academic workplaces – and of campaigns becoming sectionalist, that is, about securing advantages for workers in a clearly delimited sector.

In my practice, I am trying to bridge this distance in various ways. I say 'trying' because the lived reality of doing research and activism is messy out of practical necessity – and not as coherent as scholarly tracts like this one suggest. I am a member of the GLU network, and I have been teaching on the MA programmes for labour activists and trade unionists that the GLU provides. Part of the GLU experience is surely that there is space for exchanging different types of knowledge, and that students are asked to share, time and again, their practical experience from the worlds of trade unionism and labour activism and link them to the course content (see Hoffer, 2006: 31; Fichter et al, 2014: 567; Scherrer, 2020: 291). As a scholar interested in strikes, I have benefited significantly from frequent conversations with the labour practitioners who are part of the network – in class, at GLU conferences and at alumni workshops – and my own research on strikes has been influenced significantly by these conversations. Furthermore, I am a member of the Working Group on Labour Struggles (AK Arbeitskämpfe) of the German Association for Critical Social Research, which is a network of scholars based in the German-language area. This network also aims to facilitate conversations between academic workers and organic intellectuals, and all members are committed to reflecting critically and systematically on the world of work and actively working to change it. I have discussed my research at several points at meetings of the committee.

At the same time, I believe that my decision to research non-industrial strikes chimes with strategic debates among labour activists in different parts of the world. To me, the question of how to articulate struggles across diverging sectors, among them the public and service sectors, is of key strategic importance to present-day labour movements. It goes to the heart of the question of how to reverse the decline of organized labour in processes of deindustrialization, and where opportunities for the development of worker agency lie. As I show in this book, reports on the death of organized labour – to paraphrase Mark Twain – are a wild exaggeration. Indeed, I wager that we are witnessing a new chapter in the history of organized labour worldwide, and that the academic worker is a model that has a part to play in that story.

3

The Challenge of Strategic Research: A Critical Engagement with the Power Resources Approach*

A low-threshold research approach

If we take the normative foundation of global labour studies seriously, the aim is to produce knowledge that is strategically relevant for workers. Consequently, it makes sense to focus on their collective agency, that is, on their capacity to actively shape the social world through joint action. The strike weapon is risky to use but forceful. Workers across the globe are resorting to it time and again – and have done so since labour movements emerged in the context of early industrialization. As such, it is of high strategic relevance – and ideally suited as a research object for global labour scholars. But the question remains what kind of categories are needed to analyse it systematically.

An obvious choice for this endeavour is the PRA. It represents the most elaborate attempt to date in the field to develop a research framework that can be used to produce strategically relevant knowledge. Furthermore, it is a low-threshold approach. It works with clearly defined, parsimonious categories and thus is easy to use. The use value of the PRA is reflected in a plethora of studies based on it, which are usually aimed at identifying strategies for labour revitalization.[1] A significant number of students in German GLU programme, most of whom are union officials or labour practitioners, employ it in their coursework and dissertations. In my view,

---

* In this chapter, I partly draw upon an earlier, shorter article entitled 'Class power and union capacity: a research note on the power resources approach', which was published in the *Global Labour Journal* in September 2018.

[1] See, for example, the *Trade Unions in Transformation* project of the Friedrich Ebert Foundation or the special issue on the PRA in the *Global Labour Journal* from May 2018.

Stefan Schmalz, Carmen Ludwig and Edward Webster are right to argue that the PRA crosses the divide between academia and activism (2018: 113). Consequently, it is well-suited for intellectual practices in the 'organic academic' and 'academic worker' mould.

Nevertheless, an open question remains. If the normative foundation of global labour studies consists in a principled critique of class domination, it follows that contributions to the field should discuss how workers negotiate class relations. This in turn requires a careful conceptualization of class. In this chapter, I discuss whether the PRA meets this exigency. In this sense, I continue my discussion of how to do justice – in our conceptualizations – to the normative foundations of the field.

The compartmentalization of workers' power

According to Schmalz et al, '[t]he PRA is founded on the basic premise that the workforce can successfully defend its interests by collective mobilisation of power resources in the structurally asymmetric and antagonistic relation between capital and labour' (2018: 115). In other words, the approach is about highlighting potentials that can be used by workers to enhance their collective agency. At the same time, it is informed by a Marxian understanding of class as a structurally conditioned relation of power and conflict. According to Schmalz et al, class power is exercised by workers jointly mobilizing their resources while facing capitalists – and the latter enjoy structurally inscribed advantages in confrontations. Furthermore, the existence of an antagonist suggests that the relationship of forces between both sides impacts on how resources can be mobilized, and what kind of strategic choices are available.

Crucially, Schmalz et al implicitly transform this structural-relational notion of power into a compartmentalizing one through how they understand power resources. They speak of 'levels of labour power'[2] – that is, a neatly defined number of capacities at the disposal of workers when they are trying to advance their interests. 'Structural power' refers to their ability to disrupt

---

[2] It is surprising that Schmalz et al have chosen this term to refer to the capacity of workers to act collectively – and have done so without commenting on this terminological choice at all. In the Marxian tradition, the expression 'labour power' has been figuring, for more than a century, as the translation of the German word *Arbeitskraft*, which refers to a universal, transhistorical capacity of human beings: They are able to carry out work. This is of course not the same as the capacity of waged workers in the capitalist mode of production to join forces and forge coalitions around joint needs and interests. Obviously, Schmalz et al are free to use terminology in ways they see fit. But they explicitly build on the Marxian tradition, as their reference to 'the antagonistic relation between capital and labour' demonstrates (see also Schmalz et al, 2018: 118). Consequently, their usage of 'labour power' is prone to give rise to confusion. Hence, I contend that speaking of 'workers' power' is more appropriate, and I use this term in what follows when I refer to what Schmalz et al call 'labour power'.

'the valorisation of capital'; 'associational power' means that they have the option of forming 'workers' associations'; 'institutional power' consists in using 'legally fixed rights' to their advantage; and 'societal power' reflects the fact that they can gain strength through interacting 'with other social actors' (Schmalz et al, 2018: 119; see also AKSU, 2013: 347–63). Consequently, the exercise of power consists in the use of a range of quantifiable capacities that are possessed by the side of labour. Workers' power is now described as something that workers and their movements and organizations 'have' – and what matters, first and foremost, is whether they use this possession efficiently and effectively to reach their goals. The focus, in this type of analysis, is on how power is 'used', and not on what power is 'used for'.

Importantly, this amounts to a rupture with the structural-relational understanding of class set out in the beginning. If that route was taken, any collective activity of workers would have to be assessed in terms of how it deals with structurally inscribed opportunities and constraints – and how it reflects, and impacts on, the underlying class relations of forces (see Marticorena and D'Urso, 2021: 194; Nowak, 2021b: 16–19). This would include examining what kind of effects the goals of workers' movements and organizations have on the relations of forces if they are achieved.

The limitations of the compartmentalized conception of class power can be illustrated by looking in more detail at associational power. For Schmalz et al (2018: 118), unions are organizational pools of workers' power, supplying workers with a range of capacities that they would not possess if they were not organized. It follows that successful unions are instances of workers making good use of their associational power.

Undoubtedly, unions have greatly contributed to strengthening labour vis-à-vis capital in many situations. But the conceptualization of the PRA has the problematic consequence that any strategy of unions where stated aims are achieved can be declared a successful exercise of workers' power – no matter what the effects are of this strategy on workers as a class. Sectionalism and collusion with management or with pro-business governments on the side of unions have delivered, in certain cases, some benefits for the rank-and-file of the organizations in question. However, they also usually deepen divides with workers outside the constituency represented by the organizations in question and thus have a potential for weakening the overall position of labour (see Nowak, 2018: 353; 2021b: 16).

Furthermore, unions – in particular in countries in the Global South with huge informal sectors – often struggle to reach beyond very narrow constituencies. In these settings, union strategies may be geared to a small minority of workers and obstruct working-class formation in the sense of a process in which the collective agency of workers as a class and an antagonist of capital is strengthened (see Atzeni, 2020: 312–13; 2021: 1352, 1358; Nowak, 2021a: 1337). Finally, there is the persistent issue of union and party-political corruption, which contributes greatly to turning workers away from organized labour. In a nutshell, unions can play an important part, under certain circumstances, in dividing workers and weakening them as a class.

In 2008, to provide just one example, the leaderships of the German transport union GDBA and the railway union Transnet cooperated closely with the management of Deutsche Bahn, the national railway service. Together, they set out a plan for a partial privatization of the German railways (which was shelved in the end because the financial crisis hit the country). At the time, the unions claimed that their approach was successful insofar as Deutsche Bahn agreed as part of the deal that there would be no job losses due to privatization until 2023. From a power resource perspective, one could see the agreement as resulting from an effective use of associational power: the unions used their weight to win a job guarantee and avert the worst. But arguably, this contributed to producing deep divisions among railway workers, many of whom were opposed to privatization. The opposition against the deal grew even stronger once it became known shortly after it had been struck that the leader of Transnet during the negotiations, Norbert Hansen, would become the chief human resources officer at the company and a member of its executive board. Indeed, Hansen's decision to join the ranks of top-level management was seen as an act of betrayal by many workers opposed to the plan. It strengthened a competitor of the two unions, the Union of German Train Drivers, which was known for its confrontational stance towards management and its willingness to engage in industrial action (see Bönstrup and Döbler, 2008; Kalass, 2012: 132; Hürtgen, 2016: 63; Volume 2, Chapter 5).

The example shows that it is not just necessary to discuss whether the GDBA and Transnet won concessions thanks to their associational power. It is also necessary to examine the deal they made by putting it into in a broader context. This includes asking what the unions used their organizational capacities for, and what the effects were for workers in the sector and for the side of labour more generally (see Nowak, 2018: 353–4; 2021a: 1339; 2021b: 16–17; Marticorena and D'Urso, 2021: 194).

The mutation model of workers' power

The need for considering context is also visible when we look more closely at how the different power resources are connected. Klaus Dörre and Stefan Schmalz refer to the historical development of labour relations to explain this. In their view, 'it is possible to argue that in the countries undergoing early industrialisation there occurred, up until the 1880s, a shift from structural to organisational power, and, later, to institutional power' (2013: 19).

This suggests that one type of power resource gets translated into another over time: initially, workers went on strike spontaneously; once they started to form unions, they did not stop striking but the conditions of struggles changed due to the existence of organizations. Finally, labour relations became institutionalized through the emergence of regulations and trade union law at the level of the capitalist state, which provided labour with certain avenues for organization and collective action but closed off others. Correspondingly, the Jena group highlights that the institutionalization of labour relations at the level of the state and the integration of unions through this process should be seen as resulting from past mobilizations of power, which means that they reflect primary power resources (AKSU, 2013: 356; see also Schmalz et al, 2018: 121).

Nevertheless, institutions whose existence is guaranteed by the state work according to their own logic and with their own temporality so that they have effects on the primary power resources, which remain inexplicable with reference to the primary resources themselves. This is visible in the diverging ways in which power resources change over time: a union may still dispose of institutional power resources even if union density has gone down significantly. This is due to institutional inertia, that is, the fact that institutional safeguards are often enshrined in law and thus cannot be removed easily. Over the medium term, however, the developments affecting primary resources will also start impacting on institutions as a secondary resource, which is why the Jena group argues that the former can still have a significant effect on the latter. In their view, a union without an organizational base will eventually be stripped of its institutional capacities (Dörre and Schmalz, 2013: 358; see also Schmalz et al, 2018: 122).

The result is a mutation model of workers' power: the character of the power resources at the disposal of labour changes considerably through struggles; in turn, these changes, which consist in organization and institutionalization, impact strongly on the modalities of the struggles (see AKSU, 2013: 352). The Jena circle exemplifies this scenario with reference to recent developments in the German system of labour relations. As Ulrich Brinkmann and Oliver Nachtwey argue (2013: 39–47; see Dörre and Schmalz, 2013: 22–4), the structural and the organizational power of German trade unions has been eroding for four decades thanks to rising unemployment, internationalization, precarization and the rise of the service sector. Nevertheless, unions managed to protect skilled workers for a long time – they were able to achieve substantial wage increases for this group through the existing institutions of collective bargaining up until the mid-1990s. In other words, the German unions pursued a corporatist strategy that heavily relied on the mobilization of institutional power resources; they refrained from tackling the erosion of primary powers, which would have required a more confrontational approach. This was successful for a certain time, but in the end the Schröder government decided to remove institutional safeguards that protected workers from attacks by capital. It did so by limiting entitlements to unemployment benefits, weakening the protection from unfair dismissal and rolling out temporary work. This 'amounted to a reduction of industrial citizenship rights' (Brinkmann and Nachtwey, 2013: 41). In their original form, the latter had not just protected the socioeconomic positions of workers but had also created more favourable conditions of struggle for labour. The union leaderships, on the whole, did not respond to this attack with industrial action (Brinkmann and Nachtwey, 2023: 41). In fact, the so-called Hartz commission, which produced a report that served as the foundation for restructuring the labour market and reducing the social wage, had 15 members, two of whom were officials from the two largest German unions IG Metall and ver.di (*Tagesspiegel*, 2002; see Heinrich, 2004).

Inherent in the mutation model is a tension: On the one hand, all the different power resources are presented as facilitating the exercise of workers' power, which is visible in the fact that members of the Jena circle usually portray 'union power' as an instance of 'workers' power' (Dörre and Schmalz, 2013: 16; see also Schmalz et al, 2018: 116). On the other hand, strategies of labour that are based on institutionalization are said to change the modalities of the mobilization of workers' power, which suggests that they can produce obstacles to its exercise. In fact, it may be the case that they weaken the position of labour vis-à-vis capital. According to Brinkmann and Nachtwey, this is what happened in Germany during the global economic crisis, which hit the country in 2008: The unions operated on the grounds of a form of 'crisis corporatism', which involved tripartite negotiations. They were able to secure short-time compensation and the institution of a car scrappage scheme, which protected jobs (Brinkmann and Nachtwey, 2013: 43). However, this strategy came at a price:

> Works councils' and trade unions' strategy during the crisis to accept concessions led to an undermining of their own power resources in the long-term through the extension of temp and other forms of precarious work. The underlying problem is related to the institutional basis: Institution stabilizing policy, although leading to short-term stability, in the long term, however, leads to further institutional destabilization. (Brinkmann and Nachtwey, 2013: 44)

In a nutshell, institutional strategies seem to be a double-edged sword for unions. If institutional power resources are mobilized successfully by unions to safeguard achievements or even secure improvement for core workforces, this may weaken labour altogether over the medium term, not only 'peripheral', precarious workers. Against this backdrop, the Jena circle qualify the workings of institutional power somewhat:

> Since institutional power results from antagonistic class relations, a 'double character' is inherent in it. It grants far-reaching rights to unions, but also restricts their agency. In this respect, the mutual concessions between capital and labour have an ordering function for the accumulation of capital – even if the representation of the interests of wage dependent people is at the same time improved in this logic. (AKSU, 2013: 356–7; see also Schmalz et al, 2018: 121; 2019: 87)

This can be illustrated with reference to trade union law, which tends to favour the reproduction of capitalist class domination. It creates a divide between legitimate and illegitimate forms of labour struggle and thus criminalizes illegitimate forms. On the one hand, it provides workers with secure ways of voicing their discontent. On the other hand, labour unrest is decelerated and formalized, making it predictable and controllable (see Esser, 1982: 232; Althusser, 2014: 103). In numerous countries, political strikes are banned, and certain groups of workers, for example police or public sector workers more broadly, are not allowed to go on strike.

Labour scholars Joseph McCartin, Erica Smiley and Marilyn Sneiderman share a 'story of constriction' that shows how legalization impacts on worker agency. In 1965, there was a strike in New York City by people working for the social services, who demanded that the local welfare system be reformed. After the strike, the authorities imposed a set of rules. 'The codification of public sector collective bargaining', McCartin et al observe, 'had a dual effect: it stabilized public sector unions as entities whose future was assured; at the same time, however, it limited what unions could bargain over, denying them the right to bargain over their agencies' policies' (2021: 167).

Similarly, Josef Esser, one of the eminent figures in postwar West German materialist state theory and labour studies, describes how the institutionalization of class struggle stabilized the capitalist social formation in West Germany in the postwar decades:

> The structurally inscribed, permanent conflict between capital and labour ... is recognised politically in institutions such as the freedom of collective bargaining, the Work Constitution Act and legally enshrined co-determination. ... The collective bargaining partners agree on a system of conflict regulation, whose standard scenario is negotiation and the preparedness to compromise and cooperate. Labour disputes such

as the strike and the lock-out are only the last resort when negotiations have failed completely. ... Content-wise, industrial conflict is limited to wages and working conditions. (Esser, 2014: 91–2)

There are situations when trade unionists defy the existing conventions and laws, in particular if they feel that there is mass support for their cause. But this does not render trade union law inoperable and comes with risks. The strategic selectivities inherent in institutions created through legal regulations and safeguarded by the state do not determine fully the strategic choices of trade unionists. But they never cease to influence the calculations behind those choices.

In my view, this observation has far-reaching theoretical implications for the mutation model of power, which are not clearly spelled out by the Jena group. If institutionalization facilitates the accumulation of capital due to its 'ordering function', it does not necessarily work in favour of labour. By implication, the same can be said about the structural and associational capacities of unions that work with institutional strategies, for example, their ability to bargain collectively and to recruit new members. After all, they may focus on making concessions and on organizing core workers. To put it bluntly, the activities of unions may enhance the power of capital under certain conditions. It follows that institutional and conjunctural conditions under which workers operate when they act collectively need to be considered in analyses of workers' power.

Against this backdrop, I propose distinguishing between:

a. potentials for exercising workers' power inherent in the capitalist mode of production and the capitalist state;
b. the ways in which the dominant state institutions and organizations in specific social formations within capitalist settings affect those potentials, including the prevailing system of labour relations as well as the capacities of unions, which may reinforce or block those potentials;
c. the impact of conjunctural factors, for example, the global financial and economic crisis or the COVID-19 pandemic, which may also influence the accessibility of those potentials significantly; and
d. workers' power as it emerges when workers act collectively in and through the organizations of labour.

In a nutshell, analysing workers' power requires contextualization. If one want to understand level (d), one needs to also consider levels (a) to (c), which describe the conditions under which power is exercised. It may or may not be possible for workers to use the potentials existing at the level of mode of production, which is why the latter should not be equated with power resources that workers possess no matter what the circumstances.

Powerful workers, powerless unions

The ambiguous class effects of institutions suggest that the capacities of unions cannot be equated with workers' power. It makes sense to see unions as institutionalized collective actors representing the side of labour in the labour–capital relation because they organize and mobilize workers and represent them vis-à-vis representatives of capital and the state. But they cannot be assumed to always make strategic choices shifting class relations of forces in favour of workers or at least consolidating or defending their position. Unions can exercise workers' power, but there is no guarantee that they do. What they do may not be beneficial for workers as a collective of people sharing the same class location, as is illustrated by the involvement of union representatives in the Hartz commission.

This calls for a systematic reflection on the nature of unions in capitalism. A useful materialist conception of trade unions can be found in the work of Esser. According to him, trade unions are 'intermediary organisations' operating between civil society and the state (1982: 244).[3] They oscillate between two contradictory tendencies – 'social autonomy and statification' (1982: 244). On the one hand, they act as 'class organisations facilitating the pursuit of the economic interests of wage dependent people' (1982: 228) and, on the other hand, as instances of 'mass integration' mediating between the interests of capital and labour in a form that is conducive to the reproduction of capitalist class domination by limiting and modifying the demands of workers (1982: 239–45). Following Esser, the functioning of unions is a reflection of both the class struggles taking place against the backdrop of the given class relations of forces and the strategic selectivities inherent in the capitalist state (1982: 239–40), for example, trade union law or the existence of forums facilitating tripartite negotiations between unions, employers' associations and governments.

The selectivities do not eradicate the antagonism between capital and labour – even bureaucratic union leaderships cannot fully insulate themselves from the interests of their members – and they do not force trade unionists to act in one way or another (see Esser, 1982: 239–40; Althusser, 2014: 103–4). Consequently, it is possible, in principle, for unions to exercise class power, in particular when the relations of forces between labour and capital are not completely unfavourable. However, the selectivities also create incentives for

---

[3]   Esser takes up this concept from Walter Müller-Jentsch, who defines trade unions thus: They are 'intermediary organisations ... whose political practice depends, on the one hand, on the interests of members and, on the other hand, on the re-valuation [*Verwertung*] of capital – and whose double character results from their role as organisations based on voluntary membership and as auxiliary organs of the state in the fields of social and economic policy' (Müller-Jentsch, 1981: 183; see also Müller-Jentsch, 1973: 224).

strategic choices that are conducive to accommodation and the reproduction of capitalist class domination. As a result of the different pressures union leaders are facing, unions are not just organizations of struggle, but also fields of struggle between competing forces of labour with different strategies. Certain aspects of their strategies facilitate class organization and others mass integration, and this can change over the life course of a single union.[4] Notably, the conditions under which unions operate are transformed all the time because the patterns of capital accumulation and class conflict constantly change. This also means that strategic selectivities inherent in the state may be contained or deflected. And yet, they never stop to exist as fundamental tendencies as long as there is no fundamental rupture with the capitalist mode of production.

In a nutshell, union capacities should not be conflated with class power. The capacities of unions are not direct reflections of the potential for workers to exercise their power inherent in the capitalist mode of production, and their activities should not, in every case, be seen as exercises of workers' power. Poulantzas famously argued that the state is neither an instrument in the hands of the ruling class, nor a subject that is above class relations (1978: 148). According to him, it has no power on its own; rather, it can be seen as a field and facilitator of class strategies (1978: 35–6). I contend that unions work in a similar way (and hence can be seen as being part of the state) (Poulantzas, 1978: 153; see also Althusser, 2014: 103–4). If they opt for institutional strategies, their activities are likely to contribute to the reproduction of capitalist class domination. At the same time, however, their mere existence creates conditions that are favourable for the

---

[4]   In response to earlier comments from me on the PRA (Gallas, 2016c; 2018b), Schmalz et al have countered this critique by arguing that the concept of the 'intermediary organisation' changed from being used to 'criticise tendencies of bureaucratisation and selective interest representation of German trade unions' in 1970s to becoming a 'structurally conservative concept' aimed at justifying the corporatist status quo (2019: 87; see Dörre, 2011: 18). This counter-critique boils down to two points: The notion of the union as an 'intermediary organisation' refers to a configuration in a specific time and place and thus should not be taken out of context, and it overlooks the potentials of unions to advance workers' interests. In my view, however, these points do not do justice to what Esser says. He uses the concept to capture the entanglement of trade unionism in the reproduction of capitalist class domination in capitalist societies in general, which means that it is not about German corporatism in particular, and the attribute 'intermediary' highlights the fact that unions oscillate between advancing class interests and mass integration. It simply does not follow from this that unions are, by necessity, fully integrated into the capitalist status quo and cannot become vehicles for radical transformation if the circumstances are right. In my understanding, Esser's observations suggest that anyone pursuing a strategy of radical social transformation needs to be aware of the selectivities inherent in the capitalist state that work in favour of the reproducing the status quo – and these selectivities need to be addressed somehow.

formation of working-class strategies. In short, there is power in a union even though a union has no power. It follows that one should be wary, as a global labour scholar, to simply subscribe to existing union agendas, for example, by exploring how to strengthen a certain union without asking for what purposes.

In conclusion, research with the aim of identifying opportunities for workers to gain strength collectively does not just have to determine the strategic options and choices available to their organizations, but also to relate them back to the relationship of forces between labour and capital. Otherwise, it will fail to pick up on the contradictory effects of institutions. If the 'basic premise' of the PRA is taken seriously that capitalism is marked by an antagonistic relationship between capital and labour, it is not enough to enquire into how a specific union can use the resources at its disposal to achieve its aims. It also needs to be asked what the effects of achieving these aims are on class relations because the class effects of the use of resources are often contradictory. In my view, the PRA lacks conceptual tools to capture these ambivalences. Indeed, it falls short of doing the normative foundation of global labour studies justice because it does not sufficiently consider class domination – and how unions are entangled in reproducing it. Assessing workers' power requires class analysis, that is, an analysis that identifies existing class relations of forces, the economic, political and cultural class struggles that are taking place at a given time and in a given space and the class effects of strategies of workers' organizations.

PART II

Class Theory: Relations of Production, Antagonism and Social Domination

4

The Ontology of Class: Moving beyond Inequality and Identity

Segmentation versus class identity

In Part I of this volume, I argued that there is a normative foundation for labour studies, which consists in the assumption that class domination is an obstacle to human flourishing. Furthermore, I problematized how scientific knowledge production is implicated in capitalist class domination, and I criticized the proponents of the PRA for not sufficiently recognizing the relevance of class relations in their attempts to develop a framework for empirical research. I argued that it is impossible to assess whether union activities improve the lot of workers without considering how they affect class relations of forces. All of this calls for firmly linking global labour studies in general, and strike research in particular, with class theory. This is what I do in this part of the book. Drawing upon authors writing about class theory from a Marxist angle and about questions of ontology, epistemology and methodology from a critical realist perspective, I take a somewhat irreverent approach. I build an argument that is my own, but that is still indebted to ideas that I have inherited from these other authors.

I proceed in this part by systematically developing the concept of class. In this chapter, I discuss the ontological question of what kind of entity it refers to. I contrast two different conceptions, one centred on socioeconomic resources, and the other on identity, and explain to what extent they subscribe to a form of material and ideational reductionism, respectively. As an alternative, I present a critical-realist, materialist conception of class that highlights its intransitive dimension and the fact that it is an effect of the organization of work. From this very general issue, I first move, in the next chapter, to the issue of class in capitalism, and then to working-class formation, in the two remaining chapters contained in this part.

'Class' is a term that can be heard fairly frequently in everyday conversations, but more so at certain times and in certain spaces than in

Table 4.1: National Readership Survey social grades

		% of population
A	Higher managerial, administrative and professional	4
B	Intermediate managerial, administrative and professional	23
C1	Supervisory, clerical and junior managerial, administrative and professional	28
C2	Skilled manual workers	20
D	Semi-skilled and unskilled manual workers	15
E	State pensioners, casual and lowest grade workers, unemployed with state benefits only	10

Source: NRS, January to December 2016. Available from: http://www.nrs.co.uk/nrs-print/lifestyle-and-classification-data/social-grade/ [Accessed 14 October 2022].

others. Accordingly, an easy way to start conceptualizing class is to examine everyday understandings of the term. When people refer to 'class', they often imagine society in analogy with tangible physical objects composed of several layers, for example, rock formations, soils or cakes. In these descriptions, people are classified as belonging to one of those layers – usually with reference to their income and wealth.

Such notions of class are operationalized for social research by distinguishing social groups with different socioeconomic resources. We can speak of 'class-as-segmentation' approaches. They highlight economic inequality, that is, differences in access to material aspects of the social world understood as tangible or intangible economic goods that enable people to do certain things.

An example is a classification system from Britain called 'National Readership Survey (NRS) social grade'. It originates from market research but is oft-used in policy advice and academic discussions.[1] 'Social grades' emerge from identifying different occupational groups; the implicit assumption is that one's occupation determines, to a strong degree, one's access to socioeconomic resources – and this, in turn, conditions one's capacity to actively shape one's social surroundings and the social world more broadly. The categories used as well as data that refer to Britain can be found in Table 4.1.

The significance for social scientists of 'social grades' lies in supplying information on the distribution of different types of work within a clearly delimited political-economic space. In this case, the space is the British

---

[1] Some random recent examples are Greenwood and Twyman (2020), Kenward and Brick (2021) and Sounderajah et al (2021).

national economy, but social grades could easily be used to analyse other country cases. If we use an everyday understanding of the term 'working class' and assume that it refers to groups consisting of people who are manual labourers or have low incomes, we can simply add up C2, D and E and end up with the claim that 45 per cent of people surveyed belong to the working class.

However, this approach to identifying classes immediately raises a range of questions: Does C2 really belong to the working class? Or is it a class group that has more in common – as the lettering suggests – with C1, which would imply that it should be seen as part of the middle class? Does it make sense at all to aggregate the different 'social grades' into larger class groups? Or should we simply accept that there are six different categories? It becomes clear that the classification system as such tells us nothing about the relationships and interactions between the 'social grades' identified, which would be important for understanding how societies marked by class divisions develop over time, and which kind of conflicts emerge that are linked to differences in access to socioeconomic resources.[2]

Importantly, the framework also does not include a category for owners of capital. If we take seriously the normative foundation of global labour studies, the assumption that class domination is an impediment to human flourishing, this is a critical problem. After all, class domination refers to the hierarchical connections between one or several dominant classes and one or several dominated classes, which suggests that class is a relational concept. Against this backdrop, it becomes clear that the ownership of capital is a crucial issue to be considered when we talk about class; the 'class-as-segmentation' approaches are incomplete.

Applied to the field of strike research, segmentation approaches are of limited use. It may be possible to map, with their help, the development of incomes within class groups and social mobility across them in conjunction with strike incidence. But we learn nothing about the relationship between capital and labour, which is crucial for understanding how strikes affect the obstacles to human flourishing that workers are faced with in capitalist societies. And unless we make the simplistic presumption that people possessing the same set of resources automatically stick together (in ever so many cases, they do not), we are unable to explain why solidarity among workers expressed in strike action exists at all. 'Social classes are not empirical

---

[2]   This critique also applies to standard approaches to gauging economic inequality, which measure differences in income or wealth and identify social groups on those grounds. These approaches supply us with valuable information on differences in access to economic resources in present-day societies, their changes over the time, and the effects of redistributive measures. But they tell us little about inter-group dynamics, which is why their use value for the issues discussed in this book is limited.

groups of individuals, social groups, that are "composed" by simple addition', as Poulantzas observes (1974: 17).

In a nutshell, class-as-segmentation approaches constitute a form of material reductionism. They do not consider sufficiently joint practices of people – and people's reasons to engage in those practices. For this purpose, we also need to consider ideational factors, that is, the way people make sense of the world, and their place in it.

An alternative route is offered by many forms of contemporary political activism and social theory that talk about class, often in conjunction with other categories referring to social domination such as race and gender. According to this discourse, class is first and foremost an identity, which is formed through acts of referring to oneself and others in class terms (Bettie, 2000; Gibson-Graham et al, 2000). If the segmentation approaches can be seen as highlighting material aspects of class by focusing on access to economic goods or the lack thereof, class identity approaches focus on ideational aspects, that is, on meaning-making practices that 'classify' people.

Importantly, the latter make some suggestions on how to conceptualize class domination. Following J.K. Gibson-Graham, Stephen A. Resnick and Richard D. Wolff, people create social hierarchies and opportunities for economic exploitation through engaging in acts of classification that concern themselves and others (2000: 3). Their practices, which include speech acts, lead to the identification of individuals with groups that are placed in a hierarchical order. In analogy to racism and sexism, class-based practices of discrimination by people in privileged positions can be described as 'classism' (Kemper, 2015: 25; Seeck and Theißl, 2020: 11). One may conclude that we are dealing here with three forms of social domination that are created, in the first instance, through meaning-making practices, and that become entangled in the process.

The strength of such identity-centred conceptions lies in elucidating how ideas play a part in producing and reproducing class relations, and how this produces entangled yet differentiated forms of social domination. Nevertheless, I have chosen against using them in this book. In my view, the existing approaches tend to exhibit what can be called ideational reductionism. By this, I understand a mode of reasoning about the social world assuming that the latter is constituted primarily through meaning-making, that is, through the meanings people create to make sense of their practical experiences. Accordingly, Gibson-Graham et al focus on the 'languages of class' (Gibson-Graham et al, 2000: 3), and Andreas Kemper writes about the 'endless number of derogatory concepts, with the help of which classist labelling takes place' (2015: 27).

This strong focus on ideas becomes a critical problem if we compare socioeconomic data with people's conceptions of their position in the social fabric. According to a Gallup poll conducted across the US, 55 per cent of respondents identified either as 'middle' or 'upper-middle class' (Newport, 2018). In contrast, in a British social attitudes survey conducted a few years ago, 60 per cent of respondents stated that they were 'working class'; and 40 per cent said that they were 'middle class' (Evans and Mellon, 2016). Notably, the US – according to World Bank data – is a society marked by higher economic inequality than Britain, which is difficult to square with people's self-conceptions as measured by asking people about which class they belong to.[3] This suggests that class identity and material positions can diverge quite considerably. Mismatches of this type are often held against approaches that display forms of material reductionism, which assume that ideas are simply reflections of the observer-independent world.[4] But the argument can also be turned on its head: The social world is not solely a collection of ideas; the patterns of inequality cannot be explained by primarily looking at practices of meaning-making that concern class identity. What is not considered, in ideational reductionist accounts, is how there are mechanisms at work in the social world that are not transparent to the actors affected, that is, that either do not figure in their discourses at all or in ways that only point to their existence in indirect and implicit ways. Accordingly, observations on

---

[3]   Data source: World Bank, Gini Index, https://data.worldbank.org/indicator/SI.POV. GINI?locations=US-GB&name_desc=true [Accessed 9 October 2022].

[4]   Obviously, this is a charge often held against 'Marxism' (see, for example, Laclau and Mouffe, 1985: 84). It is justified in the case of some varieties of Marxist thought, most importantly Marxism-Leninism, the official doctrine of Soviet-type, authoritarian socialist regimes in Eastern Europe and beyond. In *Dialectical and Historical Materialism*, the founding document of this doctrine, Josef Stalin says: 'Whatever is the being of a society, whatever are the conditions of material life of a society, such are the ideas, theories, political views and political institutions of that society' (Stalin, 1938). Importantly, however, it would be a gross misrepresentation to claim that 'Marxism' (in the singular) subscribes to material reductionism. There is a variety of Marxisms that outrightly reject it. Around the same time as Stalin, Antonio Gramsci developed an anti-reductionist take on the relationship between the material and the ideational. He proceeded from the assumption that an observer-independent, material world conditions how we can construe our social environment, yet acknowledged an independent role played by ideas in processes of construal. This is visible in the following passage from the *Prison Notebooks* (Gramsci, 1971): 'Obviously, East and West are arbitrary and conventional, that is historical, constructions, since outside of real history every point on the earth is East and West at the same time. This can be seen more clearly from the fact that these terms have crystallised not from the point of view of a hypothetical melancholic man in general, but from the point of view of the European cultured classes who, as a result of their world-wide hegemony, have caused them to be accepted elsewhere. Japan is the Far East not only for Europe but also perhaps for the American from California and even for the Japanese himself, who, through English political culture, may call Egypt the Near East. … And yet these references are real; they correspond to real facts, they allow one to travel by land and by sea … to objectivise reality, to understand the objectivity of the external world. Rational and real become one' (Gramsci, 1971: 447–8).

the workings of social structures that produce differences in the access to material resources play a marginal role in identity-centred accounts of class. Poulantzas offers a thought experiment illustrating this point:

> [I]t is clear that, even on the absurd assumption that from one day to the next, or even from one generation to the next, the bourgeoisie would all take the places of the workers and vice versa, nothing fundamental about capitalism would be changed, since the places of bourgeoisie and proletariat would still be there. (Poulantzas, 1974: 33).

For my research, identity-centred accounts are of limited use. Workers are embedded in a material social environment when they go on strike, which makes itself felt in the 'economic damage' caused by stoppages. In other words, they exercise power by blocking the use of certain economic resources. It follows that the dynamics of strikes and their impact on class relations cannot be assessed by starting from the making of meanings through practices. What also matters greatly are the material effects of strikes as a key item in the repertoire of protest practices that is available to workers. Indeed, strikes may shift the relations between capital and labour without the words 'working class' being uttered once – and the majority of strikes discussed in Volume 2, Part 2 was not discussed by those involved with the help of a language of class (see Poulantzas, 1974: 17; Goes, 2019: 86). It follows that it is necessary to move beyond both class-as-segmentation approaches that focus on economic inequality and identity-centred approaches that highlight practices of self-labelling and labelling others. There is a need for an anti-reductionist approach that enables us to discuss material and ideational factors in their articulation.

The intransitive dimension of the social world

In my view, key contributions to Marxist class theory (Poulantzas, 1974; 1978; Carchedi, 1977; Wright, 1978b; see also Marx, 1976: 340–416) offer important insights on how to understand the articulation between material and ideational aspects of the social world in an anti-reductionist manner. This may be a surprising thing to say. After all, many Marxists refer to themselves as 'materialists', which could be read as a commitment to material reductionism. In my view, however, Marxist materialism offers a nuanced anti-reductionist ontology based on a distinct notion of 'materiality'. Accordingly, my concern in this section will be to explain what I mean by this. The relevance of this concept for strike research lies in elucidating how strikes are conditioned by class relations, and how they retroact on the latter.

To be clear, questions of identity are of secondary importance for the line of Marxist class theory discussed here. In this sense it is not different from material reductionist approaches. It starts from the assumption that what matters, first and foremost, for the constitution of class is how work is organized across society, and how people are placed in the resultant division of labour. Put differently, class relations are relations of production, which contain different locations for actors. In capitalist societies, the key locations are wage labour and capital. Workers and capitalists are entangled in historically specific class relations – and this happen no matter whether they refer to themselves or others in class terms. It follows that the existence of class relations does not hinge on the question of whether people see themselves or others as members of a class – or if they deny altogether any class belonging.

And yet, it should not be inferred that meaning-making is irrelevant for the constitution of the social world. Indeed, the relations of production only exist if people have certain conceptions of the world. Under capitalist conditions, these conceptions may consist in the assumptions that one needs to make a living by 'getting a job', or that it makes sense to accept the 'rule of law'. Importantly, not each and every individual living in a capitalist society will share these assumptions – quite a few people may choose not to work, and others may have little regard for the law. The point is that a capitalist society can only exist if a certain set of assumptions has reached a degree of dominance. But – and this is the key critique of identity-centred conceptions of class – there is no necessity for this set of assumptions to contain any direct references to 'class', and they do not have congeal into a class identity.

It follows that Marxist class theory, at least in the understanding used here, goes against the material reductionist view that perceptions are by and large adequate reflections of an observer-independent social reality. Indeed, perceptions can cover up, to a degree, this reality, which was visible when I discussed the divergence of class identities from socioeconomic conditions in the UK and the US, and they can also cause people to act in ways that create aspects of the social world. In other words, ideas can have independent effects on the emergence and reproduction of class relations. It makes a difference for the politics of labour, for example, how working people refer to themselves, and whether pro-worker intellectuals speak of them as 'proletarians' or as 'employees'.

This raises the questions of what the attribute 'material' means. In my understanding, it does not necessarily refer to socioeconomic resources, as it is understood not just in everyday language, but also in conceptions of class focusing on economic inequality. It points to the fact that there are social relations (or aspects thereof) that exist no matter whether, and how, the actors implicated in them are aware of them. These can be economic, but also political or cultural relations.

In the philosophy of the social sciences, this is a position taken by critical realism (Collier, 1994). In contrast to ideational reductionists, critical realists assume that there is a material or 'intransitive' dimension of the social world – a dimension that may exist and have effects without being discernible by observers (Bhaskar, 1979: 11; see also Collier, 1994: 51). They subscribe to 'ontological realism' (Bhaskar, 1979: 57) – the idea that there is an observer-independent reality that affects how we perceive our social surroundings and how we act. But in contrast to material reductionists, they also accept 'epistemic relativity', that is, the assumption that observers construe the material world in different ways, and that these different construals also have significant effects on the social world (Bhaskar, 1979: 62). The attribute 'critical' refers to the fact that emerging construals reflect a social context, and that they involve interpretations because the social world is not transparent and can only be grasped with the help of other existing construals (Owens, 2011: 8).

Importantly, relativity is not the same thing as relativism. The point of the critical realists is not that any view of how the social world works is as plausible any other; just that there is no knowledge about it that does not reflect, in some way or another, the specific socio-historical and socio-geographical conditions under which it was produced. If we assume that such contexts differ, it follows that there is a wide range of construals. Reflecting the different social situatedness of observers, these are incomplete and biased – but some explain social reality better than others, which can be gauged by their 'practical adequacy', that is, their capacity to 'generate expectations about the world and about the results of our actions which are actually realized' (Sayer, 1992: 67). On the grounds of the existing data and observations of the social world, it appears more convincing to argue, for example, that income distribution reflects, by and large, macroeconomic mechanisms rather than individual efforts.

Critical realists contend that ontological realism and epistemic relativity are fully compatible with one another. This claim is in line with a range of implicit assumptions that inform our everyday practices. Without taking a critical realist position, it is hard to argue that people can err or misconceive something (see Sayer, 1992: 67; 2000: 53). Likewise, it is hard to defend the maxim implicit in numerous academic practices (from classroom discussions to paper presentations at conferences) that scholarly debate somehow contributes to the production of knowledge.

Against this backdrop, the question emerges what the 'materialist' aspect of Marxist class theory is. In my view, materialism in this context refers to two assumptions. The first one is that the social world is constituted, in the first instance, through the organization of work (see Buckel, 2015: 33). The second assumption is that this organization has an intransitive dimension. Accordingly, there are locations in the social fabric whose occupation entangles people in social relations that they do not necessarily understand, but that have considerable influence on what they do and think. Coming back to the examples of Britain and the US, an exclusive focus on class identity would possibly cover up a range of mechanisms that affect people due to how they are implicated in the social division of labour. It follows that it makes sense to start one's theorization of class with the conceptualization of material locations in the social fabric, that is, with the relations of production. This is a move with important implications for strike research. It sensitizes us for the fact that strikes are conditioned by broader ensembles of social relations, and that striking workers are entangled in them without necessarily being fully aware of what they are.

Modes of production, social formations and conjunctures: towards a stratified ontology

The conceptual basis for Marxist class theory is the critical theory of capitalism developed by Marx in his *Critique of Political Economy*. The discussion of critical realism raises the question of how Marx's theory can be reconstructed on the grounds of the ontological assumptions discussed. If, as Lindner suggests, critical realism can be used to make sense of Marx's thought (2013: 14), it should be possible to find lines of arguments in it that are similar to those put forward in the preceding section.

Marx argues against a general social theory, which in his view runs the risk of being ahistorical and ageographical. In the three volumes of *Capital* (1976; 1978; 1981), Marx develops a critical theory of capitalism. Accordingly, he determines, in the very first sentence of the first volume, an object with temporal and spatial boundaries that are clearly definable, the 'capitalist mode of production' (Marx, 1976: 125). Marx assumes that through understanding the capitalist organization of work in its historical and geographical specificity, he has laid a foundation for explaining how capitalist societies work. This suggests that understanding the dominant mode of production is a key prerequisite for grasping not just the economic, but also the political and cultural determinations of a society. Following this line of argument, it is impossible to make sense of parliamentary politics or of monotheistic religions in present-day societies if we do not consider the social division of labour, and how it is produced and reproduced. To be sure, understanding the mode of production is a necessary, but not a sufficient, way of explaining the social world.

With the attribute 'capitalist', Marx signals that he is interested in the features of the organization of work that define capitalist societies as being capitalist – aspects that they share, and that set them apart from non-capitalist societies. Wage labour, for example, is characteristic of the capitalist mode of production; serfdom or slavery are not. As Marx makes clear, he identifies these features through 'the power of abstraction' (Marx, 1976: 90), that is, through disregarding any aspects of the social world that are not universal to capitalist societies; and through conceptualization, that is, through creating a system of concepts that describes, in their 'inner connection' (Marx, 1976: 102), the universal features.

In other words, Marx's object is historically and geographically specific. The capitalist mode of production is fundamentally different from the feudal mode of production (Marx, 1976: 915–16), which was dominant in Europe in medieval times, and it has not always existed. According to Marx, it first emerged in Italy (1976: 876) – presumably a reference to Tuscany, where early forms of capitalist production came into being in the 13th and 14th centuries (see Hilton, 1952).[5] Marx is also clear that the concept refers, in his life and time at least, to Western Europe (Marx, 1976: 646). Today, one can argue that thanks to the expansive tendency of capital accumulation, the capitalist mode of production can be found across the globe.

Marx's heavy emphasis on the mode of production raises the question of what its relationship to society in its entirety is. He gives a clue in the first sentence of the first volume of *Capital* (1976): 'The wealth of societies in which the capitalist mode of production prevails appears as an immense collection of commodities' (Marx, 1976: 125). Marx here distinguishes the capitalist mode of production from societies operating under the dominance of this mode, or from 'capitalist social formations', as Poulantzas calls them (1968: *passim*). Following this line of argument, early industrial capitalism in England could be seen as a social formation, or capitalism in the EU in the aftermath of the sovereign debt crisis, because they institutionalize the mode of production in distinctive ways.[6] Furthermore, Poulantzas suggests that these social formations exist in and through different conjunctures, that is, different moments with distinct configurations of social forces, which follow one another. In his words, the concept of the 'conjuncture' refers to the

---

[5]   The claim that the transition to capitalism consisted in the emergence of early forms of manufacture in cities has been contested. Various authors claim that capitalism in England emerged in the countryside and was initially a form of agrarian capitalism. For an overview of the debate, see Ellen Meiksins Wood (1999), who shares the view that agriculture was the first site of the transition to capitalism in England.

[6]   Poulantzas refrains from discussing the issue of scale in this context. For the moment, it suffices to say that there may be overlapping and interlinked social formations, which exist on different scales. Consequently, I contend that contemporary capitalism is constituted by a global social formation (referring to the capitalist world order), which is linked with networks of macroregional and national social formations (such as the EU and Britain, Germany and Spain, respectively).

'present moment' (Poulantzas, 1968: 41). Accordingly, we may distinguish, in the case of the post-crisis EU, the conjuncture of όχι from the conjuncture of Brexit. In a nutshell, we are dealing with different levels of abstraction when we distinguish the mode of production from social formations and their different conjunctures.[7]

The relationship between the levels is where critical realist concepts come in. In line with the assumption that there is an intransitive and a transitive dimension of the social world, critical realism proposes a 'stratified

---

[7]   The term 'prevails' in Marx's statement indicates that there can be several, coexisting modes of production in a social formation, one of which is dominant. This can be exemplified with reference to Harold Wolpe's work, who argues that the South African social formation in the era of 'racial oppression' (Wolpe, 1972: 426) rested on three modes of production: The capitalist mode of production, which was dominant; the 'African redistributive economies' based on kinship and the communal ownership of land; and 'the system of labour-tenancy and crop-sharing on White farms' (Wolpe, 1972: 431). He shows how the initial stage of capitalist development in South Africa between the 1870s and 1930s was based on holding wages for black migrant workers at the level of the *individual* cost of reproduction because family members were catered for through the African redistributive economies in the countryside (Wolpe, 1972: 432–4). This system was sustained through a 'policy of segregation' (Wolpe, 1972: 425), which grouped the population according to race and created 'Reserves' for the Black population, where the African redistributive economies were still in existence. According to Wolpe, this arrangement came under pressure through increases in the population, soil erosion and a loss of productivity in those areas, which resulted in 'a decrease in the agricultural product' (1972: 444). What ensued was 'the virtual destruction of the pre-capitalist mode of production of the African communities in the Reserves' (Wolpe, 1972: 428). The Apartheid regime emerged in this context of people finding it ever more difficult to sustain themselves through the African economies and industrial migrant workers trying to push up their wages. It amounted to an intensification of coercion. Wolpe comments: 'Thus the policy of Apartheid developed as a response to this urban and rural challenge to the system which emerged inexorably from the changed basis of cheap labour-power. What was at stake was nothing less than the reproduction of the labour force, not in general, but in a specific form, in the form of cheap labour-power. Within its framework Apartheid combined both institutionalizing and legitimating mechanisms and, overwhelmingly, coercive measures' (1972: 446). The relevance of Wolpe's article for my particular project does not lie in its empirical content – it is quite clearly about a topic that differs substantially from mine – but in illustrating a number of theoretical moves that are characteristic of a Marxian theory of capitalism. On its grounds, the relationship between the modes of production and social formations can be explained. In a first step, Wolpe focuses on conceptualizing the capitalist mode of production plus the mode of production of the African redistributive economies, which he presumes to be highly relevant for 20th-century South African politics. Subsequently, these conceptualizations serve him as orientation marks that guide him in his analysis of South African politics, which take place at the level of the social formation. Here, he focuses on the distinct articulation of the two modes, its development over time and its political effects. In a nutshell, the concepts describing the two modes of production can be used to develop an analytical framework allowing us to analyse shifts in South African politics, most importantly the passage from Segregation to Apartheid.

ontology' (Ackroyd and Fleetwood, 2000: 13). According to it, there are three 'domains' of ontology: the 'empirical', the 'actual' and the 'deep'. The first refers to 'experiences, perceptions'; the second to 'events and actions'; and the third to 'structures, mechanisms, powers relations' (Ackroyd and Fleetwood, 2000: 13).

Importantly, the critical realist understanding of the term 'the empirical' goes against common usages. It designates the rather chaotic, unordered observations we make in everyday life, not the data we examine in research processes. The purpose of the distinction between the three domains is to highlight the need to distinguish not just between events and practices and our observations of what is going on, but also take into consideration the latter's conditions of existence, which consist in powers and structures that are activated or not.

In a nutshell, the stratified ontology of critical realism lies in assuming that there are structures (the deep) causing events and actions (the actual) that we observe (the empirical) (Ackroyd and Fleetwood, 2000: 13; Sayer, 2000: 11–12). The 'deep' dimension of the social world is intransitive and material in the sense that it has effects on people even if they do not recognize it – and if it does not figure in their interpretations of what is going on.

Against this backdrop, it can be argued that whereas 'modes of production' are situated in the domain of the deep, social formations and conjunctures are located in the domain of the actual. In other words, social formations refer to how deep structures are actualized through distinct institutions and modes of collective action in a real-concrete, delimited territory during a specific era, and conjunctures to moments characterized by specific, situational factors in the evolution of social formations. Importantly, there is a causal relation between the domain of the real and the domain of the actual – in the sense that mechanisms at the level of the deep contribute to producing the events and actions taking place at the level of the actual.

The notion of causation at work here is fundamentally different from the positivist understandings that dominate the natural and social sciences. According to the latter, causation can be understood as a regularity of observed events, which allow us to identify a cause bringing into existence an effect (see Sayer, 1992: 104–5; Fleetwood, 2001). If we observe that strike incidence falls during economic downturns and increases during economic booms, we may hypothesize that the economic cycle (cause) affects the militancy of workers (effect). There is a certain plausibility to this hypothesis insofar as we may argue that the preparedness to put one's job at threat through participating in a strike may be higher if there is a boom because it may be easier in this situation to find a new job. In a second step, we can put this hypothesis to empirical tests by collecting data on economic cycles and strike incidence, and establish whether there is indeed a correlation between the two variables (economic growth and strike incidence). If there is no correlation, we may infer that the hypothesis was wrong.

Critical realists disagree with this view of causation (see Fleetwood, nd; 2001; 2011). With the help of a positivist framework of this type, we may be able to explain why workers are more prepared to 'down their tools' in certain situations than in others. But it does not tell us how potential reasons for why workers go on strike interact, and what the scope of different causal factors is. The conflictive nature of the labour–capital relation, for example, is a very general causal factor that is effective wherever capitalist relations of production exist; the fact that the owner of firm (x) decided on day (y) not pay to her workers because she had run out of cash is highly specific to this one case.

A critical problem with positivist notions of causation is their atomistic nature. They break down the social world into separate, unconnected laws that assign one cause to one effect. These laws follow the same basic pattern: If A is the case, B is also the case (see Collier, 1994: 7). Consequently, they struggle to make sense of the interrelations between the different hypothesized laws, and of the configurations of conditions that explain why they apply – and to which degree. If we stick with the example of the economic cycle, it does not say anything about why there is conflict in the world of work in the first place, only that if there is conflict, the economic cycle might predict whether workers go on strike or not. For questions of this more fundamental type, critical realists suggest, we need to look at deep structures. If we follow the lead of Marxist class theory, workers occupy locations in the social division of labour marked by subordination, which means that individualist modes of improving one's situation have limited traction. This is an argument about structure – and it is what I have in mind when I argue that the mode of production constitutes tendencies that condition what happens at the level of the social formation. With a positivist notion of causation, one is prone to overlook more comprehensive explanations. It leads to theories with limited explanatory power that do not refer to structures.

Importantly, critical realists add a caveat when they talk about tendencies rooted in deep structures. They emphasize that such tendencies may exist without being exercised or actualized (Sayer, 1992: 106). Porcelain mugs may have the tendency to break, but if we handle them carefully, they may never do. The fact that some never break does not mean that they no longer exhibit a propensity to break; in fact, the propensity to break very much influences our handling of porcelain mugs in particular if they are not broken. In analogy, one may argue that the capitalist mode of production has a tendency for working-class formation, but that this tendency is experienced in hugely diverging ways in different capitalist social formations depending on how institutions and actors are equipped in terms of dealing with crises and conflicts, and how a distinctive social formation is positioned vis-à-vis other social formations. The Eurozone crisis, for example, led to a wave of general strikes in Greece and was hardly noticeable in Germany in the area of labour unrest, at least during its initial stages.

In essence, critical realism is characterized by a non-reductionist understanding of determination or 'a non-deterministic understanding of causality' (Lindner, 2013: 168): The deep structure does not fully determine what is going on at the level of the actual, but it also does not cease to exist and have effects if the latter are not easily discernible. In Althusser's terms, we are dealing with tendencies that are 'over-determined' (Althusser, 1969: 87–128; see Sayer, 1992: 108) – by other tendencies, by institutions at the level of the social formation and by conjunctural events. It follows that the capitalist mode of production can be institutionalized, at the level of the actual, in different ways; as a consequence, social formations share fundamental mechanisms, but they diverge considerably in terms of their institutions and actors. Consequently, the developmental paths of social formations and the dynamics of workers' struggles occurring within them differ considerably. In some social formations, workers may refer to themselves with a language of class, and there may be a high degree of collective activity; in others, this may not be the case. But the relations of production still exist in the latter case, and if that is the case, the dynamics of class and class conflict still pertain – even if they are deflected or decelerated. On these grounds, I produce a sketch of a materialist class theory in the next chapter that is based on a critical realist ontology.

5

The Constitution of Class in Capitalism: From the Relations of Production to Collective Agency

Choosing an entry point

From what I discussed in the last chapter, it follows that the overall aim of Marxist class theory is to identify features of the capitalist mode of production with class effects. Any conceptualization of class in capitalism based on a critical-realist, materialist ontology needs to have a specific entry point – a vantage point from which it is possible to discern how class relations are produced and reproduced. If we follow Marx's line of argument in the first volume of *Capital* (1976: 90), there are, at the heart of each mode of production, distinct relations of production, which concern how ownership of 'the object and the means of labour' also conditions people's relations with each other (Poulantzas, 1974: 18). Accordingly, it makes sense to start one's theorization of class from here. The capitalist relations of production entail a specific division of labour that is the foundation of class relations in any capitalist social formation (Poulantzas, 1974: 18; Marx, 1976: 415; Carchedi, 1977: 1). In a nutshell, the capitalist organization of work determines, in the first instance, how class is lived and experienced.[1] It creates a force field

---

[1] Following Stuart Hall, I speak of a 'determination in the first instance' to emphasize that class theory, in my understanding, is a materialist but anti-economistic endeavour. In his article 'The Problem of Ideology: Marxism without Guarantees' (Hall, 1986: 43), Hall calls for seeing 'the "materialism" of Marxist theory in terms of "determination in the first instance", since Marxism is surely correct, against all idealisms, to insist that no social practice or set of relations floats free of the determinate effects of concrete relations in which they are located'. This statement in fully in line with my argument that 'materialism', in the Marxian tradition, refers to the existence of an intransitive dimension of the social world. At the same time, it is a critique of the Marxist trope of 'a determination in the last instance', which goes back to Friedrich Engels. In 'Ludwig Feuerbach and the end of classical German philosophy' (2003), Engels describes the relationship between the

101

that conditions people's lives. We can call this the class structure – a term that points to pre-existing social conditions under which people encounter each other, and under which they act, which is located in the ontological domain of the 'deep'. Starting from the relations of production, I explain, in what follows, how class in capitalism can be conceptualized, that is, what the capitalist class structure looks like, and why the state plays an important role in its constitution.

The capitalist relations of production and class

Capital and labour as class locations

The capitalist relations of production can be seen as relations between two distinctive class locations, which can be called 'capital' and 'labour'. They emerge thanks to a divide reflecting the ownership and non-ownership of means of production, that is, work equipment and raw materials. If there is a capitalist mode of production, the reasoning goes, there are also people who own means of production and people who own nothing but their labour power – in brief, capitalists and wage workers (Poulantzas, 1974: 18; Marx, 1976: 272–3; Carchedi, 1977: 46).[2] The existence of the two class locations also means that there are two 'groupings of social agents' or class

---

economy and the state thus: 'But if even in our modern era, with its gigantic means of production and communication, the state is not an independent domain with independent development, but one whose existence as well as development is to be explained in the last instance by the economic conditions of life of society, then this must be still be more true of all earlier times' (Engels, 2003, translation amended). This is an economistic view insofar as it suggests that the economy, if we discount other aspects, shapes social reality. As Louis Althusser observed, 'the lonely hour of the "last instance" never comes' (Althusser, 1969: 113; see Lindner, 2013: 167) – it is hard to conceive of social situations where politics or culture do not come into play somehow (even if economic dynamics may be at the forefront). Consequently, speaking of a 'determination in the last instance' is of little use for understanding the capitalist or any other mode of production. If we follow Hall's argument, however, what can be salvaged from the Marxian tradition is that the organization of work across a society entails the existence of observer-independent, material locations that tells us an awful lot about the nature of conflict and structurally inscribed inequalities. As a consequence, starting from the relations of production is a useful entry point not just for class theory, but also for social analysis more broadly understood. Importantly – and in line with the notion of 'epistemic relativity' – I neither claim that it is the only possible entry point, nor that analyses starting from it are exhaustive. From a critical realist angle, the only general requirement arising out of ontological considerations is that one's choice of entry point should allow for unlocking deep structures. Accordingly, there is no principled reason not to start, say, from the relations of reproduction rather than the relations of production. Ultimately, one's research question should determine what kind of choice one makes.

[2] I use the term 'workers' in this chapter in a narrow sense (see Chapter 2, footnote 9). This usage includes everyone who is dependent on selling their labour power to make

groupings who occupy them (Poulantzas, 1974: 14). Notably, either side only exists if its counterpart has also come into being. Capitalists can only act as such if they can buy labour power, which is the force that sets in motion their means of production. And wage workers can only act as such if they can, in principle, sell their labour power. There is a coexistence in mutual dependence, from which it follows that class is a social relation.

Furthermore, this arrangement endows individuals placed on either side of the divide with rights. They can enter labour contracts, which instigate a transaction that consists in the sale and purchase of labour power. The existence of contractual arrangements of this type gives the relation of mutual dependency a legal status.

Accordingly, Marx argues that workers in capitalism tend to be free in a 'double sense': Their 'labour-power' is their 'own commodity', and they have 'no other commodity for sale' (1976: 272). Marx highlights, on the one hand, the freedom that comes with being owner of a commodity. A contractual relationship can only be seen as such if none of the contracting parties have been actively coerced by others to enter it. This also means that workers are, in principle, free to refrain from entering a labour contract. If they did not enjoy legal freedom, they would be slaves or serfs, and we could no longer speak of a capitalist system. At the same time, their freedom is qualified because not owning means of productions significantly limits their options when they consider how to ensure their own reproduction. They (and their dependents) will struggle to survive if they refrain from selling their labour power.

Consequently, class relations, under capitalist conditions, are not plainly economic relations. They also have a legal dimension, which concerns the conditions of the ownership, and the sale and purchase, of labour power. Consequently, class in capitalism entails the existence of a capitalist state that is imposing and securing the law and private property. If one discusses class and the capitalist relations of production, one also needs to consider the state.

It also follows that the two main class groupings, capital and labour, are not constituted through a shared identity or collective agency. The claim is just that they exist because people find themselves in opposite poles in a relationship of ownership and non-ownership, which means that each side has to operate under a distinct set of conditions. There are strong incentives to act in certain ways, but these are neither the only incentives that exist, nor do they have the same effect on anyone exposed to them.

Furthermore, the incentives may lend themselves to being interpreted with certain conceptions of the social world, but there is no claim that any

---

a living and is also subject to despotism and alienation, but not people in contradictory class locations (see Chapters 2 and 6).

specific conception must prevail. In a nutshell, the conditions attached to a class location affect the people placed in them in various ways, but they do not fully determine what they think or do. In critical realist terminology, the tendencies inherent in the relations of production influence people in the sense that they constitute preconditions of their activities – and this is the case no matter whether people see those tendencies for what they are or not.

Capitalist class domination

There are two characteristic features of the capitalist relations of production, which, combined with property rights and the freedom to purchase and sell property, characterize class in capitalism: class domination and class antagonism. The former refers to the side of capital being systematically favoured over the side of labour thanks to fundamental differences in access to material and ideational resources and the resulting capacities to make binding decisions over the organization of work. The latter is associated with an irresolvable conflict of interests between the two groupings. It can be decelerated and suppressed through institutions and interventions, but it does not cease to exist as long as the relations of production are in place.

When we talk about capitalist class domination, the differences in access to resources and decision-making capacities between capital and labour exist because one side owns, and the other side does not own, means of production. This creates hugely different conditions of action for the people belonging to either grouping. The conditions can be grouped into different dimensions, which can be captured with three Marxian concepts: 'exploitation', 'despotism' and 'alienation' (see Weeks, 2011: 21). The first term refers to the extraction, through capitalists, of surplus labour carried out by workers; the second to the control of capitalists over the work process; and the third to the fact that workers are not recognized as experts when it comes to the content of their work. This is explained in detail in Table 5.1.

It follows that the coexistence of capital and labour in mutual dependence does not mean that the two sides are on a level playing field. Individual workers put their survival (and the reproduction of their dependants) at risk if they are not hired. In contrast, individual capitalists usually employ a significant number of workers. They can hire someone else or find ways of working around a vacancy if a worker refuses to enter a labour contract with them. Capitalists and workers may be co-dependent, but the degrees of dependency diverge substantially for the two sides. Usually, the individual worker is far more dependent on the individual capitalist than the other way round (see Schulze-Cleven, 2021: 43). It follows that there is no contradiction between saying that capitalist class domination coincides with the co-dependence of capital and labour.

Table 5.1: Class domination

Concept	Description
Exploitation	Workers produce the labour product. They obtain, in the form of wages, only that share of the value they have produced needed to restore their ability to work and to do so continuously. This also means that they perform unpaid surplus labour. The value created is appropriated by the capitalists in the form of profits. The overall arrangement generates substantial economic inequality because it means that whereas workers' pay reflects a (historically changeable) minimum, profits are only limited by the need to pay this minimum (variable capital) and recover the cost incurred through investing in means of production (constant capital).
Despotism	Capitalists have the capacity to make and impose binding decisions concerning the work process and the strategy of their firm. They enjoy a relationship of command over the workers. To use a phrase common in British politics in 1970s and 1980s, they are endowed with the 'right to manage'. The fact that this commanding role may be exercised by managers who are employed does not change the basic mechanisms because the people owning a company are able to decide who is managing it on their behalf.
Alienation	Workers execute plans that have been designed under the leadership of the capitalists. Whereas the latter can thus present themselves as experts on how to 'do' business,[a] the former are relegated to a subordinate place. They tend to be seen as people in need of being instructed what to do and, as a result, become alienated from their capacities and from any meanings they attach to their work.[b] The fact that the activity of the workers is focused on execution hampers the development and use of their practical and intellectual abilities; the opposite is the case for capitalists. The division of labour creates a distinction between laypeople and experts. This constitutes a structural foundation not just for acts of justifying despotism in the workplace, but also for a 'cultural symbolism', to use a Poulantzasian term (Poulantzas, 1974: 258), that results in the degradation and marginalization of workers, poor people and people with limited formal education in everyday life.

Notes: [a] Poulantzas speaks of the 'secrecy of knowledge' linked to the 'authority and the direction of labour' at the level of the firm (Poulantzas, 1974: 31). [b] See Hürtgen (2018a) on how the capitalist relations of production create a tendency for capital reduce work to a quantifiable 'performance' that is deprived of meaning because the overall aim of production becomes securing a profit through the sale of the labour product.

Class interests and the antagonism between capital and labour

In my understanding, an antagonism is a conflict of interest caused by the deep structures of the social world that cannot be resolved or settled permanently. In other words, it only ceases to exist if the structures that give rise to it are abolished. In its capitalist form, it refers to an irresolvable conflict enshrined in the relations of production between capital and labour.

This may sound far-fetched at first. In the domain of the empirical, one may encounter that a range of motives may come into play for capitalists and workers to enter an employment agreement – a philanthropic capitalist may genuinely want to help workers to lead a better life; a criminal may seek employment to create a cover for herself; and the teenage son of a well-to-do father may work to prove that he is able to pay his own way in the world. But if we want to explore the nature of the relationship between capital and labour, we need to abstract from the needs and circumstances of specific individuals or groups and focus on what can be inferred from the existence of the two class groupings constituted by the capitalist relations of production.

If we abstract from contingent circumstances creating specific urges, we are left with basic motives that can be derived from an arrangement under standard conditions – in this case, from entering an employment agreement. From this vantage point, it can be argued that capitalists have an interest in making a profit, and workers have an interest in reproducing themselves. In critical realist terminology, we can say that these interests are tendencies constituted by a deep structure, the mode of production (and the relations of production at its heart), which also means that they may be overdetermined by other tendential interests or more specific motives of actors. They are 'immediate … class interests' (Goes, 2019: 21), which means that they are inherent in any labour contract between workers and capitalists and thus are always actualized when labour power is bought and sold.

By invoking mutual dependency once more, one could say that the two groupings come together on the grounds of their interests. Put simply, workers want to work to make a living, and capitalist want workers to work to turn a profit. One would be mistaken, however, that the labour contract, which seems to be in the interest of both sides, is a harmonious arrangement.

As Marx observes, inherent in it is a clash between two legal principles: On the one hand, there is the right of buyers to freely choose what to do with any commodity acquired. This suggests that the capitalists, as the buyers of labour power, have the right to extract surplus labour from the workers in whichever way they see fit. On the other hand, the labour contract only concerns the ownership of labour power, and not of the entire person selling their capacity to work. Otherwise, we would be talking about slavery. In this understanding, it is in the nature of the labour contract that there are limits to how the commodity of labour power can be treated by those buying it. If capitalists, as owners of this commodity, cause lasting damage by exposing labourers to conditions that impair their capacity to work, they are treating people as if they were their property. The litmus test is whether the ownership of labour power can be re-transferred unharmed to the workers when the contract between the two sides is terminated (see Marx, 1976: 342–3). The Marxian argument shows that the labour contract creates significant potentials for the two sides to clash.

And yet, identifying potential for strife is not enough to show that there is an antagonism in the sense of an irresolvable conflict of interest. To show this, one needs to consider the workings of capitalist competition. Under its conditions, individual businesses compete with one another, which means that they pose a potential threat to one another's economic survival. If we abstract from any further specifications, it is rational for the individual capitalist to attempt to gain advantages over any competitors – or even to just shield oneself from potential, future competition. Consequently, capitalists not only have an interest in making profits, but in making extra profits above average profitability. As a result, inter-capitalist competition creates incentives for capital to be accumulated – capitalists are induced 'as a means of self-preservation, and on pain of going under' to constantly reinvest and reorganize the work process (Marx, 1981: 353).

Importantly, for capitalists to make extra profits, additional surplus labour from workers needs to be extracted. Marx describes two techniques of how this can be achieved. The first one is called 'the production of absolute surplus value' (Marx, 1976: 283–428), which refers to increasing the absolute amount of labour extracted from workers while holding wages constant, most importantly through expanding working time or intensifying work without extra compensation. The second is called 'the production of relative surplus value' (Marx, 1976: 429–642), which refers to a scenario where no working time is added, but where output increases thanks to the use of novel technology. One may add a third technique where capitalists cut investment in elements of the means of production that do not affect output directly, for example, health and safety measures. All three techniques pose a threat to the ability of workers to reproduce themselves. Techniques one and two can lead to job losses and unemployment because the same amount of goods can be produced with fewer workers; techniques one and three create direct threats to the health and wellbeing of workers. The competition-induced, relentless drive for the accumulation of capital destroys 'the original sources of all wealth – the earth and the worker' (Marx, 1976: 638, translation amended).

Consequently, the mechanics of capitalist competition and the resulting need for capital to accumulate turn the potential of strife inherent in the ambiguities of the labour contract into a permanent source of conflict. Competition creates a tendency for capitalists to constantly push up profitability, which goes against the interest of workers to reproduce themselves. It follows that the interests of workers and capitalists, at the level of the capitalist relations of production, are diametrically opposed, which is what the term 'antagonism' refers to – and that there is a self-destructive mechanism inherent in capital accumulation: Capital only exists if there is a constant supply of labour power and raw materials, but accumulation depletes the resources capital needs to exist and destroys human beings and the natural environment in the process (Marx, 1976: 637–8).[3]

Marx concludes that there is permanent conflict between the two sides over how the two legal principles can be brought into agreement with each other. He says: 'There is here therefore an antinomy, of right against right, both equally bearing the seal of the law of exchange. Between equal rights, force decides' (Marx, 1976: 344). We can conclude that class antagonism, which can be seen as a conflict over the boundaries of the use of labour power in the work process, becomes visible in the form of a specific set of emergent practices – the practices of class struggle.[4]

The class antagonism in the capitalist relations of production also has three dimensions:

1. the regime of ownership, which concerns the question of which share of the labour products belongs to the capitalists, and which to the workers;
2. the division of tasks, which concerns the question of who gets to decide what concerning how the labour process is organized; and
3. the order of knowledge, which concerns the question of who has the expertise to make general strategic decisions concerning the business.

---

[3] The antagonism – or contradiction, to use another Marxian term – translates into a second contradiction if we consider that, as Marxist feminists highlight, work is needed to reproduce labour power. Relations of production only exist if there are relations of reproduction that safeguard the continuous reproduction of labour power. In social formations that are patriarchal, including capitalist social formations, much of this reproductive work remains unremunerated – and a great share of it is carried out by women. This creates a permanent tension or contradiction between the relations of production and the relations of reproduction. If male workers are unable to prevent capitalists from extracting additional surplus labour, they can compensate for this, to a degree, by burdening women with extra care work. This means that the profit motive of capital not only clashes with the reproduction motive of productive labour, but also with the reproduction motive of reproductive labour (Arruzza, 2013: 126; Buckel, 2015: 36–7; Fraser, 2016; 2017; Arruzza et al, 2019: 25; see Volume 2, Chapter 8).

[4] The violent character of the relations of production has an important implication that is at odds with the freedom of workers inherent in them. Their rights cease to exist in configurations where capital overpowers labour. In other words, the tendency for freedom for workers to sell their labour power can become compromised due to the existence of countertendencies – for example, if the capitalist mode of production becomes articulated with other modes of production that deny producers this freedom, or if state apparatuses do not enforce the rule of law. If violence eats into freedom, forms of work like slavery and bounded labour are perpetuated and coexist alongside free wage labour. And no matter how strong workers' coalitions are, there are always gaps in representation and people who are not covered, which leaves certain groups of workers particularly vulnerable, for example, migrant workers who are illegalized. From a broad historical and geographical perspective, there are multiple ways in which labour power is being commodified in capitalist social formations, and in which the relations of production are institutionalized (see van der Linden, 2008; 2014).

Table 5.2: Class antagonism

Dimension	Description
Regime of ownership	The capitalists as the owners of the means of production are entitled to appropriate whatever the surplus labour performed by the non-owners produces. From this perspective – and considering the countervailing interests of the two sides – the conflict over boundaries translates into a conflict over what the share of capitalists and the workers in the labour product is.
Division of tasks	Workers are tasked with taking care of production – and capitalists are responsible, in the last instance, for its management. Consequently, the conflict over boundaries is also a conflict over the decision-making authority of managers.
Order of knowledge	There is a distinction between conception and execution: Due to their decision-making authority, capitalists present themselves as experts capable of developing business strategies, which workers have to execute. The conflict over boundaries, from this perspective, is a conflict over the content of those strategies.

The dimensions are described, in greater detail, in Table 5.2.

And yet, it needs to be added that the production of relative surplus value is also associated with temporary and localized class compromises, which may improve the working and living conditions of workers but also help capital. Following Marx, a scenario is possible where pushes for competitive advantages of individual capitalists can indeed result in improvements to the situation of workers. This is a potential outcome of investments in new technology that result in increases in productivity (Marx, 1976: 429–38). If such investments are successful, it becomes a possibility for capitalists to share some of the gains with workers. Once that happens on a regular basis, the antagonism is rendered more manageable and the self-destructive streak of capital accumulation is moderated somewhat, which also means that the existing social formation becomes more durable (see Gallas, 2011).

It is critical to note in this context, however, that class compromises of this type only come into existence if a wide range of specific preconditions is met. Furthermore, they leave capitalist class domination intact, which still impedes the flourishing of workers (see Chapter 1). For pacts around productivity to emerge, investments in new technologies need to be successful, and unions need to be strong enough to force concessions and prevent both technology-induced job losses and competition via 'low-hanging fruit' such as wages and working conditions. Thanks to the pressures of capitalist competition, these conditions can only ever be met temporarily, which means that class compromises are always brittle. It follows that they only modify, but do not suspend, the antagonism between capital and labour inherent in the capitalist relations of production.

Class struggle and social forces

The emergence of practices of class struggle show that class, from a materialist perspective, is not just a structural and relational, but also a process-oriented, dynamic category. Accordingly, Poulantzas states:

> For Marxism, social classes involve in one and the same process both class contradictions and class struggles; social classes do not firstly exist as such, and only then enter into a class struggle. Social classes coincide with class practices, that is the class struggle, and only exist in their mutual opposition. (Poulantzas, 1974: 14)

Poulantzas here refers with 'class contradictions' to conflicting class interests – and with 'class struggle' to the collective practices based on class interests that result in confrontation. Furthermore, he introduces classes as collective actors or as 'social forces' that emerge when people make use of those practices (1974: 17). This process can be called class formation. In other words, class formation occurs if groups of workers or capitalists act in concert and on the grounds of their joint interests – and form networks, coalitions and organizations in the process, for example, trade unions and employers' associations. Put differently, classes as collective actors are not fixed entities that enter into struggle in a second step. The struggles come first.

Conversely, class struggle can also result in a loss of collective agency. If networks and organizations experience defeats, they may fall apart. In other words, capitalist social formations are characterized by both class formation and class partition. In Silver's terms, classes in capitalism are constantly 'made, unmade and remade' (2014: 48; see also Thompson, 1968: 937; Poulantzas, 1974: 23, 27; Goes, 2019: 88).

We end up with a multi-tiered description of class constitution in the capitalist mode of production. It distinguishes between static class groupings at the level of the class structure and dynamic class forces at the level of class agency, which are always in formation.[5] With reference to critical realist ontological assumptions, it can be said that there is a tendency for the emergent

---

[5] To be clear, the attribute 'static' in this context refers to the fact that the capitalist mode of production cannot exist without capital and labour. It does not follow that membership in these groupings is static – or that everyone is either located on the side of capital or on the side of labour. Quite the contrary: there are contradictory class locations (see Volume 2, Chapter 2). And if we take Marx's point about freedom seriously, upward and downward class mobility is possible, in principle, for everyone – but, importantly, not for all.

class forces to take class positions that correspond to their class locations, but there is no necessity for them to do so or to emerge in full (see Poulantzas, 1974: 15). The constitution of class in capitalism is illustrated in Table 5.3.

The state and class domination

The improbability of stable class domination

Against the backdrop of this conception of class, a specific problematic for materialist social theory and social analysis emerges. If class antagonism is at the heart of the capitalist relations of production, this gives rise to the question of how capitalist social formations reach stability at all. Using an expression coined by materialist state theorist Bob Jessop, there is an 'inherent improbability' of stable class domination (Jessop, 2002: 1; see Gallas, 2016b: 36; 2017). This resonates with general observations concerning the crisis-prone and unstable nature of capitalism: 'The idea of a self-reproducing capitalism … must be abandoned. Automatic reproduction does not follow from the establishment of key modes of capitalist societalisation' (Scherrer, 1995: 479). Why is it then that class relations continue to exist, and how do they get reproduced?

As Poulantzas argues (1974: 24–35), one needs to consider the role of the state. Importantly, he does not argue, in a functionalist manner, that the state is compensating for the instability of the capitalist relations of production, or that it is holding society together. Rather, he stresses that the issue of the reproduction of class domination is not an exclusively economic question, but that it also concerns politics and the state. In so doing, he reiterates a point originally made by Marx in the third volume of *Capital*:

> The specific economic form in which unpaid surplus labour is pumped out of the direct producers determines the relationship of domination and servitude, as this grows directly out of production itself and reacts back on it in turn as a determinant. On this is based the entire configuration of the economic community arising from the actual relations of production, and hence also its specific political form. It is in each case the direct relationship of the owners of the conditions of production to the immediate producers – a relationship whose particular form naturally corresponds always to a certain level of development of the type and manner of labour, and hence to its social productive power – in which we find the innermost secret, the hidden basis of the entire social edifice, and hence also the political form of the relationship of sovereignty and dependence, in short, the specific form of state in each case. (Marx, 1981: 924)

It follows that the state is not the answer to the question of the reproduction of class domination; it is part of the question. Put differently, it is impossible to

Table 5.3: Class constitution in the capitalist mode of production

Level of analysis	Class locations			Class interests	Class groupings
	Regime of ownership *Exploitation*	**Division of tasks** *Despotism*	**Order of knowledge** *Alienation*		
Class structure *Conditions* — **Antagonism** *Conflict over boundaries of labour power*	Ownership of the means of production ↕	Management ↕	Conception ↕	Profitability ↕	Capital (capitalists) ↕
	Non-ownership of means of production ↓	Production ↓	Execution ↓	Reproduction	Labour (workers)
Domination *Unequal material and ideational resources*	Capitalist appropriation of the labour product	Capitalist extraction of surplus labour	Capitalist claim to expertise		

Class agency *Emergent practices*

Class forces → Class formation → Class struggles (cycle)

understand how capitalist social formations are stabilized and destabilized if one does not take into account the state. Following Marx, the relations of production are intrinsically linked to the state. According to him, the organization of work across society is not just the key to understanding the economy, but also politics and, by implication, ideology, as the reference to 'sovereignty' makes clear.

Poulantzas also pursues this line of thought. Following him, the state operates at a distance to the economy but is still invested in it. After all, capitalist relations of production only exist if the status of workers and capitalists as commodity owners – owners of their own labour power and of means of production, respectively – is guaranteed. For this to be the case, there needs to be a legal system with a degree of independence from capital. And for such a legal system to exist, there also has to be a state safeguarding and enforcing the law – with the help of a political-administrative apparatus, a repressive apparatus, ideological apparatuses and, last but not least, an economic apparatus. The different apparatuses of the state are explained in Table 5.4.

In a nutshell, relations of production are class relations, and they only exist if there is a state. In other words, the existence of the capitalist type of state follows from the existence of the capitalist relations of production. Poulantzas speaks of 'the State's presence in the constitution and reproduction of the relations of production' (1978: 17, 27), but adds that there is a 'relative *separation* of the state and the economic sphere' (1978: 18; emphasis in the original).

It follows that it is wrong to see the relations of production as merely economic relations, which possibly have external connections with politics and ideology. They are, simultaneously, economic, political and ideological relations: '[P]olitico-ideological class determinations are also present "within" economic class determinations right at the heart of the relations of production' (Poulantzas, 1976: 82; see also 1974: 101). This is also visible in the fact that the law – as a medium of social coordination guaranteed by the state – is, in principle, all-pervasive. Accordingly, the activities of state apparatuses in capitalist societies affect every aspect of the social fabric. They do not just concern state spaces in a narrow sense like the political scene, the bureaucracy, the organs of repressions or the legal system, but also the economy and civil society. In brief, there are no areas in capitalist social formations that remain outside the state (see Poulantzas, 1978: 151).

Indeed, the regime of ownership, the division of tasks and the order of knowledge only exist if there is a state with capacities to legitimize and defend – if need be by resorting to overt force – the ownership of the means of production and the resulting distribution of social wealth; that safeguards the decision-making authority of capitalists at the level of the firm; and that underpins, with the help of this authority, their self-conception of being expert business people. Consequently, it is necessary to consider the political and ideological dimensions of class if one wants to discuss the reproduction of class domination. The conception of class put forward here is anti-economistic.

Table 5.4: The apparatuses of the capitalist state

Apparatus(es)*	Tasks***	Bodies (examples)
Political-Administrative**	Facilitation of official political decision-making and coordination of the different branches of the state and of the relations between the state and civil society (see Poulantzas, 1978: 245)	- Parliaments - Central administrations at the national, regional and local level - Political parties
Repressive	Imposition of the law and of government decisions with the help of force (see Poulantzas, 1978: 29)	- Ministries of the Interior - Ministries of Defence - Judiciary - Prisons - Police - Military
Economic	Management of the crisis tendencies inherent in capital accumulation and creation and administration of institutions that ensure a constant supply of labour power (see Poulantzas, 1978: 163)	- Ministries of Economics and Business - Ministries of Labour and Welfare - Ministries of Finance - Central banks
Ideological*	Institutionalization of practices and systematization of ideas that bind people to the existing social order by offering them an imaginary location in the social world and turning them into citizens and members of an imagined national community (see Poulantzas, 1974: 31; 1978: 58, 63; Althusser, 2014: 181)	- Schools and universities - Public broadcasters - Statutory religious and doctrinaire bodies

Notes:

* Note that Althusser and Poulantzas refer to 'ideological state apparatuses' (in the plural). In so doing, they highlight the fact that the latter are less centralized than other state apparatuses (see Althusser, 2014: 135–9). In the last section of this chapter, I replace 'ideological' with 'cultural' for reasons explained there.

** Poulantzas speaks of an 'administrative apparatus' (1978: 245). I have added the attribute 'political' to highlight that that this apparatus is closely tied to genuinely political bodies like parliaments. In contrast to Althusser and Poulantzas, I do not see parties as being primarily part of the ideological state apparatuses even though they institutionalize a range of practices that create and reproduce imaginary relations to the social world. This is due their close ties to state administrations, which Poulantzas also describes (1978: 234, 245).

*** Importantly, none of these tasks are exclusive to a single apparatus (see Poulantzas, 1978: 29, 33, 170). However, for every apparatus, some tasks tend to predominate over others. For example, the fact that the administrative-political apparatus notifies citizens of an upcoming election by mail can be seen as an ideological act reproducing the imaginary relationship between the citizen and the nation. But it also belongs to one of the core activities of the apparatus, which is the facilitation of official political processes.

Modes of individuality and collectivity

If one acknowledges the presence of the state in the relations of production, it also becomes clear that the tendency for the formation of class actors arising out of class antagonism and domination is complemented by other modes of individuality and collectivity with contradictory effects. These modes partly amplify and partly counteract class formation – and work, on the whole, in a manner conducive to the reproduction of class domination.

Poulantzas points to two tendencies connected with the existence of the capitalist state that work against class formation. The first one reflects the fact that people in capitalist societies connect and compete with one another in markets. This is only possible if there is a state granting rights. These rights can be limited or more expansive depending on institutions and conjunctural factors – which, not least, reflect the relations of forces between capital and labour. After all, Poulantzas defines the capitalist state as 'a specific material condensation of a given relationship of forces, which is itself a class relation' (1978: 73). What can be said is that for capitalism to exist, there needs to be a minimum set of rights focused on commodity ownership and market transactions. And as bearers of rights, people are individual citizens. Poulantzas infers that there is a tendency for the 'atomization' of people thanks to the capitalist state, which he also calls the 'effect of isolation' (Poulantzas, 1968: 130–1, 213; see also 1978: 63).

This tendency is reflected in practices such as competing with others for jobs, visiting a voting booth to cast a ballot or adopting techniques of 'self-optimization' to do better and get ahead of others in school, all of which can be articulated with one another to form individualistic ideologies such as economic liberalism. The contention that 'everyone is the architect of their fortune' – an important ideological support of the latter – is rooted in such practices. In other words, the isolation effect invites people to prioritize what they see as their individual needs, treat other people as competitors – or at least as 'bystanders' to their own existence – and adopt individualistic ways of life (for example, the goal to 'get ahead' in life through hard work or the decision to participate in politics only by voting in elections). This makes it difficult for them to identify class relations and their own class locations (see Poulantzas, 1968: 130). The isolation effect tends to work against the emergence of networks of solidarity along class lines and, thus, class formation.

The second mechanism results from the fact that there was no world state or global empire when capitalism emerged historically (see Poulantzas, 1978: 95; Bieler and Morton, 2018: 79–106). In consequence, rights are secured through national states, whose extension overlaps roughly with collectives of rights bearers (see Poulantzas, 1978: 95). They have neatly defined borders, which demarcate a territory and tend to be policed, and a population of people enjoying 'citizenship'. Following Poulantzas, the existence of the rule of law and a capitalist state underpinning it creates a tendency for the formation of a 'people-nation' (1978: 63). This also means that there is a tendency for working-class forces to be constituted at the level of the national state – even if transnational class formation is in principle possible thanks to the global extension of the capitalist mode of production (see Poulantzas, 1978: 118; Goes, 2019: 135).

Again, there are practices underpinning this tendency – from positive discrimination in the job market and access to benefits that is based on one's citizenship to travelling across borders with a passport and singing the national anthem. These practices contribute to people viewing themselves as members of an 'imagined community' (Anderson, 2006). They invite the latter to adopt nationalist ideologies that homogenize social differences and create justifications for the exclusion of those deemed on the outside of the imagined national collective, which are the roots of totalitarian practices of marginalization, persecution and violence directed against racial and ethnic minorities (Poulantzas, 1978: 107). By turning workers against one another and creating ties across class lines, this tendency usually also works against class formation.

This means that people in capitalism are entangled in practices that turn them into individual citizens and members of a national collective, which explains why individualism and nationalism play such an important role in capitalist social formations. According to Poulantzas, '[t]he national State realizes the unity of the people-nation in the very movement by which it forges their individualization' (1978: 106). It follows that the two mechanisms coincide and usually reinforce each other. They contribute to the reproduction of capitalist class domination and impede working-class formation because they cut ties between people in the same class locations and create ties across them.

Importantly, this overdetermines, but does not eradicate, the fact that there are two class groupings at the structural level, and that an order of knowledge emerges that divides people into experts and laypeople. Poulantzas points out how this division becomes an ossified division of labour thanks to different state apparatuses such as the school, the university and the army – and how this creates class-based modes of individuality that do not just shape people's mindsets but also their physiques: 'There is a bourgeois and a working-class individualization, a bourgeois and a working class body' (1978: 75). The embodiment of class also has a stabilizing effect insofar it creates avenues for naturalizing work-related hierarchies as the results of differences in 'talent' and 'intelligence'.

A unified power bloc and divisions among workers

Next to the general effects of the capitalist state on individuality and collectivity, there are class-specific ones that concern either capital or labour.

If we look at the side of capital, a starting point of Poulantzas' line of argument is Marx's observation, in the second volume of *Capital*, that the circulation of capital entails various changes of form, as is captured in the formula 'M-C...P...C'-M' (Marx, 1978: 25). These changes are conducive to the emergence of specialized circuits of capital, namely 'mercantile, industrial and financial capital' (Poulantzas, 1968: 233).

Importantly, capitalists representing these different circuits share a broad interest in accumulation, but there are also specific issues that divide them. For example, it makes sense, for export-oriented industrial capitalists, to be in favour of lower interest rates. This tends to push down the price of a national currency in the international money markets, which also means that the commodities of exporters are less expensive for their international customers. In contrast, the reverse tends to be the case for financial capitalists. High rates usually curb inflation and thus prevent the worth of assets from falling in real terms. This is why one can argue, with Poulantzas, that there is a tendency for the formation of different fractions of capital, which coalesce around similar economic practices and worldviews concerning economic policy in a broad sense. Again, it is by no means a given that fractions corresponding to the different circuits of capital exist; indeed, class forces can emerge, on the side of capital, that unite different groups of capitalists, as was the case, for example, for agricultural and financial capitalists in England from the 17th century onwards (Gallas, 2008: 272–8; see also Poulantzas, 1974: 92).

Poulantzas argues that the existence of the capitalist state is conducive to uniting the different fractions of the capitalist class under the leadership of a hegemonic fraction into a power bloc and overcoming the competition of the many capitals in the economic domain at the political and ideological level. In his view, universal suffrage is an important mechanism for producing this unity: Its existence prevents the direct control of the executive through a specific fraction and means that the latter operates at a distance to all fractions; and it leads to the formation of governments, which, through agenda-setting, prioritize certain demands of the different fractions of capital over others and, if they gain support for their agenda, contribute to uniting the different fractions (see Poulantzas, 1978: 127). In this sense, there is a tendency for capitalist class formation to result from the workings of the capitalist state. Put differently, it tends to have a unifying effect on capital. The existence of a government addresses the competition problem by figuring as an instance that can, in principle, balance diverging views and preferences among capitalists. If all goes well for capital, the capitalist state serves as a forum where an agenda for capital can be formulated and a set of mechanisms that ensure this agenda is implemented.

Conversely, Poulantzas argues that the existence of the capitalist state is conducive to dividing workers and preventing the formation of a unified working class. The competition between workers is solidified and codified by turning people into citizens with individual rights and a political voice that is registered, in the first place, individually, for example through the existence of the institutions of representative democracy and the practice of voting in elections. At the same time, workers become members of an imagined national collective, which tends to have a divisive effect because it excludes non-members.

The divisiveness of the capitalist state is further reinforced through the mechanics of the accumulation of capital. Due to competition and the interest of individual capitalists in gaining advantages over their competitors, the labour process is constantly being revolutionized. This also means that workforces are not stable, and that individual capitalists tend to engage, time and again, in practices of hiring and firing workers. It follows that workers are constantly grouped together and redivided – and that capitalists can make use of existing social differences to create internal divisions, which impede class formation: Workers are 'continually repelled and attracted, slung backwards and forwards, while, at the same time, constant changes take place in the sex, age and skill of the industrial conscripts' (Marx, 1976: 583).

In a nutshell, the mechanics of capital accumulation create incentives for capitalists to take advantage of the existing social differences between workers and reinforce the latter. It is possible to create hierarchies among workers, for example, through the appointment of overseers and supervisors, or through dividing them into permanent and temporary workforces. As a result, there is ample room for capitalists to grant material and ideational advantages to certain groups of workers and deny them everyone else – and to do so by creating, dissolving, reproducing and thus perpetuating gendered or racialized divisions of labour among workers as a class grouping (see Weeks, 2011: 9–10; Arruzza, 2013: 89; Roediger, 2017: 12). Marx's point about the 'industrial conscripts' is a revision of what he and Engels had suggested decades earlier in the *Communist Manifesto* (Marx and Engels, 1959) – that capitalism is a great leveller creating a simplified social order where 'all fixed, fast-frozen relations, with their train of ancient and venerable prejudices and opinions, are swept away' and 'all new-formed ones become antiquated before they can ossify'.

The capitalist mode of production is 'dirty', to use Sonja Buckel's expression (2015), in an analytical and a normative sense: In an analytical sense because class domination in capitalism is always overdetermined by other forms of social domination. Thanks to capital accumulation, social relations in capitalism constantly undergo processes of transformation and rearticulation. Consequently, they exhibit a multiplicity of partly overlapping modes of individuality and collectivity, which cannot be reduced to class forces. In a normative sense because the accumulation of capital tends to reproduce not just class domination, but all other forms of social domination, most importantly patriarchal and racist domination. It perpetuates unequal access to material and ideational resources as well as working and living conditions that prevent people from flourishing – and creates disunity among workers. This has important implications for class political projects aiming to shift the class relations of forces profoundly in favour of labour and move beyond the dominant mode of production: 'If class politics is not feminist and anti-racist, it will not be capable of shattering capitalist domination', as Thomas Goes, a German social scientist and political activist, observes (2019: 16).

To summarize, the workings of the capitalist state tend to unify capitalists, which is reflected in the emergence of a power bloc, and to separate workers from one another. It is improbable for workers to develop a homogeneous class identity, and it is more likely for capitalists because they are fewer people in numbers, and there is less of a contradiction, on their side, between individualistic aspirations and class belonging. Consequently, I argue against the idea that classes as collective actors emerge out of a joint identity. My anti-identitarian, work-based understanding of class is based on a critical realist ontology, which means that class locations do not create class positions that are fixed once and for all.

Furthermore, it would be wrong to infer from the existence of the capitalist state and its effects on class relations that the capitalist mode of production is integrated in a functional manner and thus a self-reproducing entity. The accumulation of capital is dynamic and crisis-prone, and the class antagonism inherent in the capitalist relations of production is a constant source of conflict. Put differently, the latter can be seen as a necessary contradiction of capitalism, that is, as a relationship between two co-dependent forces that work against each other. As long as capitalism exists, this contradiction cannot be resolved, but can only be managed and moved around. This also means that a range of conditions must be met for the mode of production to get reproduced, which cannot be assumed to occur automatically.

Accordingly, it can happen that power blocs enter a state of fragmentation – but this also means that the mode of production is in an organic crisis threatening its continued existence. And it is also possible that working-class forces coalesce around a joint agenda and there is an all-encompassing form of unity and solidarity – but this is only the case if there is a revolutionary conjuncture. Importantly, neither situation is compatible with the continued existence of capitalism.

The segmentation of class struggle

According to Poulantzas, the tendential separation of the state and the economy, which is enshrined in the capitalist relations of production, entails a tendential separation of economic, political and ideological or cultural class domination (Poulantzas, 1974: 15). The ownership of the means of production does not entitle one to take a key role in government – and the holder of an important government job is not necessarily at the forefront of producing imaginary relations to the social world. In other words, the CEO of Microsoft is usually not the president of the US, and the latter usually not a director working with one of the big Hollywood studios, at least not simultaneously.[6]

In keeping with the Marxist tradition, Poulantzas uses the concept of 'ideology' frequently. He refers to practices embedded in state apparatuses with ideational and material aspects that create imaginary relations between people and the social world. A typical example for such a practice is attending school. Students learn about the world and are invited to adopt worldviews that place them in an imagined relationship with other people and society. In what follows, I will take the freedom to speak of 'culture' instead of 'ideology'. The reason is that ideology is often counterposed to truth or science or imaginaries that contest social domination, which seriously limits the extension of the concept. In contrast, culture is a more open concept referring to, in their entirety, imaginary relations and practices producing and reproducing them. This means that both imaginaries stabilizing capitalist class domination and those questioning it can be captured with it.[7] This is obviously relevant for class theory because imaginaries are constantly mobilized when people negotiate class relations.

Due to the existence of class antagonism, class struggles cannot be fully suppressed no matter what the institutional make-up of the social formation is. And yet, the existence of an ensemble of state apparatuses operating at a distance to the economy result in them being segmented and channelled. Following Poulantzas, economic, political and cultural class struggles can be distinguished (1974: 15; see also Goes, 2019: 46). He does not provide careful definitions, but gives us some hints as to how this can be done. It appears that the different modes of class struggle can be determined by differentiating between objects of struggle: Economic class struggles are struggles over the

---

[6] This does not mean that leading capitalists cannot be become heads of state or government, as the examples of Elizabeth II, Donald Trump and Silvio Berlusconi demonstrate. It means that their responsibilities in office differ fundamentally from their tasks as owners of capital, which is demonstrated by the endless discussions, in the case of the latter two, over conflicts of interest.

[7] My notion of culture is compatible with a definition provided by Althusser in a short, unpublished note (2022: 486; emphasis in the original): 'It would seem that we can take the *culture* of a given social formation by which people live, reproduce and produce their relations to their conditions of existence, both social and natural.' He adds, in a second version of the note: 'Roughly speaking, these *reflected forms* can be ranged under the following rubrics: *language, knowledge* (scientific, technical, empirical, ideological), and the corresponding *practices*.'

labour product; political class struggles concern the question of who has the authority to make binding decisions concerning the way society is organized; and cultural class struggles relate to the issue of whether dominant social imaginaries and conceptions of expertise are valid representations of the social world. This is described in detail in Table 5.5.

Table 5.5: Economic, political and cultural class struggles

Dimension and contested object	Description
Economic *The production and distribution of the labour product*	Poulantzas argues that '[t]he economic sphere is determined by the process of production' (1974: 17–18), and that the latter has, at its heart, the 'extraction of surplus value' (19) and the exploitation of workers. This in turns gives rise to 'social inequalities' (20). It follows that economic class struggles can be understood as struggles around the conditions of the extraction of surplus labour. The standard practice of economic class struggle on the side of workers is the *strike*.
Political *Decision-making authority*	Poulantzas refers to political and ideological class relations resulting from the presence of the state in the capitalist relations of production (1974: 21, 25). Translated into the language of political science, political class struggles can be seen as struggles over who has the capacity to make binding decisions concerning work (see Poulantzas, 1974: 229). They take on the form of political disputes 'over the organisation of society' (Lindner, 2006: 585) in areas where class relations are negotiated – and involve politicians and political parties, but also trade unions, employers' associations and civil society organizations.
Cultural *Imaginaries and expertise*	Following Poulantzas (1970: 17, 76), ideological practices deploy imaginary relations to the world conducive to reproducing class domination. In turn, ideological state apparatuses such as schools invite people to adopt such practices. Importantly, ideology can be contested by non-ideology, that is, imaginary relations to the world contesting class domination, for example scholarly and journalistic practices that criticize capitalism and the social division of labour. The existence of two sides indicates that there is a dimension of the social that encompasses both ideological and non-ideological imaginary relations and practices. In my view, it can be called 'the cultural'. Accordingly, cultural class struggles are battles between intellectuals over the dominance of ideological or non-ideological imaginaries and over the divide between expertise and non-expertise that sustains them. Following Poulantzas, dominant notions of expertise reflect the ideological relations enshrined in the relations of production insofar as the latter are based on the division between mental and manual labour (1974: 230). In my terms, the capitalist relations of production entail an order of knowledge that tasks people on the side of capital with 'conception', and people on the side of labour with execution.

The distinction between the three dimensions of the class struggle is complicated by the fact that it is primarily analytical. In real-concrete situations, they are not clearly separated. A very common form of the strike is the strike over higher wages, which falls into the area of economic class struggle because it primarily concerns the remunerative aspect of the organization of work. But it also touches upon the decision-making authority and the expertise of capitalists – the aim is to force them to reconsider their decisions concerning wages and to question their capacity to plan and strategize over remuneration. This is consistent with Poulantzas' claim that the relationship between the state and the economy is, simultaneously, one of separation and presence. In my view, this complicated configuration can only be disentangled if we distinguish the three dimensions, but also account for the presence of the other two dimensions in any one dimension we are looking at. This can be done by creating a three-by-three matrix, which creates space for the presence of all three dimensions in each single one of them. The implication is that economic class struggles over the distribution of goods are of course dominantly economic, but they also have political and cultural aspects – and the same can be said about the two other dimensions. The matrix is explained further in Table 5.6.

Notably, the segmentation of class domination tends to have a stabilizing effect (Poulantzas, 1974: 17; Jessop, 1978: 29; Goes, 2019: 46). If economic struggles are struggles over wages and working conditions in which workers do not pursue more far-reaching, political goals, they tend to pose less of a threat to class domination than would be the case if they were based on demands that questioned the decision-making authority of capital. Conversely, if parties representing working-class interests make demands at the political level following the procedures of representative democracy,

Table 5.6: Dimensions of the class struggle

	Object	Economic	Political	Cultural
Economic	The production and distribution of the labour product	Producing and distributing labour products	Making and imposing decisions at the company level	Strategic planning at the company level
Political	Decision-making authority	Intervening in the economy and redistributing wealth	Imposing binding decisions at the societal level	Setting out strategies and agendas at the societal level
Cultural	Imaginaries and expertise	Creating criteria for work performances and merit	Codifying expert knowledge	Producing imaginaries of a good society

and these demands are not sustained by mobilizations of workers at the level of production, it is probably easier for the forces defending the status quo to reject them. And likewise, struggles over imaginaries are often confined to the media and academic discourses – and thus are far less forceful than interventions that are taken up in, and are transformed through, economic and political struggles. It is all good and well to write 'interesting' books about strikes, but if they do not somehow connect with workers' movements and mobilizations outside of academic discourses, their impact will remain limited. In short, working-class struggles are only likely to forcefully challenge capitalist class domination if they combine economic, political and cultural demands and practices of contestation.

6

Making, Unmaking, Remaking: Working-Class Forces in Formation

The emergence of working classes

What I need to discuss in greater detail, for the purposes of this book, is working-class formation. After all, the key theoretical argument put forward in it for the analysis of strikes is that they facilitate working-class formation. So far, I have not addressed this issue.

In this context, it is worth turning to Althusser, who argues that there are roughly two different conceptions of working-class formation, which differ in terms of their sequencing. Following him, the first is what can be called a 'reformist' conception:

> Let us take a simple example, and suppose that we are dealing with just two classes. For reformists these classes exist before the class struggle, a bit like two football teams exist, separately, before the match. Each class exists in its own camp, lives according to its particular conditions of existence. One class may be exploiting another, but for reformism that is not the same thing as class struggle. One day the two classes come up against one another and come into conflict. It is only then that the class struggle begins. They begin a hand-to-hand battle, the battle becomes acute, and finally the exploited class defeats its enemy (that is revolution), or loses (that is counter-revolution). However you turn the thing around, you will always find the same idea here: the classes exist before the class struggle, independently of the class struggle. The class struggle only exists afterwards. (Althusser, 1976: 49)

In my terminology, this conception is based on the following causal chain:

  (a) Class locations → (b) class formation → (c) class forces → (d) class struggle

If we accept Althusser's metaphor, what we are seeing is an 'association football' conception of class relations: Capitalism can be seen as a game in which there are two teams, both proudly wearing their colours and trying to defeat each other. It is clear for each and every player on the field where its boundaries lie; what the rules of the game are; which side they belong to and who their opponent is; and how they are supposed to contribute, as individuals, to the efforts of their teams. The process of class formation consists in 'football training': People learn the rules of the game and the skills they need to play; in the process, the two coaches select their squads, develop a match plan including a formation and assign to their players different roles on the field. After this process is completed and the two teams have taken their positions on the field, the actual game starts. Althusser calls this conception 'reformist' because of its political implications for the side of labour. Labour politics becomes a waiting and a training game; political leaders have to educate the masses and gather them behind their agenda so that the conditions 'ripen' for class struggle to break out. In other words, the first conception lends itself to political passivity.

Following Althusser, it is possible to distinguish the 'association football' conception from what can be called, with a hint of irony, the 'mob football' conception:[1] there is a match involving two sides, but it is neither clear where the pitch ends or starts nor who is playing. Importantly, some of the players possess far more physical strength than others or use armour – and they enjoy the additional advantage that their goal is up on a hill, which makes it much harder for their opponents to score. At the beginning, it is not quite clear who is on which side. Indeed, there are a lot of bystanders, but the situation is becoming polarized over time, which draws some of them into the two more clearly demarcated camps that are emerging. Importantly, however, even in this situation there may be people who are passive or are trying to calm things down. Althusser sees this as the revolutionary conception:

> Revolutionaries ... consider that it is impossible to separate the classes from class struggle. The class struggle and the existence of classes are one and the same thing. In order for there to be classes in a 'society', the society has to be divided into classes: this division does not come

---

[1] 'Association football' is the modern game that we know today as 'football' or 'soccer'. It goes back to 1863, when the (English) Football Association convened to lay down the original 'Laws of the Game'. 'Mob football' refers to a range of games played in Europe in medieval times that involved a great number of players, who possibly hailed from neighbouring villages, kicking around a ball. In comparison to the modern game, it had few rules and was very violent (see Wilson, 2018: 15–18).

later in the story; it is the exploitation of one class by another, it is therefore the class struggle, which constitutes the division into classes. For exploitation is already class struggle. You must therefore begin with the class struggle if you want to understand class division, the existence and nature of classes. The class struggle must be put in the front rank. (Althusser, 1976: 50; see also Poulantzas, 1978: 27)

In the 'mob football' conception, the elements (b) and (c) of the causal chain are reversed:

(a) Class locations → (b) class struggle → (c) class formation → (d) class forces

It follows that the class struggle is always ongoing. '[T]here is no need for there to be "class consciousness" or autonomous political organizations for the class struggle to take place, and to take place in every domain of social reality', as Althusser's friend and interlocutor Poulantzas observes around the same time (1974: 17).[2] The political implication is that it is worth getting involved in struggles because they facilitate class formation, and that political passivity does not pay off.

Importantly, Althusser is selecting a theoretical position here on the grounds of political expediency. His considerations are useful because they allow us to clearly distinguish two different takes on class formation. But they tell us little about why the different stages should evolve in a certain way, and what the analytical value-added of the second conception is. What is needed is a theoretical discussion of the consistency and explanatory power of the two positions.

For the purposes of such a discussion, I examine, in this chapter, the writings of two eminent figures in early 20th-century Marxism that represent either side of the debate: Nikolai Bukharin and Rosa Luxemburg. Whereas the former has discussed the question of class formation in detail in his book *Historical Materialism: A System of Sociology* (2021; originally published in 1921), the latter is not known for her class theoretical work. Nevertheless, Luxemburg's political writings, in particular her famous tract *The Mass Strike* (2008; originally published in 1906), offer acute observations on class relations. Indeed, Luxemburg is particularly relevant for this book because she is interested in the connection between working-class formation and strikes. My wager is that it is possible to draw out some of the implicit theoretical assumptions informing her tract and her other political analyses to outline a distinct approach to working-class formation.

---

2   See Gallas (2017) on the relationship between Althusser and Poulantzas.

The limitations of evolutionism

Nikolai Bukharin's book can be seen as the standard account of Marxist social theory in the early 20th century. He was a leading Russian revolutionary, a fierce critic of Luxemburg's theory of imperialism and one of the scholars laying the foundations for Marxism-Leninism, the official justification doctrine of the Soviet Bloc. His text was highly influential for materialist class theory insofar as it approaches the question of class formation with the oft-discussed distinction between 'class-in-itself' and 'class-for-itself', which he derives from Marx's *Poverty of Philosophy* (2009b). Bukharin states:

> [A] class discharging a definite function in the process of production may already exist as an aggregate of persons before it exists as a self-conscious class; we have a class, but no class consciousness. It exists as a factor in production, as a specific aggregate of production relations; it does not yet exist as a social, independent force that knows what it wants, that feels a mission, that is conscious of its peculiar position, of the hostility of its interests to those of the other classes. As designations for these different stages in the process of class evolution, Marx makes use of two expressions: he calls class 'an sich' (in itself), a class not yet conscious of itself as such; he calls class 'für sich' (for itself), a class already conscious of its social role.[3] (Bukharin, 2021: 337)

This framework is based on the assumption that under capitalist conditions, the formation of the working class is proceeding in three stages: 'class-in-itself', where the working class is just an aggregate of people sharing the same place in the relations of production – or a class location, in my terminology; 'class-for-itself', where the working class becomes a self-aware collective actor that has recognized its interests; and revolution, where the working class overthrows the rule of the capitalist class. Importantly, in the passage from the first to the second stage, class struggle emerges as a mode of action:

> [L]et us consider the example of a movement for higher wages among the wage workers of a factory. If all the other workers in the country

---

[3] Importantly, Marx does not use the exact terminology ascribed to him by Bukharin. In *The Poverty of Philosophy*, he says: 'Economic conditions had first transformed the mass of the people of the country into workers. The combination of capital has created for this mass a common situation, common interests. This mass is thus already a class as against capital, but not yet for itself. In the struggle, of which we have noted only a few phases, this mass becomes united, and constitutes itself as a class for itself. The interests it defends become class interests. But the struggle of class against class is a political struggle' (Marx, 2009b: 79).

remain calm, we have only the promise of a class struggle, for the class as yet is not kindled. Let us consider, however, the case of a 'strike wave'. This is class struggle: one class stands opposed to the other. We are no longer dealing with the interests of the group impelling another group, but with the interests of a class impelling another class. (Bukharin, 2021: 343)

Following Bukharin, society is in constant evolution thanks to technological-economic development, which consists in the 'growth of the productive forces' (Bukharin, 2021: 283). And this growth is also the driver behind the transition between the three stages. Under capitalist conditions, technological-economic development simplifies the class structure and thus gives rise to conflicts in which workers learn about the nature of capitalism. In other words, the emergence of the working class as a unified and a revolutionary actor is a by-product of the evolution of capitalism, which has a clear direction: It has a neatly defined end-goal, which is also the end-goal of working-class formation: 'We may also speak of the historical necessity of socialism, since without it human society cannot continue to develop. If society is to continue to develop, socialism will inevitably come' (Bukharin, 2021: 283).

Admittedly, Bukharin introduces a qualification to this line of argument. He stresses that inequalities between workers continue to exist despite the simplification of the class structure – first of all due to differences in their 'brain power and ability'; second because of sectoral differences; and third because people with different class backgrounds continue to be proletarianized (Bukharin, 2021: 350). These differences, however, do not obstruct working-class formation. This is because a vanguard party emerges, which 'best expresses the interests of the class' and serves as the 'head' of the class 'body'. The party is not a collection of free-willed individuals, which can take the class into different political directions. It ensures that the political leaders of the working class act in line with its interests and thus acts as a catalyst for the evolution of society towards a simplified class structure. So despite the persisting internal differentiation of the working class, the overall direction of history is still set in stone: The party is facilitating working-class formation and will eventually lead the working class into revolution and end bourgeois rule.

This is an evolutionist, technologist-economistic, deterministic, teleological and vanguardist account of working-class formation: history is made thanks to a single driver (evolutionism), which is the development of the productive forces (technologism-economism); people's individual and collective activities are fully determined by this mechanism (determinism), which is why history has socialism as its clearly defined goal (teleology); and there is a clearly defined distinction, once a politics of the working class emerges, between the party as an organization of leaders and the workers outside of the party who are in need of being led (vanguardism). In many ways, Bukharin's position is compatible with textbook interpretations of Marx (see Bruce, 1999: 63–4; Browne, 2011: 404), which is unsurprising given that his book was a canonical text that influenced considerably how Marx was read in subsequent decades. Ironically, Bukharin's take on working-class formation – despite its emphasis on revolution – is compatible with the reformist position described by Althusser: It is based on the assumption that class struggles only emerge once the conditions are ripe for it, and his classes-for-themselves are the two football teams.

There are at least five critical problems with Bukharin's account. First of all, capitalist development across the globe is, by all we can say from today's vantage point, not marked by a simplification of class structures into two main classes, quite the contrary. In the 1970s, materialist class theorists were grappling with the fact that new middle classes had emerged whose existence needed to be accounted for in theoretical terms (see Poulantzas, 1974: 191–336; Wright, 1978b: 30–110). Furthermore, there has been a deepening of the transnational division of labour in recent decades, which was driven by the use of new technologies in processes of production and distribution. Arguably, the emergence of transnational production networks has contributed to a reconfiguration of the internal fractioning of working classes. In light of this, the assumption that the passage from working-classes-in-themselves to working-classes-for-themselves is the product of technological-economic development seems questionable, to say the least.

Second, there is what I would call, somewhat polemically, the Jehovah's Witnesses fallacy. It is fairly straightforward to argue that working-classes-for-themselves, as defined by Bukharin, are hard to track down anywhere in the world today. Obviously, individuals and organizations of the working class exist that have a mission and are aware of their class interests as well as their antagonism to capital. However, it is hard to argue that this type of consciousness extends to working classes in their entirety. Admittedly, one could respond that capitalism has not yet evolved sufficiently for this to occur. But this is where the fallacy is committed: It is always possible to find reasons why a predicted end result has not emerged yet, and why it will still emerge – including the end of the world. Bukharin made his prediction roughly a century ago and working-classes-in-themselves have only emerged, so far, for a limited time and under very specific historical conditions. It is fair to say that there is little empirical evidence that his prediction is correct.

Third, and related to the second point, there is a danger of not taking seriously counterattacks by capital and setbacks experienced by workers in the class struggle if one assumes that the overall direction of class formation is clear from the outset. There have been, in recent decades, fierce attacks of capital on organized labour, for example the Thatcherite offensive in Britain or the attacks on unions in the US in the Reagan era (Cohen, 2006: 53–74; Gallas, 2016b), which have contributed to undermining the organizational foundation of the working class and the capacity of workers to act in concert. Consequently, the assumption that the forward march of labour cannot be halted seems tenuous. Furthermore, there is an implication of Bukharin's account of the class struggle that appears to be questionable in this context: If class struggle only comes into existence once there are fully-fledged classes, what are attacks on the remnants of trade unionism if they take place when organized labour has already been weakened considerably?

Fourth – and here I am already invoking a point made by Luxemburg – the implication of seeing 'class consciousness' as a precondition for the emergence of classes as collective actors downplays the importance of spontaneous eruptions of protest and struggles that do not necessarily have a clear direction or goal from the outset. Luxemburg underlines how important these kinds of struggles were in the process leading to the first Russian Revolution in 1905, and how they can contribute to working-class formation under the right circumstances by speeding up the revolutionary process:

> The element of spontaneity … plays a great part in all Russian mass strikes without exception, be it as a driving force or as a restraining influence. … [I]n Russia the element of spontaneity plays such a predominant part not because the Russian proletariat is 'uneducated,' but because revolutions do not allow anyone to play the schoolmaster with them. (Luxemburg, 2008: 148)

Against this backdrop, Bukharin's vanguardism should be questioned. The three-stage model invites representatives of working-class organizations such as trade unions and parties to look down on unorganized workers as being behind; it cannot envisage scenarios where the latter drive forward and even take the lead in movements against capital. Luxemburg, in contrast, acknowledges the stabilizing and educational function of working-class organizations and their usefulness for exercising leadership in situations of confrontation (Luxemburg, 2008: 122), but she also emphasizes that spontaneity can have the positive effect of undermining rigidities and certainties blocking the advancement of the working class and triggering learning processes on the side of the organized workers (2008: 128).

Fifth, there appears to be no guarantee whatsoever that socialist revolutions will take place, and that they will be victorious. Obviously, it is possible to argue that there is no way for working classes to escape class domination if capitalist relations of production are not overthrown. From this, one could infer that workers as a class have a collective interest in abolishing the capitalist mode of production – an observation that is in keeping with the normative considerations laid out in Chapter 1. However, there are important qualifications to be made to this statement: As long as there is no plausible alternative to the capitalist status quo, it does not make much sense for workers to pursue their collective interests – and interests emerging at the individual, sectional or national level may override them. Indeed, there can be settlements that considerably improve the living standards of individual workers or groups of workers under conditions of capitalist class domination – in particular if capitalist strategies emerge that are based on increasing productivity or what Marx calls the production of relative surplus value. As a result, there are numerous reasons for workers to arrange themselves with the capitalist status quo even if this goes against their class interest.

In conclusion, Bukharin's conception of working-class formation is questionable, and much of the critique revolves around the fact that it is based on a deterministic, teleological narrative assuming that the three stages follow one after the other with iron necessity. This raises the question what an alternative conceptualization would look like.

The importance of class struggles

Luxemburg is a precursor of a theoretical-political project that I call 'Conjunctural Marxism', which emerged in the late 1960s and was shaped by Louis Althusser and Nicos Poulantzas (Gallas, 2017). I mention this line of thinking here because it is strictly anti-deterministic and anti-teleological: Revolutions are not the outcome of iron laws of history, but of conjunctures, that is, highly specific, situational articulations of contradictions (see Althusser, 1969: 178–9). Obviously, such articulations are also conditioned by deep structures such as the capitalist mode of production, in particular the fact that it is characterized by class antagonism and domination, and that it is crisis-prone. But it is also necessary to ask whether the conflict-inducing effects of these structures are blocked or activated through factors emerging in more specific spatio-temporal contexts.

This can be demonstrated with reference to Luxemburg's famous pamphlet on *The Mass Strike* (2008), in which she provides a nuanced account of the struggles of workers in the run-up to the first Russian Revolution in 1905 and draws out the strategic implications of the events for the labour movement in Germany and beyond. She highlights the general importance of capitalist class domination as a factor in creating situations of revolutionary rupture. In those conjunctures, workers experience 'the chains of capitalism' as being no longer tolerable (2008: 129).

Furthermore, Luxemburg suggests that the Russian working class became a revolutionary force in the run-up to the events in 1905 in confrontation with an absolutist state. According to her, things played out differently in the West because the state workers encountered was capitalist (Luxemburg,

2008: 162). This suggests that institutions specific to social formations matter – in this case, the institutions characteristic of capitalism in Russia in the early 20th century.

Finally, Luxemburg also discusses unpaid, 'compulsory holidays', which employers in St Petersburg imposed on workers on the occasion of the coronation of Tsar Nicholas II in May 1896 (2008: 121). This decision triggered a general strike in the city, whose historical significance lies in setting a precedent for a later wave of mass strikes across the country. It follows that situational factors located at the level of the conjuncture also matter greatly. Conjunctural factors can change all of a sudden, which is why labour unrest and revolutionary situations tend to occur unexpectedly. Accordingly, Kim Moody argues, with reference to Eric Hobsbawm, that there are 'explosive and usually unpredictable strike "waves" or "leaps"' or, in short, 'class "explosions"' (2017: 71, 174). And likewise, Althusser explains in a conjunctural manner how revolutionary situations emerge:

> If this contradiction [the class antagonism inherent in the capitalist relations of production] is to become 'active' in the strongest sense to become a ruptural principle, there must be an accumulation of 'circumstances' and 'currents' so that whatever their origin and sense … they 'fuse' into a ruptural unity: when they produce the result of the immense majority of the popular masses grouped in an assault on a regime which its ruling classes are unable to defend. (Althusser, 1969: 98)

If we take seriously the conjunctural nature of labour struggles, it follows that there is a degree of openness to history.

Importantly, a detailed theorization of working-class formation does not exist in the Conjunctural Marxist literature. Luxemburg also provides little in the way of class theoretical arguments, which is unsurprising given that her articles on labour struggles mostly focus on questions of political strategy. But she offers something else, namely, detailed descriptions of labour struggles using class terminology. In my view, these can count as descriptions of working-class formation even if they are not marked as such. Indeed, it is possible to close the gap in the literature with the help of Luxemburg's observations, which is what I will show in this section. This has the additional advantage of linking the two fields of scholarship that are discussed in this book – class theory and labour studies.

To address this gap in Conjunctural Marxism, I will present passages in Luxemburg's writings that are relevant from a class theoretical perspective – and compare them with Bukharin's observations. My aim is to show that her theoretical assumptions, argumentative patterns and empirical observations are distinctive, and that they can be used to sketch out a theory of working-class formation. Accordingly, I will not reconstruct, word for word, Luxemburg's lines of argument – in particular their political-strategic content. In keeping with the other chapters of the book, I will treat her writings in an irreverent and creative manner.

A useful starting point is a passage where Luxemburg describes the strikes in Russia in the run-up to the revolution:

> The general strikes of January and February broke out as unified revolutionary actions to begin with under the direction of the social democrats; but this action soon fell into an unending series of local, partial, economic strikes in separate districts, towns, departments, and factories. *This is a gigantic, many-colored picture of a general arrangement of labor and capital that reflects all the complexity of social organization and of the political consciousness of every section and of every district*; and the whole long scale runs from the regular trade-union struggle of a tried and tested troop of the proletariat drawn from large-scale industry to the formless protest of a handful of rural proletarians, to the first slight stirrings of an agitated military garrison; from the well-educated and elegant revolt in cuffs and white collars in the counting house of a bank to the shy-bold murmurings of a clumsy meeting of dissatisfied policemen in a smoke-grimed dark and dirty guardroom. (Luxemburg, 2008: 128; own emphasis)

In this passage, Luxemburg speaks of labour struggles of different types that culminate in 'almost the entire proletariat' moving collectively in the spring and summer of 1905. The struggles take on differentiated but connected forms, and what emerges is a general confrontation between labour and capital that is also discernible as such for the individuals involved in the struggles. This can be seen as an almost prototypical process of class formation.

At the same time, it is striking how strongly Luxemburg's account diverges from Bukharin's theorization. She moves against his narrative in five significant ways. The general gist is that it is wrong to assume that economic-technological development simply translates into working-class formation because the latter depends on institutional and, to a large degree, on conjunctural factors.

The most fundamental difference concerns the ways in which the two authors conceptualize the class struggle. For Bukharin, the class struggle only properly emerges once the working class has become a class-for-itself; confrontations between workers and capitalists taking place before this point are only embryonic or 'latent' forms (Bukharin, 2021: 342). The implication is that the class struggle has no role to play in class formation; the latter is a by-product of technological-economic development. Correspondingly, Bukharin is a committed determinist who denies the existence of a 'freedom of will' and of agency as a capacity of individual and collective actors to actively make history (2021: 48).

In contrast, Luxemburg uses expressions in her treatise such as 'the history of class struggle' (Luxemburg, 2008: 112), 'the present phase of the class struggle' (117), 'conditions of the class struggle' (118), 'the stages of development of the class struggle' (170) and 'the modern class struggle' (175). Her usage of the term suggests that class struggle is a constant occurrence in societies marked by class domination – and that it is a driver of history, which is entirely in line with the revolutionary position described by Althusser. In fact, Luxemburg's description of the struggles in 1905 quoted earlier shows that for her, class formation results from class struggle: The unity of labour visible in the 'uninterrupted strike of almost the entire proletariat against capital' is the outcome of the various confrontations of workers with capital that took place over the preceding months. The argumentative pattern at work here is that capitalist relations of production entail permanent class conflict, which is visible in the fact that labour struggles are ubiquitous in capitalist societies, and that class conflict is the driver of class formation. Workers make experiences in confrontations with capital that result in seeing connections between their situation and the situation of other workers; in other words, they undergo learning processes that help them to develop unity and collective strength. It follows that under conditions of polarization and confrontation, class struggle can produce inclusive solidarity along class lines.

The second difference concerns the factors facilitating class formation. In Bukharin's framework, it is technological-economic development that simplifies class relations and makes workers understand the nature of their oppression. For Luxemburg, this is different. Of course, working-class formation will not take place if there is no capitalist mode of production with its dynamic economic effects, most importantly capital accumulation. But capitalist development does not neatly translate into working-class formation. Luxemburg highlights, for example, how economic and political development can be out of sync with each other: Whereas the revolutions in the West resulted, first of all, in the emergence of novel liberal-constitutional political systems and, in a second step, in capitalist industrialization, the sequence was reversed in the Russian case. On the eve of the 1905 revolution, full-blown industrial capitalism already existed, but the political system was still absolutist (Luxemburg, 2008: 162). This also means that the conditions for working-class formation were markedly different in Russia: liberalism as a pro-capitalist political ideology was weak; this allowed organized labour to form as the leading collective actor at both the economic and political level with an oppositional, revolutionary agenda – despite the fact that the capitalist state had not developed yet. In other words, the working class was at the forefront of not just of the struggle against capital, but also against absolutism. It thus propelled forward a bourgeois revolution that resulted in the 'erection of a bourgeois-parliamentary constitutional state' (Luxemburg, 2008: 160).

Luxemburg's observations suggest that working-class formation is not a regular, evolutionary process with technological-economic development as its motor; much rather, it reflects specific articulations of economic and political processes of development and stagnation with distinct temporalities. Correspondingly, she argues that the institutional specificities of the capitalist social formation in Russia played a key role in facilitating working-class formation, in particular the presence of an absolutist state. Furthermore, conjunctural factors also matter greatly for class formation, which can be inferred from her account of the events in St Petersburg in 1896. The compulsory holidays imposed on workers fed into a general strike, which in turn paved the way for a long strike wave that culminated in a revolution. Put differently, a specific event triggered a process of working-class formation.

The difference between a deterministic-teleological and a conjunctural understanding of working-class formation is also visible when we look at the issue of geography and the question of the politicization of struggles. In Bukharin's framework, there is a clearly defined pattern: the transformation of a class-in-itself into a class-for-itself also entails the transformation of local, economic struggles (or labour struggles) into national, political struggles (or class struggles) and the simplification of the class structure into two camps. Again, Luxemburg's account is vastly different. Following her description of the Russian Revolution, there is no clearly defined direction of working-class formation because national struggles can disintegrate into localized struggles and political struggles can be transformed into economic struggles without interrupting the overall process. Following the earlier quote, class struggles move in both directions. Likewise, they do not entail a simplification of the class structure. In the Russian case, as is discussed in the quote, members of the Lumpenproletariat and milieus representing the middle classes joined forces with the working class in its struggle. Luxemburg suggests here that class struggle and the polarization it brings can cause, under certain circumstances, inclusive solidarity not just among workers safely located in the camp of labour, but even beyond that, presumably because a situation of confrontation and crisis makes new alignments possible. It follows that working-class formation can take place in the context of the emergence of a popular bloc based on alliances between working classes and other subaltern forces.

A third difference concerns the specific difference between the first and the second stage in Bukharin's framework. According to him, the key distinction between classes-in-themselves and classes-for-themselves is that while the latter possess class consciousness, the former do not. In other words, class consciousness is the medium through which class formation occurs. Again, Luxemburg's account of the Russian Revolution does not conform to Bukharin's script. The concept of class consciousness indicates that the awareness of the class character of capitalist societies is growing until there is a qualitative shift in its perception on the side of workers, which then leads them to embrace socialism as an alternative to capitalism and, in the end, to take revolutionary action. Luxemburg paints a very different picture: there are phases of spontaneity that are not marked, to a strong degree, by workers embracing a consistent worldview and phases of organized action where workers act on the grounds of socialist ideas. Importantly, both phases can contribute, in their different ways, to the expansion of class agency and thus to class formation. What matters is not so much a fixed worldview, but the 'class feeling' on the side of workers, that is, a sudden, intuitive understanding that capital and labour are two sides in struggle, and that capital is 'on top' in this struggle and can only be countered efficiently through collective action. Luxemburg describes 'class feeling' thus:

> The sudden general rising of the proletariat in January under the powerful impetus of the St. Petersburg events was outwardly a political act of the revolutionary declaration of war on absolutism. But this first general direct action reacted inwardly all the more powerfully as it for the first time awoke class feeling and class consciousness in millions upon millions as if by an electric shock. And this awakening of class feeling expressed itself forthwith in the circumstances that the proletarian mass, counted by millions, quite suddenly and sharply came to realize how intolerable was the social and economic existence that they had patiently endured for decades in the chains of capitalism. Thereupon, there began a spontaneous general shaking of and tugging at these chains. All the innumerable sufferings of the modern proletariat reminded them of the old bleeding wounds. (Luxemburg, 2008: 129)

Admittedly, Luxemburg here speaks both of 'class feeling' and 'class consciousness' and uses the two terms interchangeably. But against Bukharin and other deterministic-teleological accounts of class formation, I propose to stick to using the former term. In my view, it captures something that is specific about Luxemburg's observations: Class feeling is not an accumulation of experiences that results in a fixed, socialist worldview – as Bukharin describes class consciousness. Much rather, it emerges as a sudden reaction to shifted social conditions in which frustrations and indignation caused by one's working and living conditions crystallize in a political stance. This stance may be vague in terms of its political goal and justifications, but it is clear-cut in that it sees society as socially divided and rejects the domination of those 'above'. In this sense, class feeling is not a stable by-product of class struggle or capitalist development; it emerges when there are profound shifts at the level of the conjuncture. By implication, class feeling can also evaporate again when conditions change. Luxemburg's account is innovative insofar as she introduces a conjunctural concept when she refers to the ideational elements of class formation, which is in line with her description of the latter as a process that does not follow a clearly defined path. By speaking of a 'feeling', she highlights – in contrast to conceptions of class consciousness – that ideational representations of the social world build not just on ideas, but also on emotions. It follows that working–class political strategies need to be sensitive to the possibility that situations shift drastically in terms of people's preparedness to take action, and that they need to take into account that the latter is driven by emotional motivations.[4]

If the path of class formation is not predetermined, it can either be slow and gradual, or it can take place quite suddenly – and it can be halted and reversed. In other words, there are not just processes of class formation but also of class partition, which reflect changes in the conditions of struggle, active interventions of the other side or strategic and tactical choices of the movements representing the class-in-formation. If class formation consists in a process whereby workers increasingly act in concert and in line with their interests, class partition consists in a decrease in joint activity. It is a reflection of divisions that emerge between people similarly placed in the relations of production. Luxemburg's account of labour struggles in the early 20th century is fully compatible with Silver's view developed a century later. Silver captures the back-and-forth between class formation and class partition by speaking of a constant 'making', 'unmaking' and 'remaking' of classes (Silver, 2014: 49).[5]

The fourth difference emerges when we look more closely at Bukharin's assumption that there is an end goal of the process of class formation, which consists in a revolution instigated by the organizations of the working class against the rule of capital. His account is teleological insofar as there are laws in history that prescribe an outcome of historical development, which is socialism. In contrast, Luxemburg stresses class agency, that is, the capacity of class actors to actively make history. Accordingly, history is an open process

---

[4]   Building upon Lenin, Poulantzas describes a scenario which is also informed by this conjunctural understanding of popular worldviews: even if the working class adopts bourgeois ideas, its 'economic existence' is 'expressed in certain specific material politico-ideological practices which burst through its bourgeois "discourse": this is what Lenin designated, if very descriptively, as class instinct' (1974: 16–17).

[5]   Importantly, strikes of very privileged groups of workers can also lead to class partition, in particular if they disregard or even override the interests of other workers when they act together. Put differently, a strike can contribute to class partition if the action is not expandable beyond a core constituency of workers in a specific sector. In particular, this is the case if it is based on exclusive solidarity, that is, on a form of solidarity that only extends to a closed in-group and keeps other workers at a distance and even goes against their interests.

to her whose outcome cannot be predicted. This is visible in the following, famous statement, which she made during the First World War:

> Thus we stand today, as Friedrich Engels prophesied more than a generation ago, before the awful proposition: Either the triumph of imperialism and the destruction of all culture, and, as in ancient Rome, depopulation, desolation, degeneration, a vast cemetery; or, the victory of Socialism, that is, the conscious struggle of the international proletariat against imperialism, against its methods, against war. This is the dilemma of world history, its inevitable choice, whose scales are trembling in the balance, awaiting the decision of the proletariat. (Luxemburg, 2003: 18)

It is clear from this statement that there is no necessity for socialism at all; in fact, without what she calls here 'the conscious struggle of the international proletariat', and it making the right 'decision', there will be no socialism. This suggests that class formation consists in the expansion of class agency in an emphatic sense, that is, the capacity of workers to actively shape history through acting in concert and in line with their interests.

Importantly, Luxemburg's statement should not read as being voluntarist in the sense that the working class as a collective is acting without any constraints. She highlights that the conjuncture is characterized by the existence of a critical historical juncture with broadly two options, which is only possible if there are social conditions that somehow influence and narrow down the choices of class actors. This conception of history and of agency brings to mind Marx's dictum in the *18th Brumaire* (2006) that '[h]uman beings make their own history, but they do not make it as they please; they do not make it under self-selected circumstances, but under circumstances existing already, given and transmitted from the past' (Marx, 2006; translation amended). It follows that in Luxemburg's framework, class formation is the process whereby class agency is expanded, and class partition the process whereby it is constrained. This goes against deterministic-teleological views à la Bukharin and suggests that class agency – the capacity of people sharing class locations to act collectively and transform the social conditions under which they operate – develops in struggles. In this sense, her account of class formation is not oriented towards an end-goal, but towards process. What emerges is a position fundamentally different from Bukharin's (see Table 6.1).

What speaks for seeing class formation in a Luxemburgian fashion is that it addresses all five critical problems of Bukharin's conception. First of all, Bukharin assumes that the class structure will simplify through technological-economic development – an assumption that is not in line with empirical developments. If one embraces a process-oriented view of class formation, it is in no way necessary to defend this assumption. The same is true of the second problem, which I called the Jehovah's Witnesses fallacy. There is no

Table 6.1: Conceptions of working-class formation

	Bukharin	**Luxemburg**
Focus	End-goal	Process
Mode of development	Technological-economistic and evolutionist	Political-economic and conjunctural
Theory of history	Deterministic-teleological	Agency-centred
Political strategy	Vanguardist	Grassroots-oriented
Driver	Technological-economic development	Class struggle
Medium	Class consciousness	Class feeling
Sequence	Relations of production	Relations of production (class locations)
	↓	↓
	Class in itself	Class struggle (class feeling)
	↓	↓
	Technological-economic development (simplification of class structure/ economic conflicts)	Class formation/partition (expansion/restriction of class agency)
	↓	⋮
	Class consciousness	Revolutionary conjunctures
	↓	
	Class for itself	
	↓	
	Class struggle/political struggle (party/vanguard)	
	↓	
	Revolution	

need at all from a Luxemburgian standpoint to predict an end-goal of the process of class formation. Third, the Luxemburgian conception takes class partition seriously, which enables one to account for successful offensives of capital. Likewise, and fourth, it emphasizes the importance of spontaneous protests – and does not have buy into the principled privileging of organized class struggle that Bukharin stands for. Fifth, from a Luxemburgian standpoint, there are no iron laws of history. Socialism is a conjunctural possibility, not a historical necessity. All of this suggests that the Luxemburgian conception represents an important class theoretical advance over Bukharin's conception.

To highlight the conjunctural nature of class formation, I refrain from using Bukharin's distinction between 'class-in-itself' and 'class-for-itself' and the notion of 'class consciousness'. Obviously, terms can be used in different ways, and there may be attempts to interpret them in a non-deterministic and non-teleological manner. Nevertheless, due to invoking a progression from a first to a second stage and to being derived from Hegel, who had a deterministic-teleological understanding of dialectics as a progression of the spirit in historical stages, this manner of speaking lends itself to a Hegelian understanding (see Poulantzas, 1974: 16). Consequently, I use alternative terminology, namely 'class grouping', to refer to collectively shared class locations in the relations of production, 'class forces' to refer to collectives acting in concert along class lines and, in keeping with Luxemburg, 'class feeling' to refer to notions on the side of workers of togetherness and of facing the same opponents (see Poulantzas, 1974: 14, 17).

In conclusion, it becomes clear, with reference to Luxemburg, that the capitalist relations of production give rise to class struggles between representatives of the side of capital and representatives of the side of labour – and in this process, working-class agency can be expanded. In other words, struggles and strikes tend to contribute to working-class formation. There is a tendency for working-class formation inherent in the capitalist mode of production that consists in the unifying effects on workers of struggles emerging out of the capitalist organization of work.

From class groupings to class forces

In textbook interpretations, Marx is presented as having a simplistic conception of class. If there are capitalist relations of production, two classes will emerge, which are collective actors constituted of people sharing the same class location – a capitalist class acting and thinking about the world in line with the interests of capital, and a working class acting and think about the world in line with the interests of labour. In a nutshell, Marx is portrayed as a determinist who reads off collective agency from structures and assumes that there are only two classes (see Bruce, 1999: 63–4; Browne, 2011: 404).

With reference to Luxemburg's account of the Russian Revolution of 1905, I object to this understanding of class. There is a lack of historical evidence for this being the standard configuration of class in capitalism. There may be conjunctures in which it works as a rough guideline for making sense of class relations – and this in particular applies to the industrialized parts of Western Europe in the late 19th and early 20th century, where there were strong, proletarian labour movements organized in trade unions and mass parties with hundred thousands of members plus well-integrated networks of capitalists. But frequently, it has been difficult, in the history of capitalism, to identify the working class in particular as a clearly demarcated, collective actor (see Hobsbawm, 1984: 182; Gallas, 2019). As I have discussed in the last chapter, this reflects the workings of the capitalist state. Indeed, the existing alliances, settlements and processes of fragmentation create a rather messy picture, at least at first sight.

At the same time, and this is why I strongly defend materialist class theory against its detractors, capitalist social formations in all their variety are marked by disputes around work. It makes sense to describe them as class struggles because they tend to concern the extraction of surplus labour; control over the work process and expertise – as well as social hierarchies that can be understood as forms of class domination. What is needed, then, is an anti-deterministic conception of structural determination. In my view, this is offered by critical realism as an ontology that emphasizes how deep structures determine the social world through exhibiting tendencies, which are overdetermined by other tendencies and can remain inactivated thanks to countertendencies, institutions and conjunctural events.

In my view, the concept of 'class formation' is particularly useful in this context. I follow E.P. Thompson here, who highlights that class formation takes place in processes of class struggle:

> [T]he notion of class entails the notion of a historical relationship. ...
> And class happens when some men, as a result of common experiences
> ... feel and articulate the identity of their interests as between
> themselves, and as against other men whose interests are different
> from (and usually opposed to) theirs. The class experience is largely
> determined by the productive relations into which men are born – or
> enter involuntarily. (Thompson, 1968: 8–9)

Readers well-versed in the ins and outs of postwar Western Marxism may be surprised that I quote a staunch critic of Poulantzas in this Poulantzasian tract. But in my view, this definition is entirely compatible with the Poulantzasian conception of class presented in the preceding chapter. Indeed, it may have been to the lasting detriment of materialist class theory that neither Poulantzas nor Thompson seem to have been particularly interested in a dialogue (see Poulantzas, 1967; Thompson, 1978). They might have discovered some common ground.

The Thompsonian and Poulantzasian views of class formation refer to conflicts over work through which, over time and in delimited spaces, classes as collective actors emerge, that is, as actors sharing certain patterns of action and worldviews. In my terms, class formation refers to processes whereby class forces emerge that possess collective agency. There is, under conditions of the dominance of the capitalist mode of production, a class structure containing two class locations. This means that there is a tendency for the formation of class forces in the form of power blocs as well as working-class forces. I do not claim that the emergence of collective actors along class lines is an unavoidable necessity.

Importantly, this anti-deterministic understanding of class determination is fully compatible with Marx's line of argument in *Capital*. Against textbook interpretations, he highlights the weight of competition, which affects both the capital and labour and leads to fragmentation and disunity, at least at an initial stage, on both sides. The competitive pressures faced by capitalists go as far as threatening their economic existence, and there are competition-induced races-to-the-bottom among workers that affect the condition of the extraction of surplus labour (1976: 462, 546–7, 558, 601, 697, 789; 1981: 353). If we take competition seriously, neither the side of capital nor the side of labour can be assumed to automatically reach a state of unity (see Poulantzas, 1974: 60; Erd and Scherrer, 1985: 117). At the same time, Marx also points out, with reference to concrete conjunctures, how class conflict facilitates the unification of class forces. In chapter 27 of *Capital* volume 1, he relays how the 'glorious Revolution' in late 17th-century England, which was directed against parts of the aristocracy and a king seen as ruling against parliament, allowed 'the landed and capitalist profit-grubbers' to take power (Marx, 1976: 884). This can be seen, with a reference to Poulantzasian terminology, as the emergence of a power bloc (see Gallas, 2008). Likewise, in chapter 10, he discusses how a 'working-class movement on both sides of the Atlantic, which had grown instinctively out of the relations of production' emerges through workers fighting for a legal regulation of the working day (Marx, 1976: 415). It follows that the processes of the unification of individuals into class forces needs to be explained – and this can only be done with reference to historical and geographical circumstances that are specific to a social formation and conjuncture.

Against this backdrop, the question emerges how the class effects of the state play out in real time and real spaces – or how class forces emerge out of class groupings. The distinction between the 'capitalist mode of production' and 'capitalist social formations' is useful for discussing this question. Following Poulantzas, we need to distinguish two different levels of abstraction in our conceptualization of class. First, there are the 'structural determination of classes' containing class locations at the level of the mode of production, which reflect the nature of the capitalist relations of production. Speaking in critical realist terms, this is the deep structure of capitalism, which serves as the foundation of the class theoretical argument put forward here. But second, there is also a variety of 'class positions' or, in my terms, class forces (Poulantzas, 1974: 15). In contrast to the class groupings at the level of the deep structure, these are visible collective actors in a given conjuncture of a social formation. It follows that class locations at the level of the mode of production condition processes of class formation at the level of conjuncture (of a social formation). Class struggles trigger processes of class formation, which solidify into class forces. And these feed back into the class struggle, in which the forces can become liquefied again.

Correspondingly, class forces do not neatly reflect the structural determinations. Otherwise, there would be no need to distinguish the two levels at all. The claim of materialist class theory is not that the structural determinations or class locations are simply mirrored by class forces, as textbook interpretations of Marx have it. Much rather, structural determinations produce a specific field of conflict and hierarchy conditioning the formation of class forces, which takes place in real time and in real places. Put differently, there are constant struggles between capital and labour, in which more stable forces tend to emerge. If we speak of 'class formation', we can think of capitalists and workers starting to build associations and alliances in the process and developing collective agency. Due to the diverging effects of the existence of the capitalist state on the two sides and the vast differences in the access to material and ideational resources, this tends to be a lot easier for the former than the latter. Whereas the side of capital tends to display a degree of unity, the side of labour tends to be characterized by divisions. Working-class formation is always an uphill battle, and the working class, as a unified entity, does not exist. As long as capitalism prevails, workers will be divided to a degree, but these divisions change over time and diverge considerably depending on conditions at the level of the social formation and the conjuncture.

Accordingly, there are conjunctures in which the reproduction of class relations is characterized by deepening splits and an erosion of class agency. With reference to such processes, I propose to speak of 'class partition'. The splits are usually on the side of workers – the limits to access in resources make it harder to cut out competition among them, and while some workers may rally around a cause, others may refrain from doing so because they want to hold their head below the parapet or believe in finding individual arrangements that preserve the status quo. But they can also emerge on the side of capital, in particular in situations where there are disagreements over whether to take a hard line or seek accommodation with workers. Even more importantly, there are situations of deep crisis, where it may be difficult for capitalists to find a clear line. The rhythms and patterns of class struggle vary, which also means that class forces can emerge and disappear again over time.

Poulantzas summarizes the class effects of the existence of the capitalist state at the level of the mode of production on capitalist social formation thus:

> The articulation of the structural determination of classes and of class positions within a social formation, the locus of existence of conjunctures, requires particular concepts. I shall call these *concepts of strategy*, embracing in particular such phenomena as class polarization and class alliance. Among these, on the side of the dominant classes,

is the concept of 'power bloc', designating a specific alliance of classes and fractions; also on the side of the dominated classes, the concept of the 'people', designating a specific alliance of these classes and fractions. These concepts are not of the same status as those with which we have dealt up until now: whether a class, fraction or stratum forms part of the power bloc, or part of the people, will depend on the social formation, its stages, phases and conjunctures. (Poulantzas, 1974: 24; emphasis in the original)

The antagonism between capitalists and workers as class groups at the level of the mode of production translates into the relationship between a power bloc and the people (or an ensemble of popular forces) at the level of the social formation. The working class, if it exists in the singular at this level, is a mosaic of working-class forces that form part of this ensemble and can give it strategic direction (see Urban, 2009). Due to the divisive mechanisms inherent in the mode of production and the capitalist state, it is often the case that the picture created by this mosaic is pretty fuzzy, and in some conjunctures there is not much to see. Accordingly, the configuration of class forces at the level of the social formation can take on a huge variety of forms depending on alliances and ruptures specific to the formation and to conjunctures within the formation, but there are always sites of class conflict and struggle. We arrive at a conjunctural understanding of class, where class formation is conditioned by the mode of production, but is also dependent on the institution of the social formation and factors specific to the conjuncture. It follows that the working class is a collective project and aspiration, which is in the process of being made, unmade and remade as long as the capitalist mode of production continues to exist.

Adsorption: contradictory class locations and working-class formation

What further complicates the pictures is that in the capitalist mode of production, as I have argued with reference to academics in Chapter 2, there is space for 'contradictory locations within class relations' (Wright, 1978b: 74). It is easy to identify groups of people working in a capitalist environment who do not neatly fit on either side of the capital–labour divide. This does not just concern plumbers, shopkeepers, psychotherapists or graphic designers who run their own businesses but do not have employees. Executive managers, for example, exercise control over the work process and orchestrate processes of planning and conceptualization, which allows them to claim expertise. But unless they are owner-managers, their relationship to the means of production is somewhat opaque because they are employed. Similarly, engineers, supervisors and foremen and -women are wage-dependent, but usually have a considerably higher degree of control over the means of production than unskilled workers. Furthermore, they are usually able to present themselves as people possessing a specific form of expertise. All these groups defy a neat categorization in terms of their class location because it is hard to say which side they belong to based on my three criteria – the regime of ownership, the division of tasks and the order of knowledge. This is relevant for the question of working-class formation – not least because some of the workers in contradictory locations do indeed organize and mobilize around their work and are very active strikers, and others do not. In abstract terms, it can be said that those workers are arranged, depending on factors specific to the social formation and the conjuncture, in different distances and proximities to the antagonism between capital and labour (see Poulantzas, 1974: 23).

Engineers, for example, usually do not own the means of production, but they exercise a degree of control over their own work, and they are involved with conceptual work. This means that they tick one out of three boxes belonging to the side of labour, and two belonging to capital. In other words, there are two mechanisms that drag engineers towards capital (control over the work process and expertise) and one that pushes them towards labour (wage dependency). In many workplaces, they may closely collude with management. But there are also cases of workplaces where engineers are heavily unionized, and where they have been going on strike (see Edwards, 1982; Imberman, 2001). The more likely scenario is that engineers are on the side of capital or that they chose to sit on the fence. In the end, institutional and conjunctural factors determine whether they are on side, and which one it is.

Institutional factors could be the system of labour relations, the presence or absence of a union that caters to engineers, and its affiliation or distance to unions umbrellas that have a broad working-class base. The existence of a union that is institutionally linked to other unions representing workers with a consistent class location tends to facilitate inclusive solidarity and working-class formation. If it does not exist, inclusive solidarity is much harder to achieve because there are institutional obstacles that need to be overcome – either through other institutional factors that cancel out those obstacles, for example the existence of civil society networks that create links between engineers and other workers, or through conjunctural factors. Examples of the latter can be found in the cited case studies of strikes of engineers. The latter show that inclusive solidarity can result from the failure of management to recognize the strong identification of engineers with their work and their unwillingness to accept managerial control. Last but not least, it may also be the case that there are strong professional networks leading workers in contradictory locations to adopt conceptions of their own position in society that highlight their difference to both labour and capital. For many professions, there are associations fostering such occupational identities.

If uni-directional tendencies for class formation arise out of consistent class locations, it follows that multi-directional tendencies emerge in the case of contradictory locations. People finding themselves in contradictory locations are subjugated by certain aspects of class domination and benefit from others. Consequently, they are not subject to a single tendency that pulls in a certain direction but may be blocked thanks to divisive mechanisms, institutions or conjunctural factor in the class struggles; they are subject to tendencies pulling them in two different directions. Depending on circumstances at the level of the social formation and the conjuncture, they can either remain in a state of division or become part of a class force – and this class force can either be on one side of the class antagonism or operate at a certain distance to it. In particular if there is a polarization between capital and labour, it is likely that forces arising out of contradictory class locations are pulled onto a side (see Goes, 2019: 149).

It follows that there is a possibility of the adsorption of forces emerging out of contradictory class locations into working-class networks and vice versa. The term 'adsorption' refers to the adhesion of a gaseous or liquid molecules to a surface of a solid body. It can be contrasted with 'absorption', where the molecules enter the body (Encyclopaedia Britannica, 2013). I use the term to refer to processes where forces emerging out of one distinct class location are integrated into class forces representing another. I use adsorption, not absorption, to highlight the fact that the integration of these forces tends to be more fragile than the integration of forces arising out of the same location. After all, the access to material and ideational resources and the immediate interests of the adsorbing and the adsorbed forces diverge. Consequently, it is likely that conjunctural shifts, in particular crises, result in the emergence of tensions and ruptures. If follows that class forces, over time, are adsorbed, released and re-adsorbed (see Poulantzas, 1974: 15–16, Goes, 2019: 140). In fact, it is possible that adsorbing and adsorbed forces trade places if circumstances change. In cases where the power bloc drags other class forces to its side, I speak of co-optation. In so doing, I highlight the fact that subaltern forces tend to remain in subaltern positions vis-à-vis the power bloc even if they cooperate closely with business leaders and governments.

Importantly, Luxemburg reminds us that there is a connection between strikes and processes of adsorption. Her example is the wave of strikes in the run-up to the 1905 Russian Revolution. These involved, according to her, 'the entire proletariat', which consisted not just of factory workers, but also of 'bourgeois and liberal professions, commercial employees, technicians, actors, and members of artistic professions' as well as 'the domestic servants, the minor police officials, and even … the stratum of the lumpenproletariat' (Luxemburg, 2008: 128). This suggests that workers from contradictory class locations were adsorbed into the working-class network behind the revolution. More recent examples include the waves of strikes and student protests that occurred in the late 1960s and early 1970s in many countries; the general strikes against austerity in Western Europe in the early 2010s, which involved public sector professionals; the *estallido social* [social outburst] in Chile in 2019 and 2020, a series of protests against inequality and neoliberalism that included a general strike; and the feminist strikes taking place around the globe since the mid-2010s (see Volume 2, Chapter 8).

In conclusion, researchers in the field of class analysis carry a burden of proof: They need to show empirically how the tendencies for class formation at the level of the mode of production are activated or obstructed. The conceptualization of class at the level of the mode of production identifies basic tendencies concerning class formation. But there can be countertendencies, that is, mechanisms and events obstructing them at the level of the mode of production, the social formation or the conjuncture. In a nutshell, the working class is a collective actor-in-emergence. It consists of an ensemble of forces that are usually located on the side of labour. And to some degree, it can also adsorb associations emerging out of contradictory class locations.

Between Representation and Intermediation: The Double Character of Workers' Mass Organizations

The institutionalization of class struggle

Luxemburg shows how class struggles act as a catalyst of class formation. She highlights the importance of often localized and sectoral labour struggles and argues that they became interlinked in the revolutionary conjuncture of Russia in 1906. According to her, these struggles can be both spontaneous and the result of the strategic calculations and tactical considerations of mass organizations, and the latter can be revitalized through their involvement in struggles (Luxemburg, 2008: 128, 135). This suggests that there is a specific strategic role for mass organizations in facilitating advances of labour, which raises the question of how they advance or block processes of working-class formation.

As I have argued in Chapter 5, there is a tendential separation of economic, political and cultural class struggles in capitalism, which has a stabilizing effect on capitalist class domination. Connected to this separation is the official recognition of class struggle, that is, its legalization and institutionalization. In a broad understanding, any activity with direct, unidirectional class effects can be seen as constituting an instance of class struggle. But if a capitalist state under the rule of law exists, 'official' procedures of the class struggle tend to emerge. These are legally enshrined mechanisms that institutionalize collective action. They invite negotiations between capitalists and workers over the distribution of material and ideational resources and the organization of society, whose outcomes are relevant for the class relations of forces.

There are three sets of mechanisms that are particularly important in this context: the regulations surrounding labour disputes (economic dimension); political procedures that create binding decisions concerning the way society is run (political dimension); and the rules and conventions sustaining public fora in which battles over imaginaries and ideas take place (cultural dimension) (Table 5.6; see also Althusser, 1969: 96; Poulantzas, 1974: 15; Esser, 1982: 232–5). Historically, these mechanisms emerged as a result of class struggles that had not yet been channelled. They are based on settlements between capital and labour where the acceptance of the rule of law and the existing order is traded for the legal recognition of mass organizations of the working class (see Althusser, 1969: 95). Marx demonstrated this in the first volume of *Capital* (1976) with reference to the successful struggles of workers over the legal limitation of the working day in mid-19th-century England (Marx, 1976: 340–416). On the one hand, the emergence of legal regulations often protected the organizations of workers; on the other hand, they tended to decelerate the dynamics of workers' struggle and to render them predictable and manageable for capital, at least to a degree (Kelly, 1988: 77). This suggests that class struggles *both* stabilized the capitalist mode of production and forced capital to accept that workers had a collective voice.

Importantly, this is not meant to suggest that every instance of collective action is necessarily an 'official' form of class struggle (see Esser, 1982: 242–3). The point is that norms and rules emerge that determine what are portrayed, by societal forces in favour of the status quo, as 'legitimate' ways of rallying around class interests. This affects significantly what kind of patterns of collective activity emerge. There tends to be a need for people to justify themselves if they operate outside the 'official' forms – and this need can be stronger or weaker depending on how stable the institutions in question are. If union density in a sector is low, it may be seen as less of a problem if workers bypass existing unions and set up rank-and-file networks instead; if the reverse is the case, their activities are usually seen as a form of inter-union competition and possibly as a threat by those representing the official organizations, which is why their activities become loaded through the context in which they take place.

In the economic domain, 'legitimate' activities emerge where organized labour and organized capital encounter each other as collective entities, most importantly the activities and procedures surrounding collective bargaining (see Esser, 1982: 228–33; Kelly, 1988: 183). These are usually conducted by unions on the side of labour and employers or employers' associations on the side of capital. Legally, collective bargaining tends to be enshrined through provisions guaranteeing 'freedom of association' – for example, through Article 11 of the European Convention of Human Rights. Under conditions of a capitalist democracy, going on strike is usually considered a legitimate part of the collective bargaining process – as long as certain rules are observed.[1]

---

[1] For example, the German Federal Labour Court observed in 1980 that 'collective bargaining without the right to strike would be, in general, not more than "collective begging"' (Bundesarbeitsgericht, 1980: 11).

This institutionalization tends to render the trajectory and outcomes of labour disputes predictable and, from the standpoint of power blocs, manageable. There is a 'ritualistic' aspect of confrontations between capital and labour (Hyman, 1989: 83), which reflects the existence of clear-cut rules and expectations that guide interactions between the two sides. Examples are union recognition and balloting procedures or 'peace obligations' and 'cooling off' periods when workers are not allowed to go on strike legally. Indeed, the German language contains the term *Tarifritual*. It can be translated loosely as 'collective bargaining ritual'.

The claim that collective bargaining is an instance of class struggle comes with the important caveat that not every single activity of a trade union can be seen as being in favour of working-class interests. Some unions pursue sectionalist strategies that go against the interests of other groups of workers, and in some cases, union officials seek personal or organizational favours through colluding with management (Kelly, 1988: 77, 136). In line with my critique of the PRA, processes of collective bargaining have to be assessed in terms of their effects on class relations of forces before they can be identified as instances of class struggle.

Importantly, institutionalization is never complete, which reflects the unstable, crisis-prone nature of social relations in capitalism (see Hirsch, 1994: 175). The encounters between capital and labour at the economic level can take on collective but more spontaneous forms that emerge outside institutionalized labour relations. Businesses may choose to operate outside employers' associations and not coordinate their strategy vis-à-vis labour with their competitors; workers may resort to wildcat strikes and forms of rank-and-file networks that are rather loose. Nevertheless, institutionalization matters because it creates a point of reference for any kind of activity in the particular domain. The strategic significance of wildcat strikes can be assessed only if it is considered what 'regular' labour relations are.

In the political domain, the picture is more blurred because the class effects of political processes are more opaque. If we take one of the pertinent political issues in Western Europe in recent years, Brexit, it is far from clear what its implications are for workers. There is the argument that Britain leaving the EU has amounted to an onslaught on workers' rights because some of them are enshrined in EU law. A counterargument is that a socialist government project in Britain is only possible if the country is no longer bound by EU law because the latter prevents far-reaching interventions in property relations and the nationalization of key industries.[2]

---

[2] On the different scenarios of how Brexit is going to play out for workers, see Gumbrell-McCormick and Hyman (2017) and Teague and Donaghey (2018).

Similarly, the effects on workers of mandatory vaccination against COVID-19 either for certain sectors or for everyone, which has been implemented in various countries around the globe to combat the pandemic, are controversial.

There are, however, political conflicts whose class relevance is obvious. Against union protests, the Austrian government decided in 2018 to raise the legal limitation of the working week to up to 60 hours – an intervention that altered the conditions of the production of absolute surplus value in the country. Likewise, the Modi government in India has been working, in recent years, to streamline and liberalize labour law, to which trade unions have responded with protests and mass strikes (see DW, 2018; Gallas, 2020: 182–3, 196). Such disputes about the organization of society with direct class effects can be seen as political class struggles. Both government projects or protests by the parliamentary opposition or extra-parliamentary force can form part of them. Again, institutionalization is far from complete, but it establishes norms that affect how those disputes play out (see Althusser, 1969: 96; Esser, 1982: 232–3).

In the cultural domain, things are also less clear-cut than in the economy. Arguably – and reflecting the effect of isolation – civil society is even more fragmented in class terms than the economy and the political sphere. Here, class struggle is about the production and reproduction of class-relevant ideas and imaginaries, that is, collective practices laden with meanings that concern people's places in the world, for example, the attendance of an elite university or the support for a local football club in an industrial area. The resulting imaginaries do not just facilitate the formation of economic and political mass organizations that mobilize people along class lines, most importantly trade unions and workers' parties (see Althusser, 1969: 95). They also contribute to the emergence of networks in civil society, for example, religious organizations or clubs and associations dedicated to community issues. Consequently, the mass organizations reflecting the three dimension of the social world diverge considerably – both in terms of their main activities and their primary field of operation (see Table 7.1).

Importantly, none of this meant to say that class struggles necessarily take on a legal and institutionalized form, and that they do not potentially pose a threat to capitalist class domination. My point is that the emergence of legal forms of the class struggle creates strong incentives for workers to adopt them, and that considerations of legality and legitimacy at the level of collective practices of workers reflect selectivities inherent in the capitalist state favouring the reproduction of capitalist class domination (Esser, 1982: 229). Put differently, the claim that the legal recognition of organized labour contributed to the stabilization of capitalism should not be taken to imply the complete integration of the working class into the capitalist mode of production, as has been claimed, among others, by Moishe

Table 7.1: Institutionalized avenues of the class struggle

Dimension	Mass organisation	Legally enshrined mechanism	Official procedures
Economic	Trade unions	Regulations surrounding unions and labour disputes	Collective bargaining (including strikes)
Political	Workers' parties and social movements	Procedures of political decision-making	Parliamentary and extra-parliamentary negotiations over the organization of society
Cultural	Civil society networks of clubs, media and intellectuals	Rules and conventions concerning civil society	Battles over ideas and imaginaries

Postone (1993: 314–24).[3] In line with my critical realist ontology, I contend that the integration is tendential and – thanks to the antagonistic nature of the capitalist mode of production – never complete.

Conversely, there are conjunctures in which a genuine rupture with capitalist class domination becomes a historical possibility. This happens when mass mobilizations take place, in the context of an economic, political and cultural crisis, that activate, align and heighten contradictions emerging out of the mode of production in a way that poses a threat to the control of the power bloc over the social formation (see Althusser, 1969: 95–101). Mass mobilizations of this type usually involve a broad coalition of forces that manages to overcome the tendential separation of struggles and the latter's containment in a specific domain, as Luxemburg observed with reference to Russia. Historical examples of conjunctures of mass mobilization and labour unrest in capitalist centres where a revolutionary rupture seemed possible are the 1926 General Strike in Britain or May 1968 in France.

Trade unions between class organization and mass integration

In the context of this book, unions deserve specific attention because they are the most important organizational body addressing the economic conditions of wage workers in the capitalist centres. They represent the standard form, in the economic domain, in which class agency tends to get stabilized and institutionalized. This happens thanks to the official recognition of workers'

---

[3] For a more detailed critique of Postone's line of argument, see Gallas (2006; 2011).

coalitions through state authorities. But there is an important twist: Due to state regulation, class agency tends to get modified in the process of union recognition insofar as it produces predictable and manageable outcomes that are not threatening to class domination (see Esser, 1982: 228–32; Kelly, 1988: 293). Indeed, Hyman argues that this is where the 'central paradox of trade unionism' lies (Hyman, 1989: 40). On the one hand, union recognition amounts to a victory for workers because it enables them to legally contest some of conditions under which surplus labour is extracted, most importantly wages and working times; on the other hand, it also plays into the hands of capital because it tends to fortify the status quo in the sense of creating general acceptance of capitalist class domination.

The first thing to note is that trade unions are located primarily in the economy. They represent coalitions of workers aiming to suppress competition among themselves (see Poulantzas, 1968: 275; Erd and Scherrer, 1985: 117; Hyman, 1989: 38). This strengthens their hands in negotiations with capitalists (see Erd and Scherrer, 1985: 117; Lüthje and Scherrer, 2003: 105; Hürtgen, 2018a: 248). Accordingly, the primary task of unions is to conduct processes of collective bargaining on behalf of their members. In so doing, they can counterbalance, to a degree, the dominance of capital over the work process and the labour market. Accordingly, an incentive exists for unions to work along class lines (Esser, 1982: 228). The broader the constituency of organized labour, the easier it is to cut out competition among workers. In principle, the capitalist relations of production invite inclusive solidarity, that is, forms of solidarity that do not operate on the grounds of creating clearly demarcated in-groups and out-groups. This is visible in the existence of general unions, union federations and union internationals.

And yet, there are four countertendencies, which pose obstacles to class organization. First, if competition between workers is fierce and deeply engrained in their subjectivities, it may be difficult for unions to overcome it. There can be situations where individual workers may find it more plausible to fend for themselves – because they are resigned to the fact that it will not be possible to build strong solidarity, because they are worried that joining forces with other workers may lead to retributive action from the side of management, because they do not plan to stay in their job for long, or because they believe in meritocracy and individual advancement.

Second, collective bargaining over wages and conditions often takes on the format of negotiating on the ground of 'fair comparisons' (Hyman, 1989: 27). This Hymanian term refers to the fact that certain groups of workers make claims by saying that they deserve more than other groups. Obviously, such an approach does not preclude and can even encourage other groups of workers to make equally forceful demands, which means that 'fair comparisons' can, in principle, lead to shifts in the class relations of forces in favour of labour. But if workers construe their grievances solely on the grounds of comparisons with other workers, mobilizations along class lines are obstructed.

Third, some unions opt for strategies against this backdrop that are based on exclusive rather than inclusive solidarity, that is, on representing a clearly demarcated constituency and keeping everyone else out. There are unions with strong sectional and occupational identities or with a business orientation (Hyman, 2001: 6–16; Schroeder and Greef, 2014). They may exploit the fact that they represent workers employed by firms earning extra-profits, which allows them to fight for getting an additional share of the labour product not available to other workers. Or they may use the fact that they operate in 'closed' sectors or occupations with high entry thresholds to their advantage and reduce competition by marginalizing outsiders. Divides between workers may reflect informal personal networks or differences in skills or qualifications. But in many cases, they are also the product of racism, patriarchy or other forms of social domination (see Weischer, 1988: 126). Importantly, there are countless configurations in which forms of inclusive and exclusive solidarity get mixed up in the day-to-day practices of trade unions (see Hyman, 1975: 41).

Fourth, there are situations where union leaders collude with management to such a degree that they can no longer be said to be representing the interests of workers. In some cases, this may be the result of outright corruption. But personal ties, a lack of internal democracy, networks of cooperation with business and an interest in protecting the union as an organization can also play a role (Kelly, 1988: 160–78).[4]

All of this suggests that even if there is a strong tendency for unions to operate along class lines, not all unions act as class organization all of the time. Consequently, union activities cannot be equated with being instances of the exercise of working class power per se, as the PRA suggests. They need to be contextualized in a broader analysis of class relations to identify their class effects.

In addition, it needs to be considered that the capitalist state contains a range of selectivities that tend to circumscribe the activities of unions. They create obstacles to advancing working-class interests beyond the realm of the economy and limit what are considered legitimate interventions by unions. Most importantly, capitalist relations of production entail the existence of a legal system, which enshrines the principle of private property

---

[4] In the German system of co-determination, for example, works councillors, who are elected by everyone working in a given business unit (including people who are not union members), are obliged by law to cooperate with management. At the same time, the main German unions see works councils as an important space for their activities (Dribbusch and Birke, 2012: 11). This means that many union activists are also works councillors who on occasion have to collaborate with management.

in a constitution and legitimizes a monopoly of violence to protect it. In so doing, it lays the foundation of the repressive state apparatus, which is tasked with defending private property – and this, of course, includes private property in means of production and the sale and purchase of labour power (see Poulantzas, 1978: 39, 81). Accordingly, there are clearly demarcated lines that workers cannot overstep when they act together. They cannot take control of the work process without encroaching on the capitalists' 'right to manage', which results from the latter's ownership of the means of production and the workers' labour power. Correspondingly, trade union law in the capitalist centres prescribes a range of conditions that have to be met before workers can go on strike legally – for instance, union recognition and balloting procedures or strike bans imposing mandatory 'cooling off' periods, 'protecting' specific sectors or affecting specific types of stoppages such as solidarity strikes or political strikes (see Renneberg, 2014: 174–7).

Furthermore, the existence of a separate political scene based on representative democracy works to delegitimize the general political activity of unions, in particular if instruments are used that are seen as belonging in the realm of 'labour disputes'. In other words, if unions go on strike for political goals, they run the risk of being criticized for acting in an undemocratic manner. This is despite the fact that there is a range of channels used by corporations to influence the political process and the outcomes of political decision-making (see Abendroth, 1954: 59; Hensche, 2012: 221–2).

Finally, the mode of production contains a mechanism, the production of relative surplus value, that invites class compromises around the creation of productivist cycles. Combined with the selectivities at the level of the state, this creates a strong incentive for unions to come to settlements with capital. These consist in trading general acceptance of the capitalist social order (including capitalist class domination and the 'right to manage') for union recognition and the right of unions to bargain on behalf of their members.

It follows that there is a 'double character of trade unions' (Müller-Jentsch, 1981; 2003: 654; see also Hürtgen, 2018b), which means that unions operating under capitalist conditions tend to play two different roles at the same time: On the one hand, their leaderships are incentivized to adopt strategies that stabilize capitalist class domination. Under conditions of stable capital accumulation and entrenched class domination, these strategies tend to carry far less of a risk to both the organization and individual union members than revolutionary adventures. On the other hand, unions are still accountable to their members; rank-and-file experiences of class antagonism and domination tend to feed into the choices of their leaders, and there may be conjunctures – in particular if there are crises – in which these inform union strategies to a stronger degree than the incentives to opt for stabilization. It follows that the double role for unions consists in them operating as 'intermediary organisations' between civil society and the state

(Esser, 1982: 244). They are 'class organisations facilitating the pursuit of the economic interests of wage dependent people' (Esser, 1982: 228), but also instances of 'mass integration' that channel class conflict by operating through what are seen as legitimate and legal forms of negotiating with capital. In this sense, they represent the interests of labour but are also forced to mediate them with those of capital (Esser, 1982: 245). It follows that trade union officials tend to act both as 'class warriors' and 'managers of discontent' (Mills, 1948, cited in Hyman, 1989: 40).

Trade unions and strikes

Reflecting the double character of unions, their activities vis-à-vis employers can be seen as both exercises of working-class power and practices that render worker discontent manageable. In many cases, the two sides coexist; they cannot be separated out neatly. What can be said is that the repertoire of action available to unions is a continuum between persuasion and force, whose components can be used in different combinations. Union activities range from campaigning, negotiations and peaceful demonstrations on the side of persuasion to boycotts, overtime bans, go-slows, strikes, occupations of workplaces and riots on the side of force (see Gall, 2014: 210–29). Social partnership approaches are based primarily, but not exclusively, on forms of persuasion; in contrast, militant trade unionism is primarily but not exclusively focused on the mobilization of force (see Cohen, 2006; Dribbusch and Birke, 2012: 13).

Importantly, the divide between class struggle and the management of discontent is not congruent with the divide between persuasion and force. Unions may use limited, symbolic stoppages as a 'safety valve' (Closer, 1956; cited in Costa and Dias, 2016: 145), that is, an activity allowing workers to let off 'steam'. There have been claims (Philipps, 2011; Karyoti, 2012: 168), for example, that the string of one- or two-day general strikes against austerity in Greece that occurred in the wake of the Eurozone crisis from 2010 prevented more forceful action from workers, namely, open-ended strikes. Conversely, there are many instances of unions negotiating improvements for workers without resorting to open force, for instance the successful, union-supported campaign in Germany that led to the introduction of a statutory minimum wage in 2015 (Nowak, 2015: 366–71). And what also has to be considered is that the dynamic of strikes can change. It may be the case that the polarization brought by a 'safety valve' strike turns it into an instance of working-class resistance – or the other way round (see Fantasia, 1988: 187–8). In other words, it would be wrong to assume that strikes are, in each and every case, instances of the exercise of working-class power, but the reverse also holds true. It follows that it needs to be assessed empirically what the class effects of individual strikes are.

At the same time, strikes are still 'the most important of trade union form of struggle' (Müller-Jentsch, 2001: 732; see Hürtgen, 2018a: 249). One can argue that stoppages tend to be more costly to employers than other forms of forceful action because they aim at fully halting economic processes and thus hit employers particularly hard,[5] and that they differ from other activities because of the magnitude of the disruption that they can cause – not just in economic terms, but also in politics and everyday life. Consequently, strikes, more than other forms of action, shape labour relations, class formation and, by implication, class relations, which is why they are the focus of this book.

Importantly, unions do not have a monopoly on conducting strikes. Indeed, it is also the case that civil society networks resort to the strike as a means of protest.[6] And admittedly, union density has been dwindling across the globe in recent decades – and in some cases quite dramatically (van der Linden, 2016: 202). But in many countries that are hubs of global capitalism, unions still have thousands, and in some cases, millions of members, which is why they represent the main mass organization of workers.[7] Next to their mass base, unions also have at their disposal considerable material resources (Willman, 1990; Dribbusch and Birke, 2012: 5–6). Obviously, figures vary significantly between countries and sectors, but as organizations collecting

---

[5] Public sector strikes are a notable exception because striking public sector workers do not have to get paid. This decreases public expenditure and thus reduces costs for those in charge of public coffers.

[6] Arguably, the most prominent example in recent years is the wave of feminist general strikes, which have been taking place in a range of countries, among them Argentina, Poland and Spain (see Volume 2, Chapter 8). These strikes do not just condemn violence against women, but also criticize the position of women in the labour market. Besides, there are of course spontaneous stoppages or wildcat strikes, which are led by rank-and-file networks, and not by clearly defined organizational bodies (see Schumann et al, 1971; Fantasia, 1988: 75–120; Birke, 2007). Recent examples are the strikes at British oil refineries in 2009, and the stoppages at the German online food delivery service Gorillas in 2021 (Gallas, 2018a: 246–7; Krantz, 2021; Ewen et al, 2022). Last but not least, strikes can be an instrument of protest used in struggles that are not directly about the organization of work, as is evidenced by the recent wave of climate strikes.

[7] In this respect, unions differ from parties, which are different not just because they participate in representative democracy and stand in elections. Whereas unions tend to focus on economic issues, parties are usually wedded to more clearly defined, political agendas. These agendas go beyond representing the needs and interests of workers in the workplace and claim to be universal in the sense that they reflect a certain vision of society (see Jäger, 2010: 251). Consequently, parties tend to have fewer members and a more clearly defined political agenda. Furthermore, they are open to people from all walks of life and are usually more heterogeneous than unions in terms of the composition of their membership. In postwar era, left-socialist and Euro-communist forces, in particular, argued that it is necessary to build broad constituencies based on class alliances that unite subaltern groups into a popular bloc (Poulantzas, 1978: 263; see also Laclau, 1977: 196).

membership fees, they usually have some funds, which can be used to hire staff and finance campaigns and strikes. By far not all unions pay strike money, but if they do, this can contribute to sustaining and consolidating strike efforts.

The stability of unions as organizations with a mass base and funds also means that they can act as containers of knowledge. Unlike some of the social movements that emerge spontaneously, unions often have a long organizational history, which means that they have detailed know-how when it comes to organizing, campaigning and going on strike. Furthermore, union activists can impart this knowledge to the rank-and-file through education drives and the creation of forums for debate, which may concern work-related skills, but also organizing and general economic and political issues (see Brinkmann et al, 2008: 122, 147; Schmalstieg, 2015: 148–52). In this sense, unions represent an important part of the cognitive infrastructure that workers can draw upon when they choose to walk out, and they create institutionalized relations between organic intellectuals and the rank-and-file (see Goes, 2019: 88). Indeed, these often become official relations of representation when the latter elect the former as shop stewards or works councillors.

Union leaders, officials and activists may contribute significantly to creating strategic orientations for workers operating collectively, and in this way facilitate the emergence of clear-cut strategies behind strikes. In other words, union activists use their organizational knowledge to conduct strategic calculations, which also means that they are well positioned to act as strike leaders (see Darlington, 2018: 620). On the one hand, this gives strike efforts stability and direction; on the other hand, it creates a split between a rank-and-file and a leadership, which can result in a weakening of the momentum behind strikes (see Darlington, 2018: 628). This does not just concern the 'Trotskyite' scenario of leaders 'selling out' and undermining strikes thanks to bureaucratization and outright corruption. It may also be the case that union officials are prepared to go further than the workers they represent, as is visible in the fairly frequent scenario of union members voting against strike action in ballots (Kelly, 1988: 156; see Gallas, 2016b: 176).

In principle, there are two dominant strategic orientations for unions when it comes to their constituency, which reflect the fact that their activities can either contribute to class formation or to class partition. In a class formation scenario, unions are guided by the principle of inclusive solidarity, which means that they cater for a broad and rather diverse constituency, are prepared to forge alliances and make expansive demands that can be transferred to other groups of workers. In contrast, class partition occurs if they operate on the grounds of exclusive solidarity, that is, on organizing a clearly demarcated constituency and remaining closed to everyone else. In this scenario, they try to make gains that are hard to transfer to other groups of workers and may even weaken the latter's position. Significantly, this clear-cut analytical distinction may be difficult to make when it comes to actual disputes. This implies that there is a need to carefully assess the class effects of individual disputes and allow for contradictions to be mapped.[8]

The role of political parties and civil society networks

In contrast to trade unions, political parties usually aim at gaining decision-making authority over the 'organisation of society' (Lindner, 2006: 585). Under conditions of capitalist democracy, they stand in elections, work in and through parliament and join governments. Furthermore, they advance agendas that tend to have a universal character. In contrast to unions, they do not have a primary focus like the workplace, and their activities address more directly the political scene and, by implication, the state (see Steckner, 2013: 224–30).

If there is universal suffrage and a large chunk of voters is wage dependent, parties tend to emerge that, in some way or another, are committed to working-class politics, most importantly, social democratic, socialist and communist parties (see Kelly, 1988: 293). Again, however, there is no guarantee for parties of this type to appear on the scene. As has been widely discussed by historians and social scientists (see Moore, 1945; Wallerstein, 1981; Cayo Sexton, 1991), there has never been, in the history of US, a dominant party with a claim to being a workers' party. And in the cases of some Western European countries, formerly strong social democratic and communist parties have been reduced to roles at the margins in recent years.[9]

As already has been discussed, there are 'isolation' and 'homogenization' effects at the level of the state inviting individualist, populist and nationalist interpellations that work against working class-based politics and explain why there are strong liberal, conservative and right-wing populist political projects in the capitalist centres. These factors may be further reinforced when organized labour, at the political level, is faced with repression, or is compromised through its collusion with business. At the same time, it also

---

[8] In Germany, there was a wave of pilot strikes in 2014 and 2015 (see Nowak, 2018: 353). In the news media, the strike wave was often portrayed as a classic example of highly qualified and privileged workers exploiting their strong negotiating hand for their own gains. However, the picture is complicated by the fact that in September 2018, pilots and flight attendants at Ryanair decided to go on strike simultaneously (Boewe et al, 2020: 24), which suggests that the stoppages of pilots did indeed have expansive effects.

[9] Note the decline of what were arguably the strongest Western European communist parties, the Parti communiste français and the Partito Communista Italiano, in the 1980s and 1990s, plus the more recent collapse in France, Greece and the Netherlands of what used to be large social democratic parties.

worth noting that similar to unions, workers' parties – in particular if they reach a certain size and political clout – have also contributed to adsorbing workers in contradictory class locations to working-class networks. This applies, in particular, to the mass parties of the 20th century like the Parti communiste français, the Partito Communista Italiano or the Partido dos Trabalhadores in Brazil.

At the political level, there are, again, selectivities inherent in the state that obstruct the forceful representation of working-class interests. Even when radical left forces enter governments, the capitalist status quo is usually still protected through constitutions, repressive state apparatuses and political-administrative apparatuses (see Poulantzas, 1978: 258–60). There is the possibility, through the interpersonal connections forming part of being in the public service, that 'parallel power networks' of politicians, civil servants and businesspeople emerge (Jessop, 2010: 45), which work in favour of the status quo. Importantly, the functioning of the capitalist state usually depends on tax income (Jessop, 2011: 14), and this creates a strong incentive in favour of pro-capitalist political decision-making that aims to 'keep the economy going'.

There is also a third type of workers' organization, the civil society network, which tends to be less clearly defined. It can consist of activists and be committed to a specific, at times localized, cause – or it can be more weakly tied to a political agenda. Its nodes are entities that in some cases benefit from public funding, but are not directly controlled by political decision-makers or bureaucrats, for example, cultural and social clubs, infrastructures of mutual help, welfare facilities and educational institutions. Usually, these entities are not mass organizations, but they can become interlinked, both through personal and organizational connections.

The emerging networks may involve large numbers of people and thus can contribute to producing stable connections between workers along class lines. A famous example from the interwar period is 'Red Vienna', the political project of building a form of municipal socialism in the Austrian capital under the auspices of a socialist-controlled city council. At the time, a tightly knit network emerged of cultural, social and sports clubs, news media and welfare facilities for workers. It is estimated that 400,000 people were part of it in the early 1930s (Opratko and Probst, 2010). Such civil society networks may operate 'at a distance' to the political-bureaucratic and repressive core of the state, but they are not located outside of it (Poulantzas, 1978: 153; see also Gramsci, 1971: 160). This is visible in the fact that 'Red Vienna' relied on public money and the city council (see Duma and Lichtenberger, 2016).

Just like in politics, however, there is no guarantee, in the domain of culture, for such webs of connections to emerge that represent workers. If they do not exist, this is not just a product of the potential strength of individualist, populist and nationalist interpellations. Their absence also reflects the fragmentation characteristic of civil society. Centripetal forces like central banks and national parliaments are missing; there is usually a diversity of initiatives, practices and worldviews. Such a diversity does not exist in the more streamlined realms of the economy and politics, where practices tend to be more goal-oriented and thus are based, to a stronger degree, on strategic calculations. It follows that it is usually harder in civil society than in the economy or state to overcome fragmentation. In addition, civil society organizations are still bound by legal regulations and often depend on state funding, which means that they are exposed, just like parties and trade unions, to selectivities that favour the reproduction of capitalist class domination.

Importantly, 'the economy', 'politics' and 'culture' are analytical distinctions, not clearly demarcated social fields that are cut off from each other (see Poulantzas, 1978: 17; Hyman, 1989: 44). Correspondingly, many unions make political demands and intervene in political debates – in particular if labour relations are directly concerned. Likewise, political parties usually have a stance on labour struggles, and cultural initiatives may support both economic and political struggles. There may be a tendency for economic, political and cultural class struggles to be separate, but they usually still influence one another. Indeed, in some countries, there are close organizational ties between trade unions and political parties – and pro-labour intellectuals are active in both types of organizations.[10] Besides, unions and parties create and reproduce imaginaries concerning the organization of society and thus are also implicated in cultural class struggles.

It follows that depending on circumstances at the level of the social formation and the conjuncture, struggles with different dimensions can be further apart or more closely aligned. In general, it is conducive to the reproduction of class domination if class struggles are segmented along the lines of their three dimensions (see Jessop, 1978: 29). After all, it is hard to forcefully contest the existence of the capitalist relations of production with just collective bargaining on the one hand and parliamentary procedure on the other hand. In those two arenas, the capitalist nature of the relations of production does not belong in the realm of the negotiable. It follows that profound shifts in the class relations of forces favouring labour tend to be premised on the close articulation of class struggles across the three dimensions.

---

[10] In Britain, for example, 11 unions were affiliated with the Labour Party in 2022, among them the three largest unions in the country, the GMB, Unison and Unite. They are represented in the party's national executive committee and their members can vote in party leadership elections. The main South African union federation, the Congress of South African Trade Unions, is in a tripartite alliance with the two parties that have been in government since the end of Apartheid, the African National Congress and the South African Communist Party.

Afterword

Throughout this first volume of my book, my intention has been to put forward an argument for the continued relevance of class – both as a relation of social domination pervading contemporary societies, and as a category of social analysis broadly understood.

In the first part, I was concerned with global labour studies as a research field. I argued that global labour scholars tend to take 'the side of workers'. This is visible in key contributions to the literature, which contain a normative-critical subtext. According to it, neoliberalism and capitalism entail class domination, and this contributes to the suffering of workers. Consequently, it would be desirable for class domination to end – and workers deserve support when they exercise their collective power to resist and challenge their own subjugation.

The implications of this normative line of reasoning for empirical research in the field are profound. In particular, they go against a key assumption of the PRA, an approach oft-used by global labour scholars. It sets out to identify sources of workers' power – and sees the activities of unions as one instance of where it is exercised. With reference to materialist state theory, I emphasized that unions have a 'double character': They are apparatuses facilitating both mass integration and the advancement of workers. I inferred, contra the PRA, that their interventions cannot simply be seen as forthright expressions of workers' power. They also invite workers to abide by the existing rules and regulations concerning collective action, and to moderate their demands accordingly. In a nutshell, they strengthen workers by allowing them to make forceful, collective demands, but they also contribute to fortifying class domination. It follows that scholarship in the field of global labour studies needs class analytical tools capable of capturing the contradictory class effects of trade union activity and the tensions surrounding it.

The second part of this volume was dedicated to developing such tools. In keeping with a Marxian understanding of materialism, I started from the wager that the social world in general should be examined, in the first instance, by looking at the organization of work. Importantly, this is an anti-reductionist endeavour. In my understanding, work should not be seen as a merely economic activity. It has political and cultural dimensions, too.

After all, it is intimately related to questions of who gets to make binding decisions over how things are run, and how we see our own positions and those of others in the social fabric.

In line with my wager, I began my conceptualization of class with examining the capitalist relations of production, which refer to general features of work in capitalism. I pointed out that they are relations with two poles or class locations, the side of capital and the side of labour, which are defined by the ownership and the non-ownership of the means of production. Furthermore, the relations of production exhibit two characteristic features: capitalist class domination, that is, the domination of capital over labour, which is reflected in the systematic inequality of the two sides in access to material and ideational resources; and class antagonism, the existence of a conflict-in-permanency between both sides over how labour power is expended in the work process, which cannot be settled for good. In summary, class in capitalism can be seen as a conflict-ridden force field marked by hierarchies and inequalities. Any actors in capitalist social formations, be they individuals or collectives, operate within this force field. It influences – but does not fully determine – their activities.

The conceptualization of class contained in this volume sets the scene for the second volume, which is dedicated to examining strikes and strike waves. But what do class theoretical concepts offer in this context? Looking back at my own research process, they primarily served me as orientation marks. In their connectedness, they constituted a roadmap for how to approach the topic of strikes, which guided me through the messiness of the empirical. As any good map, it informed me about what to look out for, namely disputes related to work, and what to circumnavigate, for example, the pitfall of equating union capacities with working-class power.

As I argued in Part II of this volume, class domination is produced and reproduced in and through conflicts over the work process – and reproduction cannot be presumed to take place automatically. Consequently, these conflicts have a specific strategic significance for how capitalist social formations are stabilized and destabilized, and how collective actors deal with the existence of social domination. Class theory shows that it is worth studying conflicts around work in capitalist settings, which is why I can say that my focus on strikes is fully in line with the insights produced through my conceptualization of class.

And as I also discussed in Part II, class formation takes place when workers develop collective agency along class lines. This occurs when they start to act in unison in the context of a dispute and create links with workers in other branches of the economy. It follows that a plausible agenda for labour research informed by materialist class theory is to trace whether processes of class formation are visible in strikes.

Of course, these are general pronouncements, from which I was able to develop a research agenda. But they leave open the question of how it is possible to operationalize class theoretical concepts, that is, how to turn them into categories that can be applied to empirical observations, how to select suitable cases, and how to do all of this from a global vantage point. This is the topic of the inaugural chapter of Volume 2. That volume contains my empirical analysis of strikes and class formation around the world in the context of the Great Crisis. In it, I map and examine what Nagelschmidt describes in the novel mentioned in the preface: The networks of solidarity of people working in non-industrial branches of the economy, which emerge in and through conflicts concerning work.

References

Abendroth, W. (1954) 'Der politische Streik', in W. Abendroth (1975) *Arbeiterklasse, Staat und Verfassung: Materialien zur Verfassungsgeschichte und Verfassungstheorie der Bundesrepublik*, edited by J. Perels, Frankfurt am Main: EVA, pp 54–63.

Ackroyd, S. and Fleetwood, S. (2000) 'Realism in contemporary organisation and management studies', in S. Ackroyd and S. Fleetwood (eds) *Realist Perspectives on Management and Organisation*, London: Routledge, pp 3–25.

Ainsley, C. (2018) *The New Working Class: How to Win Hearts, Minds and Votes*, Bristol: Bristol University Press.

AKSU (Arbeitskreis Strategic Unionism) (2013) 'Jenaer Machtressourcenansatz 2.0', in S. Schmalz and K. Dörre (eds) *Comeback der Gewerkschaften? Machtressourcen, innovative Praktiken, internationale Perspektiven*, Frankfurt am Main: Campus, pp 345–75.

Althusser, L. (1969) *For Marx*, London: Allen Lane, original work published in 1965.

Althusser, L. (1976) *Essays in Self-Criticism*, London: NLB.

Althusser, L. (2014) *On the Reproduction of Capitalism: Ideology and Ideological State Apparatuses*, London: Verso.

Althusser, L. (2022) 'How should we define "culture"?', *Décalages: A Journal of Althusser Studies*, 2(4): 485–8, original work written in 1966.

Alvaredo, F., Chancel, L., Piketty, T., Saez, E. and Zucman, G. (2018) *World Inequality Report*, World Inequality Lab. Available from: https://wir2018.wid.world/files/download/wir2018-full-report-english.pdf [Accessed 21 October 2023].

Anderson, B. (2006) *Imagined Communities: Reflections on the Origin and Spread of Nationalism*, revised edn, London: Verso.

Aristotle (1999) *Nicomachean Ethics*, Kitchener: Batoche Books.

Aron, R. (1960) 'Science et conscience de la société', *Archives Européennes de Sociologie*, 1(1): 1–30.

Arruzza, C. (2013) *Dangerous Liaisons: The Marriages and Divorces of Marxism and Feminism*, Pontypool: Merlin.

Arruzza, C. (2018) 'From women's strikes to a new class movement: the third feminist wave', *International Viewpoint*, December. Available from: https://viewpointmag.com/2018/12/03/from-womens-strikes-to-a-new-class-movement-the-third-feminist-wave/ [Accessed 6 October 2022].

Arruzza, C., Bhattacharya, T. and Fraser, N. (2019) *Feminism for the 99 Percent: A Manifesto*, London: Verso.

Atzeni, M. (2020) 'Workers' organisation in precarious times: abandoning trade union fetishism, rediscovering class', *Global Labour Journal*, 11(3): 311–14.

Atzeni, M. (2021) 'Workers' organizations and the fetishism of the trade union form: toward new pathways for research on the labour movement?', *Globalizations*, 18(8): 1349–62.

Aulenbacher, B., Burawoy, M., Dörre, K. and J. Sittel (2017) 'Vorwort', in B. Aulenbacher, M. Burawoy, K. Dörre and J. Sittel (eds) *Öffentliche Soziologie: Wissenschaft im Dialog mit der Gesellschaft*, Frankfurt: Campus, pp 11–32.

Barker, B. and Cox, L. (2000/2001) ' "What have the Romans ever done for us?": academic and activist forms of movement theorizing'. Available from: https://mural.maynoothuniversity.ie/428/ [Accessed 23 May 2022].

Beck, U. and Beck-Gernsheimer, E. (2002) *Individualization: Institutionalized Individualism and its Social and Political Consequences*, London: SAGE.

Becker, H.S. (1967) 'Whose side are we on?', *Social Problems*, 14(3): 239–47.

Bergfeld, M. (2018) 'Do you believe in life after work? The university and college union strike in Britain', *Transfer*, 24(2): 233–6.

Bettie, J. (2000) 'Women without class: chicas, cholas, trash, and the presence/absence of class identity', *Signs*, 26(1): 1–35.

Bhaskar, R. (1979) *The Possibility of Naturalism: A Philosophical Critique of the Contemporary Human Sciences*, London: Routledge.

Bieler, A. (2012) ' "Workers of the world, unite"? Globalisation and the quest for transnational solidarity', *Globalizations*, 9(3): 365–78.

Bieler, A. and Morton, A. (2004) ' "Another Europe is possible"? Labour and social movements at the European social forum', *Globalizations*, 1(2): 303–25.

Bieler, A. and Morton, A. (2018) *Global Capitalism, Global War, Global Crisis*, Cambridge: Cambridge University Press.

Birke, P. (2007) *Wilde Streiks im Wirtschaftswunder: Arbeitskämpfe, Gewerkschaften und soziale Bewegungen in der Bundesrepublik und Dänemark*, Frankfurt am Main: Campus.

Blaikie, N. and Priest, J. (2017) *Social Research: Paradigms in Action*, Cambridge: Polity.

Blaikie, N. and Priest, J. (2019) *Designing Social Research*, Cambridge: Polity.

Blair, A. and Schröder, G. (1998) 'Europe: The Third Way/Die Neue Mitte', Friedrich Ebert Foundation, South Africa Office, Working Documents, 2 June. Available from: https://library.fes.de/pdf-files/bueros/suedafrika/02828.pdf [Accessed 30 May 2022].

Blanc, E. (2019) *Red State Revolt: The Teachers' Strike Wave and Working-Class Politics*, London: Verso.

Boewe, J., Butollo, F. and Schulten, J. (2020) 'Organizing Ryanair: Die transnationale Gewerkschaftskampagne bei Europa Billigfluglinie Nummer eins', Rosa Luxemburg Foundation, Analysen, 63, December. Available from: https://www.rosalux.de/fileadmin/rls_uploads/pdfs/sonst_publik ationen/Analysen63_Ryanair.pdf [Accessed 8 October 2022].

Bönstrup, C. and Döbler, M. (2008) 'Hansen macht auf Mehdorn', *Der Tagesspiegel*, 17 May. Available from: https://www.tagesspiegel.de/wirtsch aft/hansen-macht-auf-mehdorn-1653778.html [Accessed 8 October 2022].

Bourdieu, P. (1987) 'What makes a social class? On the theoretical and practical existence of groups', *Berkeley Journal of Sociology*, 32: 1–17.

Brankovic, J. (2021) 'Academia's Stockholm Syndrome: the ambivalent status of rankings in higher education (research)', *International Higher Education*, 107: 11–12.

Brecher, J. (2009) 'The decline of strikes', in A. Brenner, A. Day and I. Ness (eds) *The Encyclopedia of Strikes in American History*, Armonk: M.E. Sharpe, pp 72–80.

Brinkmann, U. and Nachtwey, O. (2013) 'Industrial relations, trade unions and social conflict in German capitalism', *La Nouvelle Revue de Travail*, 3. Available from: https://journals.openedition.org/nrt/1382 [Accessed 8 October 2022].

Brinkmann, U., Choi, H.-L., Detje, R., Dörre, K., Holst, H., Karakayali, S. and Schmalstieg, C. (eds) (2008) *Strategic Unionism: Aus der Krise zur Erneuerung? Umrisse eines Forschungsprogramms*, Wiesbaden: Springer VS.

Brookes, M. and McCallum, J. (2017) 'The new global labour studies: a critical review', *Global Labour Journal*, 8(3): 201–18.

Browne, K. (2011) *An Introduction to Sociology*, 4th edn, Cambridge: Polity.

Bruce, S. (1999) *Sociology: A Very Short Introduction*, Oxford: Oxford University Press.

Bruff, I. (2011) 'The case for a foundational materialism: going beyond historical materialist IPE in order to strengthen it', *Journal of International Relations and Development*, 14(3): 391–9.

Buckel, S. (2015) 'Dirty capitalism', in D. Martin, S. Martin and J. Wissel (eds) *Perspektiven und Konstellationen kritischer Theorie*, Münster: Westfälisches Dampfboot, pp 29–48.

Buhlungu, S. (2006) 'Rebels without a cause of their own? The contradictory location of white officials in black unions in South Africa, 1973-94', *Current Sociology*, 54(3): 427–51.

Buhlungu, S. (2009) 'South Africa: the decline of labor studies and the democratic transition', *Work and Occupations*, 36(2): 145–61.

Bukharin, N. (2021) *Historical Materialism: A System of Sociology*, np: Cosmonaut Press, original work published in 1921.

Bundesarbeitsgericht (1980) *10.06.1080 – 1 AZR 168/79*. Available from: https://www.prinz.law/urteile/BAG_1_AZR_168-79 [Accessed 1 November 2019].

Burawoy, M. (1979) *The Politics of Production: Factory Regimes under Capitalism and Socialism*, London: Verso.

Burawoy, M. (2008) 'What is to be done? Theses on the degradation of social existence in a globalizing world', *Current Sociology*, 56(3): 351–9.

Burawoy, M. (2012) 'The roots of domination: beyond Bourdieu and Gramsci', *Sociology*, 46(2): 187–206.

Camfield, D. (2013) 'What is trade union bureaucracy? A theoretical account', *Alternate Routes: A Journal of Critical Social Research*, 24(1): 133–56.

Candeias, M., Dörre, K. and Goes, T.E. (2019) *Demobilisierte Klassengesellschaft und Potenziale verbindender Klassenpolitik*, Berlin: Rosa-Luxemburg-Stiftung.

Carchedi, G. (1977) *On the Economic Identification of Social Classes*, London: Routledge and Kegan Paul.

Carroll, W.K. (2010) *The Making of a Transnational Capitalist Class: Corporate Power in the Twenty-First Century*, London: Zed Books.

Carroll, W.K. (2020) 'Fossil capital, imperialism and the global corporate elite', in V. Satgar (ed) *BRICS and the New American Imperialism: Global Rivalry and Resistance*, Johannesburg: Wits University Press, pp 182–202.

Castells, M. (2010) *The Rise of the Network Society*, 2nd edn, Hoboken: Wiley, original work published in 1996.

Cayo Sexton, P. (1991) *The War on Labor and the Left: Understanding America's Unique Conservatism*, New York: Routledge.

Çelik, E. (2013) '"The academy and the rest"? Intellectual engagements, circulation of knowledge and the labour movement in South Africa, 1970s–1980s', *Transcience*, 4(2): 19–35.

Cohen, S. (2006) *Ramparts of Resistance: Why Workers Lost Their Power and How to Get It Back*, London: Pluto.

Collier, A. (1994) *Critical Realism: An Introduction to Roy Bhaskar's Philosophy*, London: Verso.

Connolly, H. and Darlington, R. (2012) 'Radical political unionism in France and Britain: a comparative study of SUD-Rail and the RMT', *European Journal of Industrial Relations*, 18(3): 235–50.

Cook, M.L., Dutta, M., Gallas, A., Nowak, J. and Scully, B. (2020) 'Global labour studies in the pandemic: notes for an emerging agenda', *Global Labour Journal*, 11(2): 74–88.

Costa, H. and Dias, H. (2016) 'The strike as a challenge to the North and to the South', *Workers of the World*, 8: 143–59.

Cottle, E. (2017) 'Long waves of strikes in South Africa: 1900–2015', in O. Balashova, I.D. Karatepe and A. Namukasa (eds) *Where Have All the Classes Gone? A Critical Perspective on Struggles and Collective Action*, Augsburg: Rainer Hampp, pp 146–72.

Cox, L. (2015) 'Scholarship and activism: a social movements perspective', *Studies in Social Justice*, 9(1): 34–53.

Cox, R. (1981) 'Social forces, states and world orders: beyond international relations theory', *Millennium*, 10(2): 162–75.

Darlington, R. (2018) 'The leadership component of Kelly's mobilisation theory: contribution, tensions, limitations and further development', *Economic and Industrial Democracy*, 39(4): 617–38.

Darlington, R. and Upchurch, M. (2011) 'A reappraisal of the rank-and-file versus bureaucracy debate', *Capital & Class*, 36(1): 77–95.

Demirović, A. (2020) 'Undoing Class: Warum von Klasse, Klassenkampf und Klassenpolitik reden?', *PROKLA. Zeitschrift für kritische Sozialwissenschaft*, 50(3): 429–38.

Devine, F. and Sensier, M. (2017) 'Class, politics and the progressive dilemma', *The Political Quarterly*, 88(1): 30–8.

Donovan Commission (1971) *Royal Commission on Trade Unions and Employers' Associations 1965–1968*, London: Her Majesty's Stationery Office, reprint, original work published in 1968.

Dörre, K. (2011) 'Functional changes in the trade unions: from intermediary to fractal organization?', *International Journal of Action Research*, 7(1): 8–48.

Dörre, K. (2017) 'Gewerkschaften, Machtressourcen und öffentliche Soziologie. Ein Selbstversuch', *Österreichische Zeitschrift für Soziologie*, 42: 105–28.

Dörre, K. and Schmalz, S. (2013) 'Einleitung: Comeback der Gewerkschaften? Eine machtsoziologische Forschungsperspektive', in S. Schmalz and K. Dörre (eds) *Comeback der Gewerkschaften? Machtressourcen, innovative Praktiken, internationale Perspektiven*, Frankfurt am Main: Campus, pp 13–38.

Dörre, K., Holst, H. and Nachtwey, O. (2009) 'Organizing: a strategic option for trade union renewal?', *International Journal of Action Research*, 5(1): 33–67.

Dribbusch, H. and Birke, P. (2012) 'Trade unions in Germany: organisation, environment, challenges', Friedrich Ebert Foundation, May. Available from: https://library.fes.de/pdf-files/id-moe/09113-20120828.pdf [Accessed 29 July 2021].

Dribbusch, H. and Vandaele, K. (2016) 'Comparing official strike data in Europe: dealing with varieties of strike recording', *Transfer*, 22(3): 413–18.

Duma, V. and Lichtenberger, H. (2016) 'Das rote Wien', *Zeitschrift LuXemburg*, 2: 122–30.

DW (2018) 'Österreich beschließt Zwölf-Stunden-Tag', 5 July. Available from: https://www.dw.com/de/%C3%B6sterreich-beschlie%C3%9Ft-zw%C3%B6lf-stunden-tag/a-44546989 [Accessed 9 October 2022].

Edwards, P. (1982) 'The local organisation of a national dispute: the British 1979 engineering strike', *Industrial Relations Journal*, 13(1): 57–63.

Encyclopaedia Britannica (2013) 'Adsorption', 6 August. Available from: https://www.britannica.com/science/adsorption [Accessed 16 February 2022]

Engels, F. (2003) 'Ludwig Feuerbach and the End of Classical German Philosophy'. Available from: https://www.marxists.org/archive/marx/works/1886/ludwig-feuerbach/ [Accessed 3 March 2022], original work published in 1886.

Erd, R. and Scherrer, C. (1985) 'Unions – caught between structural competition and temporary solidarity: a critique of contemporary Marxist analysis of trade unions in Germany', *British Journal of Industrial Relations*, 23(1): 115–31.

Esser, J. (1982) *Gewerkschaften in der Krise*, Frankfurt am Main: Suhrkamp.

Esser, J. (2014) 'Funktionen und Funktionswandel der Gewerkschaften in Deutschland', in W. Schroeder (ed) *Handbuch Gewerkschaften in Deutschland*, 2nd edn, Wiesbaden: Springer VS, pp 85–106.

Evans, G. and Mellon, J. (2016) 'Social class: identity, awareness and political attitudes: why are we still working class?', *British Social Attitudes*, 33: 4–22.

Evans, M. (2020) 'Navigating the neoliberal university: reflecting on teaching practice as a teacher-researcher-trade unionist', *British Journal of Sociology of Education*, 41(4): 574–90.

Ewen, J., Heiland, H. and Seeliger, M. (2022) 'Dynamiken autonomer Arbeitskonflikte im digitalen Kapitalismus: Der Fall "Gorillas"', Schriftenreihe Institut Arbeit und Wirtschaft, Universität Bremen, 33. Available from: http://hdl.handle.net/10419/249962 [Accessed 20 September 2022].

Fairbrother, P. and Webster, E. (2008) 'Social movement unionism: questions and possibilities', *Employee Responsibilities and Rights Journal*, 20: 309–13.

Fantasia, R. (1988) *Cultures of Solidarity: Consciousness, Action, and Contemporary American Workers*, Berkeley: University of California Press.

Fichter, M., Anner, M., Hoffer, F. and Scherrer, C. (2014) 'The global labour university: a new laboratory of learning for international labor solidarity?', *WorkingUSA: The Journal of Labor and Society*, 17: 565–77.

Fleetwood, S. (nd) 'Causal laws and tendencies'. Available from: http://care con.org.uk/QM/Conference%202008/Papers/Fleetwod.pdf [Accessed 10 October 2022].

Fleetwood, S. (2001) 'Causal laws, functional relations and tendencies', *Review of Political Economy*, 13(2): 201–20.

Fleetwood, S. (2011) 'Powers and tendencies revisited', *Journal of Critical Realism*, 10(1): 80–99.

Fraser, N. (2016) 'Contradictions of capital and care', *New Left Review*, II.100: 99–117.

Fraser, N. (2017) 'From progressive neoliberalism to Trump – and beyond', *American Affairs*, [online] no date. Available from: https://americanaffairs journal.org/2017/11/progressive-neoliberalism-trump-beyond/ [Accessed 9 October 2022].

Friedman, M. (1962) *Capitalism and Freedom*, Chicago: University of Chicago Press.

Gall, G. (ed) (2009) *Union Revitalisation in Advanced Economies: Assessing the Contribution of Union Organising*, Houndmills: Palgrave.

Gall, G. (2014) 'New forms of labour conflict: a transnational overview', in M. Atzeni (ed) *Workers and Labour in a Globalised Capitalism: Contemporary Themes and Theoretical Issues*, Houndmills: Palgrave Macmillan, pp 210–29.

Gall, G. (2022) 'The government has quietly stopped sharing strike data: how convenient', *Novara Media*, 15 August. Available from: https://novarame dia.com/2022/08/15/the-government-has-quietly-stopped-sharing-str ike-data/ [Accessed 3 October 2022].

Gall, G. and Cohen, S. (2013) 'The collective expression of workplace grievances in Britain', in G. Gall (ed) *New Forms and Expressions of Conflict at Work*, Houndmills: Palgrave, pp 86–107.

Gall, G. and Kirk, E. (2018) 'Striking out in a new direction? Strikes and the displacement thesis', *Capital & Class*, 42(2): 195–203.

Gallas, A. (2006) 'Subjektivität = Fetischismus? Die wertkritische Marxrezeption auf dem Prüfstand', in J. Hoff, U. Lindner, A. Petrioli and I. Stützle (eds) *Das Kapital neu lesen. Beiträge zur radikalen Philosophie*, Münster: Westfälisches Dampfboot, pp 303–23.

Gallas, A. (2008) 'Kapitalismus ohne Bourgeoisie: Die "Gentlemanly Association" und der englische Block an der Macht, in Lindner, U., Nowak, J. and P. Paust-Lassen (eds) *Philosophieren unter anderen: Beiträge zum Palaver der Menschheit*, Münster: Westfälisches Dampfboot, pp. 263–87.

Gallas, A. (2011) 'Reading capital with Poulantzas: form and struggle in the critique of political economy', in A. Gallas, L. Bretthauer, J. Kannankulam and I. Stützle (eds) *Reading Poulantzas*, Pontypool: Merlin, pp 89–106.

Gallas, A. (2014) 'The three sources of anti-socialism: a critical inquiry into the normative foundations of F.A. Hayek's politics', *Zeitschrift für kritische Sozialtheorie und Philosophie*, 2(1): 182–99.

Gallas, A. (2016a) 'Vom "Nachlaufspiel" zum multiskalaren Internationalismus: Bedingungen grenzüberschreitender Solidarität von ArbeiterInnen im globalen Kapitalismus', in U. Brand, H. Schwenken and J. Wullweber (eds) *Globalisierung analysieren, kritisieren und verändern: Das Projekt kritische Wissenschaft*, Hamburg: VSA, pp 145–62.

Gallas, A. (2016b) *The Thatcherite Offensive: A Neo-Poulantzasian Analysis*, Leiden: Brill.

Gallas, A. (2016c) 'There is power in a union: a strategic-relational perspective on power resources', in A. Truger, E. Hein, M. Heine and F. Hoffer (eds) *Monetary Macroeconomics, Labour Markets and Development*, Weimar an der Lahn: Metropolis, pp 195–210.

Gallas, A. (2017) 'Revisiting conjunctural Marxism: Althusser and Poulantzas on the state', *Rethinking Marxism*, 29(2): 256–80.

Gallas, A. (2018a) 'The politics of striking: on the shifting of dynamics of workers' struggles in Britain', in J. Nowak, M. Dutta and P. Birke (eds) *Workers Movements and Strikes in the Twenty-First Century: A Global Perspective*, London: Rowman & Littlefield, pp 237–54.

Gallas, A. (2018b) 'Class power and union capacities: a research note on the power resources approach', *Global Labour Journal*, 9(3): 348–52.

Gallas, A. (2018c) 'Precarious academic labour in Germany: termed contracts and a new Berufsverbot', *Global Labour Journal*, 9(1): 92–102.

Gallas, A. (2018d) 'Introduction: the proliferation of precarious labour in academia', *Global Labour Journal*, 9(1): 69–75.

Gallas, A. (2019) 'Klassen', in C. von Braunmühl, H. Gerstenberger, R. Ptak and C. Wichterich (eds) *ABC der globalen (Un)Ordnung*, Hamburg: VSA, pp 136–7.

Gallas, A. (2020) 'Mass strikes in a global conjuncture of crisis: a Luxemburgian analysis', in V. Satgar (ed) *BRICS and the New American Imperialism: Global Rivalry and Resistance*, Johannesburg: Wits University Press, pp 182–202.

Gallas, A. and Nowak, J. (2012) 'Agieren aus der Defensive: Ein Überblick zu politischen Streiks in Europa mit Fallstudien zu Frankreich und Großbritannien', in A. Gallas, J. Nowak and F. Wilde (eds) *Politische Streiks im Europa der Krise*, Hamburg: VSA, pp 24–106.

Gallas, A., Nowak, J. and Wilde, F. (eds) (2012) *Politische Streiks im Europa der Krise*, Hamburg: VSA.

Gallas, A., Scherrer, C. and Williams, M. (2014) 'Inequality: the Achilles heel of free market democracy', *International Journal of Labour Research*, 6(1): 143–61.

Gallas, A., Herr, H., Hoffer, F. and Scherrer, C. (eds) (2016) *Combating Inequality: The Global North and South*, London: Routledge.

Gibson-Graham, J.K., Resnick, S.A. and Wolff, R.D. (eds) (2000) *Class and its Others*, Minneapolis: University of Minnesota Press.

Goes, T.E. (2019) *Klassen im Kampf: Vorschläge für eine populäre Linke*, Köln: Papyrossa.

Gorz, A. (1982) *Farewell to the Working Class: An Essay in Post-Industrial Socialism*, London: Pluto Press.

Gouldner, A. (1968) 'The sociologist as partisan: sociology and the welfare state', *The American Sociologist*, 3(2): 103–16.

Gramsci, A. (1971) *Selections from the Prison Notebooks*, edited and translated by Q. Hoare and G. Nowell Smith, New York: International Publishers.

Greenwood, J. and Twyman, J. (2018) 'Exploring authoritarian populism in Britain', in I. Crewe and D. Sanders (eds) *Authoritarian Populism and Liberal Democracy*, Basingstoke: Palgrave Macmillan, pp. 33–48.

Gumbrell-McCormick, R. and Hyman, R. (2017) 'What about the workers? The implications of Brexit for British and European labour', *Competition & Change*, 21(3): 169–84.

Gumbrell-McCormick, R. and Hyman, R. (2019) 'Democracy in trade unions, democracy through trade unions?', *Economic and Industrial Democracy*, 40(1): 91–110.

Habermas, J. (1994) *The Philosophical Discourse of Modernity: Twelve Lectures*, Cambridge: Polity.

Hägler, M. (2021) 'VW-Betriebsratschef wechselt die Seiten', *Süddeutsche Zeitung*, 23 April. Available from: https://www.sueddeutsche.de/wirtsch aft/volkswagen-osterloh-1.5273678 [Accessed 23 April 2021].

Hall, S. (1986) 'The problem of ideology: Marxism without guarantees', *Journal of Communication Inquiry*, 10(2): 28–44.

Harvey, D. (2005) *A Brief History of Neoliberalism*, Oxford: Oxford University Press.

Hayek, F.A. (1960) *The Constitution of Liberty*, Chicago: University of Chicago Press.

Hayek, F.A. (1973–7) *Law, Legislation, and Liberty: A New Statement of the Liberal Principles of Justice and Political Economy*, London: Routledge.

Hayek, F.A. (1988) *The Fatal Conceit: The Errors of Socialism*, Chicago: University of Chicago Press.

Hayes, G. (2018) 'Regimes and spaces of austerity: inside the British university', *Lo Squaderno: Explorations in Space and Society*, 47(7): 7–12.

Hein, E. and Detzer, D. (2016) 'Financialisation, redistribution and "export-led mercantilism": the case of Germany', in A. Gallas, H. Herr, F. Hoffer and C. Scherrer (eds) *Combating Inequality: The Global North and South*, London: Routledge, pp 132–49.

Heinrich, M. (2004) 'Agenda 2010 und Hartz IV: Vom rot-grünen Neoliberalismus zum Protest', *Prokla*, 34(3): 477–83.

Hensche, D. (2012) 'Das Tabu des politischen Streiks in Deutschland. Rechtliche und politische Aspekte', in A. Gallas, J. Nowak and F. Wilde (eds) *Politische Streiks im Europa der Krise*, Hamburg: VSA, pp 219–26.

Herr, H. and Ruoff, B. (2016) 'Labour and financial markets as drivers of inequality', in A. Gallas, H. Herr, F. Hoffer and C. Scherrer (eds) *Combating Inequality: The Global North and South*, London: Routledge, pp 61–79.

Herr, H., Ruoff, B. and Salas, C. (2014) 'Labour markets, wage dispersion and union policies', *International Journal of Labour Research*, 6(1): 57–74.

Hilton, R.H. (1952) 'Capitalism: what's in a name?', *Past & Present*, 1: 32–43.

Hirsch, J. (1994) 'Politische Form, politische Institutionen und Staat', in J. Esser, C. Görg and J. Hirsch (eds) *Politik, Institutionen und Staat*, Hamburg: VSA, pp 157–211.

Hoare, Q. and Nowell Smith, G. (1971) 'Preface', in A. Gramsci, *Selections from the Prison Notebooks*, edited and translated by Q. Hoare and G. Nowell Smith, New York: International Publishers, pp ix–xvi.

Hobsbawm, E.J. (1978) 'The forward march of labour halted?', in M. Jacques and F. Mulhern (eds) *The Forward March of Labour Halted?*, London: NLB, pp 1–19.

Hobsbawm, E.J. (1984) *Worlds of Labour: Further Studies in the History of Labour*, London: Weidenfeld & Nicolson.

Hobsbawm, E.J. (1991) 'Good-bye to all that', in R. Blackburn (ed) *After the Fall: The Failure of Communism and the Future of Socialism*, London: Verso, pp 115–25.

Hodder, A., Williams, M., Kelly, J. and McCarthy, N. (2016) 'Does strike action stimulate trade union membership growth?', *British Journal of Industrial Relations*, 55(1): 165–86.

Hoffer, F. (2006) 'Building global labour networks: the case of the global labour university', *Just Labour*, 9: 16–34.

Hoggart, R. (1989) 'Introduction', in G. Orwell, *The Road to Wigan Pier*, London: Penguin, pp v–xii.

Hui, E.S. (2017) *Hegemonic Transformation: The State, Laws, and Labour Relations in Post-Socialist China*, New York: Palgrave.

Hume, D. (1888) *A Treatise of Human Nature*, Oxford: Clarendon, original work published in 1739–40.

Hürtgen, S. (2016) 'Authoritarian defense or the German model?', *Workers of the World*, 1(8): 56–70.

Hürtgen, S. (2018a) 'Gewerkschaften', in B. Belina, M. Naumann and A. Strüver (eds) *Handbuch kritische Stadtgeographie*, 3rd edn, Münster: Westfälisches Dampfboot, pp 246–52.

Hürtgen, S. (2018b) 'Kampf ums Konkrete: Der "Doppelcharakter der Arbeit" und die Gewerkschaften', *Luxemburg*, January. Available from: https://zeitschrift-luxemburg.de/artikel/kampf-ums-konkrete/ [Accessed 26 March 2022].

Hyman, R. (1975) *Industrial Relations: A Marxist Introduction*, London: Macmillan.

Hyman, R. (1989) *Strikes*, 4th edn, Houndmills: Macmillan, original work published in 1972.

Hyman, R. (2001) *Understanding European Trade Unionism*, London: SAGE.

Imberman, W. (2001) 'Why engineers strike – the Boeing story', *Business Horizons*, 44(6): 35–44.

Jäger, M. (2010) 'Machtblock und Parteien bei Poulantzas', in A. Demirović, S. Adolphs and S. Karakayali (eds) *Das Staatsverständnis von Nicos Poulantzas: Der Staat als gesellschaftliches Verhältnis*, Baden-Baden: Nomos, pp 241–58.

Jessop, B. (1978) 'Capitalism and democracy: the best possible shell?', in G. Littlejohn, B. Smart, J. Wakeford and N. Yuval-Davis (eds) *Power and the State*, London: Croom Helm, pp 10–51.

Jessop, B. (2000) 'The crisis of the national spatio-temporal fix and the tendential ecological dominance of globalizing capitalism', *International Journal of Urban and Regional Research*, 24(2): 323–60.

Jessop, B. (2002) *The Future of the Capitalist State*, Cambridge: Polity Press.

Jessop, B. (2010) 'Redesigning the state, reorienting state power, and rethinking the state', in K.T. Leicht and J.C. Jenkins (eds) *Handbook of Politics: State and Society in Global Perspective*, New York: Springer, pp 41–62.

Jessop, B. (2011) 'Reflections on the state, state power, and the world market', in P. Ibarra and M. Cortina (eds) *Recuperando la Radicalidad: Un encuentro en torno al análisis político crítico*, Barcelona: Hacer, pp 11–30.

Johnstone, F.A. (2023) *Class, Race and Gold: A Study in Class Relations of Class Relations and Racial Discrimination in South Africa*, Milton Park: Routledge, original work published in 1976.

Kalass, V. (2012) *Neue Konkurrenz im Bahnwesen: Konflikt um die Gewerkschaft Deutscher Lokomotivführer*, Wiesbaden: Springer.

Kalekin-Fishman, D. (2012) 'Words from writers: an interview with Edward Webster', *International Sociology Review of Books*, 27(2): 160–9.

Karyoti, O. (2012) 'Es ist leichter, Steine zu schmeißen, als unseren Arbeitsplatz dicht zu machen', in A. Gallas, J. Nowak and F. Wilde (eds) *Politische Streiks im Europa der Krise*, Hamburg: VSA, pp 165–70.

Kelly, J. (1988) *Trade Unions and Socialist Politics*, London: Verso.

Kelly, J. (1998) *Rethinking Industrial Relations: Mobilisation, Collectivism and Long Waves*, London: Routledge.

Kemper, A. (2015) '"Klassismus!" heißt Angriff: Warum wir von Klassismus sprechen sollten – und warum dies bisher nicht geschah', *Kurswechsel*, 4: 25–31.

Kenward, B. and Brick, C. (2021) 'Even Conservative voters want the environment to be at the heart of post-COVID-19 economic reconstruction in the UK', *Journal of Social and Political Psychology*, 9(1): 321–33.

Kollmeyer, C. (2018) 'Trade union decline, deindustrialization, and rising income inequality in the United States, 1947 to 2015', *Research in Social Stratification and Mobility*, 57: 1–10.

Krantz, P (2021) 'Gorillas delivery service fires back over workers' strike', *DW*, 8 October. Available from: https://www.dw.com/en/gorillas-deliv ery-service-fires-back-over-workers-strike/a-59445809 [Accessed 10 October 2022].

Kutun, M. and Tören, T. (2018) '"Peace academics" from Turkey: solidarity until the peace comes', *Global Labour Journal*, 9(1): 103–12.

Laclau, E. (1977) *Politics and Ideology in Marxist Theory: Capitalism, Fascism, Populism*, London: NLB.

Laclau, E. and Mouffe, C. (1985) *Hegemony and Socialist Strategy: Towards a Radical Democratic Politics*, London: Verso.

Lebovitz, M. (1992) *Beyond Capital: Marx's Political Economy of the Working Class*, Houndmills: Macmillan.

Lévesque, C., Murray, G. and Le Queux, S. (2005) 'Union disaffection and social identity: democracy as a source of union revitalization', *Work and Occupations*, 32(4): 400–22.

Lindner, U. (2006) 'Alles Macht, oder was? Foucault, Althusser und kritische Gesellschaftstheorie', *PROKLA. Zeitschrift für kritische Sozialwissenschaft*, 36(145): 583–609.

Lindner, U. (2013) *Marx und die Philosophie: Wissenschaftlicher Realismus, Ethnischer Perfektionismus und kritische Sozialphilosophie*, Stuttgart: Schmetterling.

Lodewick, C. (2022) 'The Bureau for Labor Statistics data only reported 16 strikes in 2021. A new database argues there were 14x as many', *Yahoo Finance*, 26 February. Available from: https://finance.yahoo.com/news/bureau-labor-statistics-data-only-140000185.html [Accessed 26 June 2022].

Lüthje, B. and Scherrer, C. (2003) 'Rassismus, Immigration und Arbeiterbewegung in den Vereinigten Staaten', *PROKLA. Zeitschrift für kritische Sozialwissenschaft*, 33(103): 97–118.

Luxemburg, R. (2003) 'The Junius pamphlet: the crisis of German social democracy'. Available from: https://www.marxists.org/archive/luxemburg/1915/junius/ [Accessed 1 October 2022], original work published in 1915.

Luxemburg, R. (2008) 'The mass strike', in R. Luxemburg, *The Essential Luxemburg*, edited by H. Scott, Chicago: Haymarket, pp 111–82, original work published in 1906.

Marticorena, C. and D'Urso, L. (2021) 'El poder de los/as trabajadores/as: una revisión crítica de los abordajes conceptuales para su estudio', *Revista de Estudios Marítimos y Sociales*, 18: 171–98.

Marx, K. (1976) *Capital: A Critique of Political Economy* (vol 1), London: Penguin, original work published in 1867.

Marx, K. (1978) *Capital: A Critique of Political Economy* (vol 2), London: Penguin, original work published in 1885.

Marx, K. (1981) *Capital: A Critique of Political Economy* (vol 3), London: Penguin, original work published in 1894.

Marx, K. (2005) *Theses on Feuerbach*. Available from: https://www.marxists.org/archive/marx/works/1845/theses/theses.htm [Accessed 20 September 2022], original work written in 1845.

Marx, K. (2006) *The Eighteenth Brumaire of Louis Bonaparte*. Available from: https://www.marxists.org/archive/marx/works/1852/18th-brumaire/index.htm [Accessed 20 September 2022], original work published in 1852.

Marx, K. (2009a) *A Contribution to the Critique of Hegel's Philosophy of Right: Introduction*. Available from: https://www.marxists.org/archive/marx/works/1843/critique-hpr/intro.htm [Accessed 24 March 2021], original work published in 1844.

Marx, K. (2009b) *The Poverty of Philosophy: Answer to the Philosophy of Poverty by M. Proudhon*. Available from: https://www.marxists.org/archive/marx/works/download/pdf/Poverty-Philosophy.pdf [Accessed 10 October 2022], original work published in 1847.

Marx, K. and Engels, F. (1959) 'Manifest der kommunistischen Partei', in *Marx-Engels-Werke (MEW)* (vol 4), Berlin: Dietz, pp 459–93, original work published in 1848.

Marx Ferree, M. and Roth, S. (1998) 'Gender, class and the interaction between social movements: a strike of West Berlin day care workers', *Gender & Society*, 12(6): 626–48.

Marxhausen, T. (2004) 'Historische Mission der Arbeiterklasse', in W.F. Haug (ed) *Historisch-kritisches Wörterbuch des Marxismus* (vol 6 [I]), Hamburg: Argument, pp 293–301.

Mason, P. (2015) *PostCapitalism: A Guide to Our Future*, London: Allen Lane.

McCartin, J.A., Smiley, E. and Sneiderman, M. (2021) 'Both broadening and deepening: toward sectoral bargaining for the common good', in T. Schulze-Cleven and T. Vachon (eds) *Revaluing Work(ers): Toward a Democratic and Sustainable Future*, Champaign: LERA, pp 163–78.

Metcalfe, A. and Cock, J. (2010) 'Public sociology and the transformation of the university', *Transformation*, 72/73: 66–85.

Meyerson, H. (2012) 'The state of American unions', study by the Friedrich Ebert Foundation Office in Washington, DC, February. Available from: https://library.fes.de/pdf-files/id-moe/08922-20120302.pdf [Accessed 2 February 2022].

Milkman, R. and Voss, K. (eds) (2004) *Rebuilding Labor: Organizing and Organizers in the New Union Movement*, Ithaca: Cornell University Press.

Miller, R.W. (1981) 'Marx and Aristotle: a kind of consequentialism', *Canadian Journal of Philosophy*, 7(supplement): 323–52.

Moody, K. (2017) *On New Terrain: How Capital Is Reshaping the Battleground of Class War*, Chicago: Haymarket.

Moore, B. (1945) 'The Communist Party of the USA: an analysis of a social movement', *American Political Science Review*, 39(1): 31–41.

Mountz, A., Bonds, A., Mansfield, B., Loyd, J., Hyndman, J., Walton-Roberts, M. et al (2015) 'For slow scholarship: a feminist politics of resistance through collective action in the neoliberal university', *ACME: An International Journal for Critical Geographies*, 14(4): 1235–59.

Müller-Jentsch, W. (1973) 'Bedingungen kooperativer und konfliktorischer Gewerkschaftspolitik', *Leviathan*, 1(2): 223–41.

Müller-Jentsch, W. (1981) 'Vom gewerkschaftlichen Doppelcharakter und seiner theoretischen Auflösung im Neokorporatismus', in *Gesellschaftliche Arbeit und Rationalisierung* [*Leviathan* special issue, 4]: 178–200.

Müller-Jentsch, W. (2001) 'Gewerkschaftliche Kampfformen', in W.F. Haug (ed) *Historisch-kritisches Wörterbuch des Marxismus* (vol 5), Hamburg: Argument, pp 732–6.

Müller-Jentsch, W. (2003) 'Gewerkschaften heute: Zwischen arbeitspolitischer Kompetenz und sozialer Gerechtigkeit', *Gewerkschaftliche Monatshefte*, 10–11: 654–8.

Munck, R. (2009) 'Afterword: beyond the "new" international labour studies', *Third World Quarterly*, 30(3): 617–25.

Nagelschmidt, T. (2020) *Arbeit*, Frankfurt am Main: S. Fischer.

Newport, F. (2018) 'Looking into what Americans mean by "working class"', *Gallup*, 3 August. Available from: https://news.gallup.com/opin ion/polling-matters/239195/looking-americans-mean-working-class.aspx [Accessed 2 June 2022].

Nisbet, R. (1959) 'The decline and fall of social class', *The Pacific Sociological Review*, 2(1): 11–17.

Nowak, J. (2015) 'Union campaigns in Germany directed against inequality: the minimum wage campaign and the Emmely campaign', *Global Labour Journal*, 6(3): 366–80.

Nowak, J. (2018) 'The spectre of social democracy: a symptomatic reading of the power resources approach', *Global Labour Journal*, 9(3): 353–60.

Nowak, J. (2019) *Mass Strikes and Social Movements in Brazil and India: Popular Mobilisation in the Long Depression*, Cham: Palgrave.

Nowak, J. (2021a) 'From industrial relations research to global labour studies: moving labour research beyond Eurocentrism', *Globalizations*, 18(8): 1335–48.

Nowak, J. (2021b) 'Do choke points provide workers in logistics with power? A critique of the power resources approach in light of the 2018 truckers' strike in Brazil', *Review of International Political Economy*, 29 June. Available from: https://doi.org/10.1080/09692290.2021.1931940 [Accessed 20 July 2022].

Nowak, J. and Gallas, A. (2013) 'Die aktuelle Streikwelle in Europa ist ein historischer Einschnitt', *Sozialismus*, 9: 33–7.

Opratko, B. and Probst, S. (2010) 'Sozialismus in einer Stadt?', *PERSPEKTIVEN. Magazin für linke Theorie und Praxis*, 11, 4 May. Available from: www.perspektiven-online.at/2010/05/04/sozialismus-in-einer-stadt/ [Accessed 22 October 2019].

Owens, J. (2011) 'An introduction to critical realism as a meta-theoretical research perspective', Centre for Public Policy Research Working Paper, King's College, 1, September. Available from: http://www.kcl.ac.uk/sspp/departments/education/research/cppr/workingpapers/Paper-1.pdf [Accessed 6 October 2022].

Oxfam (2020) *Time to Care*, Briefing Paper, 20 January. Available from: https://oxfamilibrary.openrepository.com/bitstream/handle/10546/620928/bp-time-to-care-inequality-200120-en.pdf [Accessed 6 October 2022].

Pakulski, R. and Waters, M. (1996) *The Death of Class*, London: SAGE.

Palley, T. (2016) 'The US economy: explaining stagnation and why it will persist', in A. Gallas, H. Herr, F. Hoffer and C. Scherrer (eds) *Combating Inequality: The Global North and South*, London: Routledge, pp 113–31.

Panitch, L. (2001) 'Reflections on strategy for labor', *Socialist Register*, 37: 367–92.

Petersen, T. and Hartmann, H. (2020) *Globalization Report 2020: How Do Developing Countries and Emerging Markets Perform?*, Gütersloh: Bertelsmann-Stiftung.

Philipps, L. (2011) 'Society-wide anger', *Red Pepper*, 18 June. Available from: https://www.redpepper.org.uk/greece-no-tahrir-here/ [Accessed 7 October 2022].

Pickett, K. and Wilkinson, R. (2009) *The Spirit Level: Why More Equal Societies Always Do Better*, London: Allen Lane.

Pickett, K. and Wilkinson, R. (2014) 'The world we need', *International Journal of Labour Research*, 6(1): 17–34.

Pieber, M (2012) 'Die erste Frage lautet bei uns in Österreich meistens: "Darf man das überhaupt?"', in A. Gallas, J. Nowak and F. Wilde (eds) *Politische Streiks im Europa der Krise*, Hamburg: VSA, pp 130–7.

Pillay, D. (2016) 'The labor movement and ecosocialist prospects in South Africa', *Socialism and Democracy*, 30(2): 171–86.

Polanyi, K. (2001) *The Great Transformation: The Political and Economic Origins of Our Time*, Boston: Beacon Press, original work published in 1944.

Postone, M. (1993) *Time, Labor, and Social Domination: A Reinterpretation of Marx's Critical Theory*, Cambridge: Cambridge University Press.

Poulantzas, N. (1967) 'Marxist political theory in Great Britain', *New Left Review*, I(43): 57–74.

Poulantzas, N. (1968) *Political Power and Social Classes*, London: NLB.

Poulantzas, N. (1970) *Fascism and Dictatorship*, London: NLB.

Poulantzas, N. (1974) *Classes in Contemporary Capitalism*, London: NLB.

Poulantzas, N. (1976) 'The capitalist state: a reply to Miliband and Laclau', *New Left Review*, I(95): 63–83.

Poulantzas, N. (1978) *State, Power, Socialism*, London: NLB.

Renneberg, P. (2014) *Handbuch Tarifpolitik und Arbeitskampf*, 3rd edn, Hamburg: VSA.

Rhodes, C. (2019) 'The motor industry: statistics and policy', House of Commons Library, Briefing Paper, 00611, 16 December. Available from: https://researchbriefings.files.parliament.uk/documents/SN00611/SN00611.pdf [Accessed 20 March 2022].

Ripple, W.J., Wolf, C., Newsome, T.M., Barnard, P. and Moomaw, W.R. (2020) 'World scientists' warning of a climate emergency', *BioScience*, 70(1): 8–12.

Rodrik, D. (2016) 'Premature deindustrialization', *Journal of Economic Growth*, 21: 1–33.

Roediger, D. (2017) *Class, Race and Marxism*, London: Verso.

Ross, A.M. and Hartman, P.T. (1960) *Changing Patterns of Industrial Conflict*, New York: Wiley.

Sayer, A. (1992) *Method in Social Science: A Realist Approach*, London: Routledge.

Sayer, A. (2000) *Realism in Social Science*, London: SAGE.

Sayer, A. (2005) *The Moral Significance of Class*, Cambridge: Cambridge University Press.

Schelsky, H. (1952) 'Die Wandlungen der deutschen Familie in der Gegenwart und ihr Einfluß auf die Grundanschauungen der Sozialpolitik', *Sozialer Fortschritt*, 1(12): 284–8.

Scherrer, C. (1995) 'Eine diskursanalytische Kritik der Regulationstheorie', *PROKLA. Zeitschrift für kritische Sozialwissenschaft*, 25(3): 457–82.

Scherrer, C. (2020) 'Das Global Labour University Netzwerk: Ein neues Lernlabor für die internationale Arbeit Solidarität?', in N. Henkel, G. Bade and B. Reef (eds) *Politische Bildung: vielfältig – kontrovers – global. Festschrift für Bernd Overwien*, Frankfurt am Main: Wochenschau, pp 290–301.

Schmalstieg, C. (2015) *Prekarität und kollektive Handlungsfähigkeit: Gewerkschaftsarbeit im Niedriglohnsektor – das Beispiel USA*, Hamburg: VSA.

Schmalz, S. and Dörre, K. (eds) (2013) *Comeback der Gewerkschaften? Machtressourcen, innovative Praktiken, internationale Perspektiven*, Frankfurt am Main: Campus.

Schmalz, S. and Weinmann, N. (2016) 'Between power and powerlessness: labor unrest in western Europe in times of crisis', *Perspectives on Global Development and Technology*, 15: 543–66.

Schmalz, S., Ludwig, C. and Webster, E. (2018) 'The power resources approach: developments and challenges', *Global Labour Journal*, 9(2): 113–34.

Schmalz, S., Ludwig, C. and Webster, E. (2019) 'Power resources and global capitalism', *Global Labour Journal*, 10(1): 86–90.

Schofer, E. and Meyer, J.W. (2005) 'The worldwide expansion of higher education in the twentieth century', *American Sociological Review*, 70(6): 898–920.

Schroeder, W. and Greef, S. (2014) 'Struktur und Entwicklung des deutschen Gewerkschaftsmodells: Herausforderung durch Sparten- und Berufsgewerkschaften?', in W. Schroeder (eds) *Handbuch Gewerkschaften in Deutschland* (2nd edn), Wiesbaden: Springer VS, pp 123–46.

Schulze-Cleven, T. (2021) 'Beyond market fundamentalism: a labor studies perspective on the future of work', in T. Schulze-Cleven and T. Vachon (eds) *Revaluing Work(ers): Toward a Democratic and Sustainable Future*, Champaign: LERA, pp 27–54.

Schumann, M., Gerlach, F., Gschlössl, A. and Milhoffer, P. (1971) *Am Beispiel der Septemberstreiks: Anfang der Rekonstruktionsperiode der Arbeiterklasse: Eine empirische Untersuchung*, Frankfurt am Main: Europäische Verlagsanstalt.

Seeck, F. and Theißl, B. (2020) 'Einleitung', in F. Seeck and B. Theißl (eds) *Solidarisch gegen Klassismus: Organisieren, intervenieren, umverteilen*, Münster: Unrast, pp 9–16.

Silver, B.J. (2003) *Forces of Labor: Workers' Movements and Globalization since 1870*, Cambridge: Cambridge University Press.

Silver, B.J. (2014) 'Theorising the working class in twenty-first-century global capitalism', in M. Atzeni (ed) *Workers and Labour in a Globalised Capitalism: Contemporary Themes and Theoretical Issues*, Houndmills: Palgrave Macmillan, pp 46–69.

Simons, H.J. and Simons, R.E. (1969) *Class and Colour in South Africa 1850–1950,* Harmondsworth: Penguin.

Sklair, L. (2001) *The Transnational Capitalist Class*, Oxford: Wiley-Blackwell.

Smyth, S. (2018) 'The UCU strikes: a battle for the future of higher education', *British Politics and Policy at LSE* blog, 27 February. Available from: http://eprints.lse.ac.uk/88779/1/politicsandpolicy-the-ucu-strikes-a-battle-for-the-future-of-higher.pdf [Accessed 7 August 2022].

Sounderajah, V., Clarke, J., Yalamanchili, S., Acharya, A., Markar, S.R., Ashrafian, H. and Darzi, A. (2021) 'A national survey assessing public readiness for digital health strategies against COVID-19 within the United Kingdom', *Scientific Reports*, 11: np.

Stalin, J. (1938) 'Dialectical and historical materialism'. Available from: https://www.marxists.org/reference/archive/stalin/works/1938/09.htm [Accessed 9 October 2022].

Steckner, A. (2013) 'Marxistische Parteiendebatte revisited: Zur Verortung politischer Parteien in der Bürgerlichen Gesellschaft', *PROKLA. Zeitschrift für kritische Sozialwissenschaft*, 43(171): 217–38.

Stützle, I. (2011) 'The order of knowledge: the state as knowledge apparatus', in A. Gallas, L. Bretthauer, J. Kannankulam and I. Stützle (eds) *Reading Poulantzas*, Pontypool: Merlin, pp 170–85.

Tagesspiegel (2002) 'Die Mitglieder der Hartz-Kommission', 24 June. Available from: https://www.tagesspiegel.de/wirtschaft/die-mitglieder-der-hartz-kommission-904396.html [Accessed 23 March 2022].

Taylor, M. (2009) 'Who works for globalisation? The challenges and possibilities for international labour studies', *Third World Quarterly*, 30(3): 435–52.

Teague, P. and Donaghey, J. (2018) 'Brexit: EU social policy and the UK employment model', *Industrial Relations Journal*, 49(5–6): 512–33.

Thompson, E.P. (1968) *The Making of the English Working Class*, Harmondsworth: Penguin.

Thompson, E.P. (1978) *The Poverty of Theory & Other Essays*, London: Merlin.

Uellenberg-van Dawen, W. (2013) 'Gute Arbeit in den Dienstleistungen', in S. Schmalz and K. Dörre (eds) *Comeback der Gewerkschaften? Machtressourcen, innovative Praktiken, internationale Perspektiven*, Frankfurt am Main: Campus, pp 397–406.

Urban, H.-J. (2009) 'Die Mosaik-Linke. Vom Aufbruch der Gewerkschaften zur Erneuerung der Bewegung', *Blätter für deutsche und internationale Politik*, 54(5): 71–8.

Urban, H.-J. (2010) 'Wohlfahrtsstaat und Gewerkschaftsmacht im Finanzmarkt-Kapitalismus: Der Fall Deutschland', *WSI-Mitteilungen*, 9: 443–50.

Urban, H.-J. (2012) 'Crisis corporatism and trade union revitalisation in Europe', in S. Lehndorff (ed) *A Triumph of Failed Ideas: European Models of Capitalism in the Crisis*, Brussels: ETUI, pp 219–41.

Urban, H.-J. (2013) 'Gewerkschaftsstrategien in der Krise: Zur kollektiven Handlungsfähigkeit im Gegenwartskapitalismus', in S. Schmalz and K. Dörre (eds) *Comeback der Gewerkschaften? Machtressourcen, innovative Praktiken, internationale Perspektiven*, Frankfurt am Main: Campus, pp 376–96.

Urban, H.-J. (2018) 'Social critique and trade unions: outlines of a troubled relationship', in K. Dörre, N. Meyer-Ahuja, D. Sauer and V. Wittke (eds) *Capitalism and Labor: Towards Critical Perspectives*, Frankfurt am Main: Campus, pp 378–99.

Vandaele, K. (2011) 'Sustaining or abandoning "social peace"? Strike development and trends in Europe since the 1990s', ETUI working paper, 2011.05, May. Available from: https://www.etui.org/publicati ons/working-papers/sustaining-or-abandoning-social-peace [Accessed 26 June 2021].

Vandaele, K. (2016) 'Interpreting strike activity in western Europe in the past 20 years: the labour repertoire under pressure', *Transfer*, 22(3): 277–94.

Van der Linden, M. (2005) 'Labour history: an international movement', *Labour History*, 89: 225–33.

Van der Linden, M. (2008) *Workers of the World: Essays towards a Global Labour History*, Leiden: Brill.

Van der Linden, M. (2014) 'Who is the working class?: wage earners and other labourers', in M. Atzeni (ed) *Workers and Labour in a Globalised Capitalism: Contemporary Themes and Theoretical Issues*, Houndmills: Palgrave, pp 70–84.

Van der Linden, M. (2016) 'Global labour: a not-so-grand finale and perhaps a new beginning', *Global Labour Journal*, 7(2): 201–10.

Van der Pijl, K. (1998) *Transnational Classes and International Relations*, London: Routledge.

Van der Velden, S. (2007) 'Introduction', in S. van der Velden, H. Dribbusch, D. Lyddon and K. Vandaele (eds) *Strikes around the World, 1968–2005: Case-Studies of 15 Countries*, Amsterdam: Aksant, pp 12–23.

Vernell, S. (2012) 'Wir brauchen eine Gesellschaft, die auf dem Prinzip der Planung beruht', in A. Gallas, J. Nowak and F. Wilde (eds) *Politische Streiks im Europa der Krise*, Hamburg: VSA, pp 179–93.

Voss, K. and Sherman, R. (2000) 'Breaking the iron law of oligarchy: union revitalization in the American labor movement', *The American Journal of Sociology*, 106(2): 303–49.

Wallerstein, I. (1981) 'The USA in today's world', *Contemporary Marxism*, 4: 11–17.

Weber, M. (1904) 'Objectivity in social science and social policy', in M. Weber (1949) *On the Methodology of the Social Science*, edited and translated by E.A. Shills and H.A. Finch, Glencoe: The Free Press, pp 50–112.

Webster, E. (1992) 'The impact of intellectuals on the labour movement', *Transformation*, 18: 88–92.

Webster, E. (2004) 'Sociology in South Africa: its past, present and future', *Society in Transition*, 35(1): 27–41.

Webster, E. (2015) 'Labour after globalisation', ISER Working Paper No. 2015/1, Rhodes University.

Webster, E. (2017) 'Partei ergreifen: Verheißungen und Fallstricke einer öffentlichen Soziologie im Apartheid-Südafrika', in B. Aulenbacher, M. Burawoy, K. Dörre and J. Sittel (eds) *Öffentliche Soziologie: Wissenschaft im Dialog mit der Gesellschaft*, Frankfurt: Campus, pp 260–73.

Webster, E., Bezuidenhout, A. and Lambert, R. (2008) *Grounding Globalization*, Malden, MA: Blackwell.

Weeks, K. (2011) *The Problem with Work: Feminism, Marxism, Antiwork Politics, and Postwork Imaginaries*, Durham, NC: Duke University Press.

Weischer, C. (1988) *Kritische Gewerkschaftstheorie: Ansätze einer Neurorientierung*, Münster: Westfälisches Dampfboot.

Wilkinson, R. and Pickett, K. (2014) 'The world we need', *International Journal of Labour Research*, 6(1): 17–34.

Willman, P. (1990) 'The financial status and performance of British trade unions, 1950–1988', *British Journal of Industrial Relations*, 28(3): 313–27.

Wilson, J. (2018) *Inverting the Pyramid: The History of Football Tactics*, new edn, London: Weidenfeld & Nicolson.

Wolf, M. (2004) *Why Globalization Works*, New Haven: Yale University Press.

Wolf, M. (2014) 'Shaping globalization', *Finance & Development*, 51(3): 22–5.

Wolpe, H. (1972) 'Capitalism and cheap labour-power in South Africa: from segregation to apartheid', *Economy and Society*, 1(4): 425–56.

Wood, A.W. (1972) 'The Marxian critique of justice', *Philosophy and Public Affairs*, 1: 244–82.

Wood, E.M. (1999) *The Origins of Capitalism*, New York: Monthly Review Press.

Wright, E.O. (1978a) 'Intellectuals and the working class', *Insurgent Sociologist*, 8(1): 5–18.

Wright, E.O. (1978b) *Class, Crisis and the State*, London: NLB.

Wright, E.O. (2000) 'Working-class power, capitalist–class interests, and class compromise', *American Journal of Sociology*, 105(4): 957–1002.

Yudken, J.S. and Jacobs, D.C. (2021) 'Worker voice in technological chance: the potential of recrafting', in T. Schulze-Cleven and T. Vachon (eds) *Revaluing Work(ers): Toward a Democratic and Sustainable Future*, Champaign: LERA, pp 141–62.

Zastrow, V. (2004) 'Gerhard Schröder: Wir waren die Asozialen', *Frankfurter Allgemeine Zeitung*, 15 December, p 3.

Index